A QUESTION OF RETRIBUTION?

THE BRITISH ACADEMY AND THE MATTER OF ANTHONY BLUNT

A Question of Retribution?

The British Academy and the Matter of Anthony Blunt

EDITED BY
DAVID CANNADINE

Published for THE BRITISH ACADEMY
by OXFORD UNIVERSITY PRESS

Oxford University Press, Great Clarendon Street, Oxford OX2 6DP

First edition published in 2020

British Library Cataloguing in Publication Data
Data available

Library of Congress Cataloging in Publication Data
Data available

Typeset in the offices of the British Academy
by Portia Taylor
Printed in Great Britain by
CPI Group (UK) Ltd, Croydon, CR0 4YY

ISBN 978-0-19-726678-6

Contents

We know no spectacle so ridiculous as the British public in one of its periodical fits of morality.

Thomas Babington Macaulay, *Critical and Historical Essays Contributed to the Edinburgh Review*, London, 1843, vol. i, p. 315

If I had to choose between betraying my country and betraying my friend, I hope I should have the guts to betray my country.

E.M. Forster, *What I Believe*, London, 1939, p. 8

Academic politics are so vicious precisely because the stakes are so small.

attributed to Henry Kissinger, and many others

At least a great number of people have now heard of the Academy who had never before done so.

Professor G.R. Elton to Sir Kenneth Dover, 24 August 1980

Preface

This year marks the fortieth anniversary of the Annual General Meeting of the British Academy, held in July 1980, when the Fellows declined to expel one of their number, Professor Anthony Blunt, the renowned art historian, who had been unmasked as a former Soviet spy by the Prime Minister, Margaret Thatcher, late in the previous year. During the intervening months, the 'Blunt affair' had received extensive coverage in the media: there were many denunciations of his life and conduct, and the Academy itself became an object of un-precedented public interest, as debate and discussion flowed back and forth among some, but not all, of the Fellowship. Should Blunt be expelled, on the grounds that his treason and treachery rendered him an unfit person to continue to be a Fellow of a great national institution, or should he be allowed to remain, since the Academy's prime concern was with scholarly excellence rather than political affiliation, and Blunt was undoubtedly a distinguished scholar? The President of the Academy was the eminent Hellenist, Sir Kenneth Dover, who was responsible for providing leadership and holding together a Fellowship that became deeply but not equally divided. Once the affair was over, Dover deposited a file with the Academy entitled 'Materials for a History of the Events Leading to the Resignation of Professor A.F. Blunt and arising therefrom, November 1979-April 1981'. Much of the text consisted of letters he had received from Fellows (and others) during the course of the affair, together with relevant Academy papers, to which he added his own accompanying narrative and explanation of events as they had unfolded.

The core of this book is a selection of letters and documents from Dover's 'Materials' that have never before been made public, linked together by a new commentary which often refers back to his earlier version. To these have been added further documents from the papers of Lord Robbins, a previous President of the Academy, who 'deplored' Blunt's conduct but wished him to remain a Fellow, and from the archive of Professor J.H. Plumb, who was one of the leaders of those Fellows who wanted him expelled. My prologue sets these primary sources in context by describing the British Academy as it then was, and by giving some account of the lives and careers of Blunt and Dover up to the time when Blunt was publicly unmasked. I have also contributed an epilogue, which reflects on the affair and the principal protagonists, and explores the lengthy afterlife of Blunt's career in fiction and the media. The selection of the documents from Dover's 'Materials' has been made, and the new linking and interpretive passages have been written, by James Rivington and Karen Syrett, while the additional research on which my prologue and epilogue draw has been undertaken by Dr Martin Spychal. I am deeply grateful to them, and also for their many helpful comments on my earlier drafts, and for their additional work in preparing the final text for publication, as well as to Portia Taylor, who was responsible for the final typesetting. I am equally indebted to Mr Peter Brown, Dr Robin Jackson, Sir Charles Saumarez Smith and Sir Keith Thomas, who read the entire manuscript, and made many valuable suggestions.

One of the surprises of working on this subject has been discovering just how many of the major actors were historians, and how many of them were already known to me at the time of the Blunt affair, or subsequently became colleagues and friends. The sight of their writing paper and calligraphy has been both reassuringly familiar and unexpectedly disconcerting. It is also a reminder that they (and I) belonged to a very small, very male, very Oxbridge-and-London dominated world which was in some respects (but not all) very different from British academe today. Professor Geoffrey Elton was a Fellow of Clare College, Cambridge, where I had read history as an undergraduate and first met him; Professor John A. Crook was a Fellow of St John's College, Cambridge, where I was later a Research Fellow and for a time lived in rooms on the same staircase as he did; Professor J.H. Plumb was Master of Christ's College, Cambridge, where I had been elected a Fellow in 1977, and it was from him that I learned what little I knew of the Blunt affair at the time (only later did I come to realise just how one-sided his account of things was). While a graduate student in Oxford, I had heard A.J.P. Taylor lecture, and my research supervisor, Professor Peter Mathias, was Treasurer of the Academy at the time of the Blunt affair (although he seems to have kept his head well down). Robert Blake, Eric Hobsbawm, Michael Howard and Hugh Trevor-Roper were historians with whose work I was already admiringly familiar, and whom I later got to know. On the other hand, I met Ian Christie only once, and

Norman Gash never, though Gash and I did have an Oxford college in common, namely St John's. Among past and future Presidents of the Academy who appear in these pages, I knew Isaiah Berlin slightly, and Owen Chadwick rather better. But I never encountered either of the two principal protagonists, Blunt and Dover, and their fields of academic interest were a long way from mine.

As I have worked on this book, I have often asked myself how I would have voted at the July 1980 AGM, had I then been a Fellow, and how I would have acted throughout the Blunt affair, had I then been President. But the times and the Academy were so different in so many ways, and the issues were so deeply felt by so many of the Fellows who had gone through the Second World War, that it is impertinent for anyone born much later to believe they can know how they would have responded, what they would have thought, and what they would have done forty years earlier. From one perspective, this may seem a petty story of academic rivalries, professional jealousies and personal antagonisms, of moral grandstanding and (as we might now say) virtue signalling, and of revenge and retribution. Yet from another, this is an account of highly educated, deeply learned and unfailingly thoughtful men and (some, but not many) women, struggling with issues of profound and abiding significance: the relationship between professional conduct and personal beliefs; the duties owed to friendship and conscience, and the obligations due to king (or queen) and country; the role, purpose and function of a learned academy in the life of a nation; and the competing claims of justice and punishment, forgiveness and mercy. There was disagreement among the Fellows of the Academy about those matters then, and since they remain issues of fundamental importance in any free (or un-free) society, they rightly deserve regular ventilation and repeated re-examination. 'If', Sir Kenneth Dover told the Fellows, towards the end of the meeting at which they had declined to expel Blunt, 'we value our independence, we cannot escape the consequences of working out our own principles of conduct.'[1] This book records the most testing and controversial episode in which the President and Fellows of the British Academy were obliged to try to do just that. Forty years on, there is still much to learn from their efforts.

David Cannadine
The British Academy
February 2020

[1] K. Dover, 'Presidential Address, 3 July 1980', *Proceedings of the British Academy*, 66 (1980), p. 83.

Note on the documents and sources

In 1981, Sir Kenneth Dover, President of the British Academy, deposited with the Academy a typed narrative and explanation, interspersed with copies of letters and other documents, entitled 'Materials for a History of the Events Leading to the Resignation of Professor A.F. Blunt and arising therefrom, November 1979 – April 1981'.

Dover's collection of 'Materials' has been the starting point for the 'Documentary narrative' now published here. 'Materials' contains just over 150 documents in full: a little under one third of those have been reproduced in this volume.

The handwritten circled numbers that can be seen on some of the documents were added by Dover, to indicate their place in his sequence of 'Materials'.[1] The discolouration on some of the facsimiles arises from Dover's use of tape to stick the documents into his typed script.

In the following text, the shorthand 'Materials' has been used to indicate elements extracted, either directly or indirectly, from Dover's own narrative.

In addition to Dover's 'Materials', further items in the British Academy's archives have been drawn upon. These include formal agenda papers and minutes that Dover did not include in his 'Materials' (of the Academy's Council and of the infamous July 1980 AGM), as well as some papers from the Secretary's files (eight documents in all). Seven documents (2, 14, 42, 44, 45, 47, 48) come from the papers of J.H. Plumb and are reproduced by kind permission of the Syndics of Cambridge University Library. Four more (22, 26, 29, 63) have been taken from the archive of Lord Robbins and are reproduced by kind permission of the LSE Library, The London School of Economics and Political Science.

Photographs of Fellows of the British Academy reproduced within the 'Documentary narrative' are from the Academy's own collection. While these images do not necessarily date from the time of the Blunt affair, the captions give the individuals' titles and honours as they were in 1979-80.

[1] Dover also assigned numbers to over 70 documents that he merely referred to in his explanatory text, which is why his own numbering sequence exceeded 200.

The British Academy is very grateful to everyone who has granted permission to publish material in this book. Whilst every effort has been made to contact all the copyright holders, if anyone has been inadvertently overlooked, the Academy will be pleased to make the necessary arrangements at the first opportunity.

James Rivington, Martin Spychal and Karen Syrett
February 2020

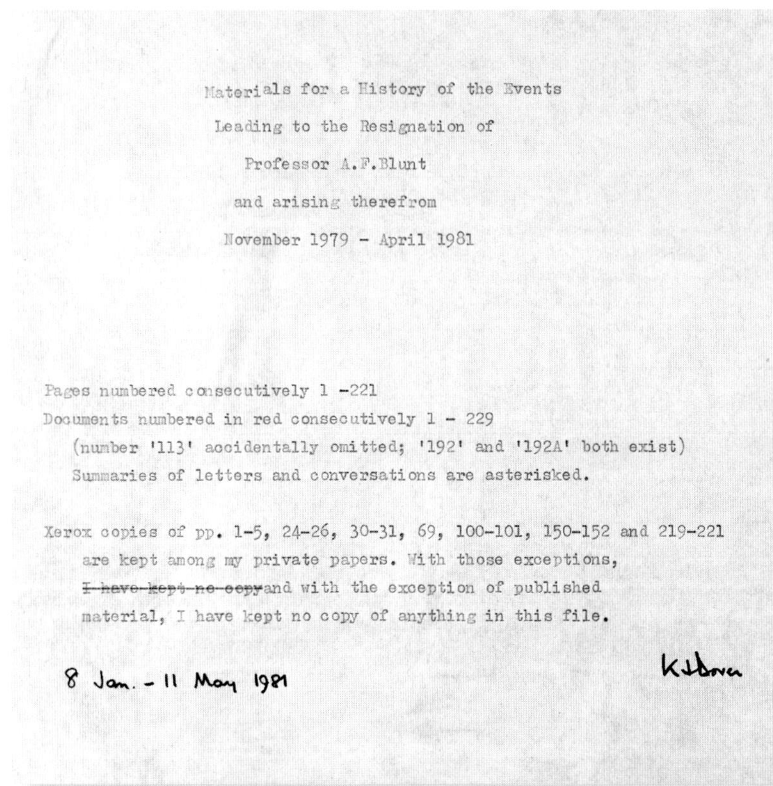

Materials for a History of the Events
Leading to the Resignation of
Professor A.F.Blunt
and arising therefrom
November 1979 - April 1981

Pages numbered consecutively 1 -221
Documents numbered in red consecutively 1 - 229
(number '113' accidentally omitted; '192' and '192A' both exist)
Summaries of letters and conversations are asterisked.

Xerox copies of pp. 1-5, 24-26, 30-31, 69, 100-101, 150-152 and 219-221 are kept among my private papers. With those exceptions, ~~I have kept no copy~~and with the exception of published material, I have kept no copy of anything in this file.

8 Jan. - 11 May 1981 KJDover

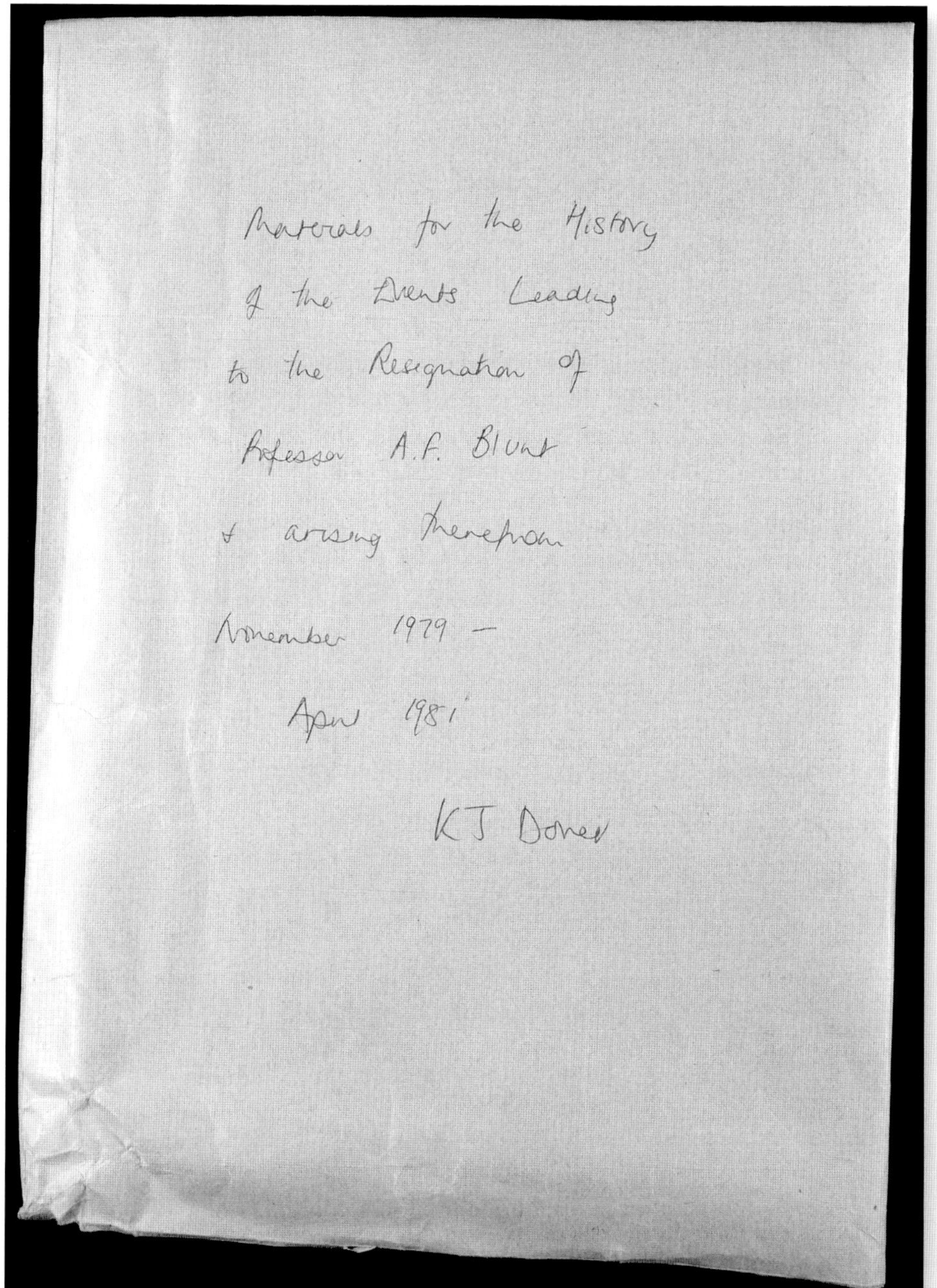

Sources

Archival collections consulted:

Lord (Noel) Annan papers, King's College, Cambridge
Sir Isaiah Berlin papers, Bodleian Library, Oxford
Anthony Blunt file, National Archives, Kew
Anthony Blunt unpublished autobiography, British Library, London
British Academy Council Minutes, British Academy, London
John Carswell papers, British Academy, London
Sir Kenneth Dover papers, British Academy, London
Federal Bureau of Investigation records: the Vault (accessed online)
Rosalind Lehmann papers, King's College, Cambridge
Sir John Plumb papers, Cambridge University Library
Prime Ministers' papers, National Archives, Kew
Lord (Lionel) Robbins papers, London School of Economics
G.H.W. ('Dadie') Rylands papers, Kings College, Cambridge
A.J.P. Taylor papers, Parliamentary Archives, London

Interviews and e-mail correspondence:

Professor Dawn Adès FBA, 30 October 2019
Mr Peter Brown, 18 February 2018
Sir Barry Cunliffe FBA, 6 November 2019
Sir John Elliott FBA, 16 October 2019
Sir Michael Howard FBA, 27 October 2019
Miss Jane Lyddon, 30 March 2020
Baroness Onora O'Neill FBA, 9 January 2020
Dr Robin Jackson, 24 October 2019
Sir Keith Thomas FBA, 4 November 2019

Sir Anthony Blunt FBA, former Surveyor of the Queen's Pictures, at Hampton Court Palace in 1975. (Photo by Chris Ware/Keystone/Hulton Archive/Getty Images.)

Prologue

In November 1979, the Prime Minister, Margaret Thatcher, named and unmasked the distinguished art historian, Professor Sir Anthony Blunt, as the 'Fourth Man', who had been one of the wartime traitors known as the 'Cambridge spies' or, eventually and ironically, as the 'Magnificent Five'. Thatcher regarded Blunt's behaviour as 'contemptible and repugnant', on the grounds that 'he had betrayed his country', and she was appalled by these latest revelations of treason and treachery in high places.[1] The first two 'Cambridge spies' to have been outed were Guy Burgess and Donald Maclean, who had defected to Russia in 1951, their departure assisted and orchestrated by Blunt, who knew that the British security services were closing in on them. The third was 'Kim' Philby, who had followed his friends to the USSR in 1963, so that he, like them, might escape prosecution in the British courts.[2] From the early 1950s, Blunt had also been under suspicion, in both the United Kingdom and the United States, and was interrogated eleven times in Britain, although nothing could be proven against him.[3] But in the light of new evidence, he eventually confessed in 1964 that he had passed on state secrets to Russia while working for MI5 during the Second World War, although he only admitted his guilt in exchange for a guarantee that he would be immune from any subsequent prosecution for the rest of his life. Since Blunt had no wish to follow Burgess, Maclean and Philby to exiled disgrace in Russia, and since, as Thatcher grudgingly admitted, there were 'no grounds on which criminal proceedings could be instituted', this meant he was free to continue living and working in Britain, where he had been Director of the Courtauld Institute of Art at the University of London, and Surveyor of the Queen's Pictures, and remained a widely-esteemed scholar and a well-connected figure at the heart of the British establishment during his retirement.[4]

[1] C. Moore, *Margaret Thatcher: The Authorized Biography*, vol. i, *From Grantham to the Falklands* (New York, 2013), pp. 483-5; *Hansard's Parliamentary Debates*, Commons, 21 November 1979, cols. 402-520.

[2] M. Carter, *Anthony Blunt: His Lives* (London, 2001), pp. 337-57.

[3] FBI Records: The Vault: Anthony Blunt file accessed online.

[4] *Hansard's Parliamentary Debates*, Commons, 15 November 1979, cols. 679-81; C.M. Andrew, *The Defence of the Realm: The Authorized History of MI5* (London, 2010), p. 429.

Although Blunt had been unmasked by Thatcher, the immunity agreement meant he would remain beyond the reach of English law. But having accumulated a glittering array of honours during his academic career, Blunt was at risk in other ways. Once he had been named, demands mounted that, while he could not be imprisoned, he should certainly be dishonoured and disgraced in the country he had betrayed, and there was ample scope for such shunning and shaming. At the peak of his renown, Blunt had been made a member of the French Legion of Honour for his work on Poussin, awarded a string of honorary degrees by British universities, and elected a Fellow of the Society of Antiquaries and an Honorary Fellow of Trinity College, Cambridge, where he had been an undergraduate. On his retirement from the Courtauld, the University of London had conferred upon him the title of Emeritus Professor, and for his work as Surveyor of the Queen's Pictures, Elizabeth II had made him a Knight Commander of the Royal Victorian Order, an honour in her personal gift, in 1956. Here was a rich field for reckoning, revoking and retribution. In the aftermath of Thatcher's announcement, the Queen immediately stripped Blunt of his knighthood, and he was subsequently compelled to resign his Fellowship at the Antiquaries and his Honorary Fellowship at Trinity, in both cases having been told that he would be expelled if he did not. But the University of London declined to rescind his Emeritus Professorship, on the grounds that, having retired, Blunt was fully entitled to it by virtue of his age, none of his honorary degrees were cancelled, and the French government did not take away his Legion of Honour.[5] These decisions were rapidly reached, with minimal public controversy. But in the case of the British Academy, to which Blunt had been elected almost thirty years before, the issue as to whether he should be deprived of his Fellowship turned out to be much more controversial, protracted and highly profiled.

***

[5] BL Add MS 88901/1: Blunt, Unpublished handwritten memoir [c. 1982], ff. 130-32; Dawn Adès interview, 30 October 2019; N. Annan, *Our Age: Portrait of a Generation* (London, 1990), p. 322.

The British Academy had been established to further the pursuit of what was then termed 'Historical, Philosophical and Philological Studies', but which we now call the humanities and social sciences, by a Royal Charter granted on 8 August 1902.[6] It was brought into being by a group of distinguished academics, scholars, writers and politicians largely in response to the creation of an International Association of Academies in 1899, on the grounds that no British organisation existed which represented what was termed 'literary' science in the way that the Royal Society spoke for the 'natural' sciences. The Academy's bye-laws were settled early in 1903, and established a basic structure of governance that was still in existence during the time when Blunt was a Fellow, and that remains essentially unaltered today. The executive business of the Academy was to be undertaken by the President, the Secretary and the Council, but they had to report to the Annual General Meeting of the Fellowship, which as the Academy's sovereign body retained certain powers, one of which was that it alone could expel a Fellow, on the grounds of no longer being a 'fit and proper person', by a majority vote of those present. The number of Fellows was originally set at one hundred, and then as now, they were elected into different 'Sections' representing different subjects. At the outset, there were only four of them: History and Archaeology; Philology (Oriental, Biblical, Classical, Medieval and Modern); Philosophy (Logic, Psychology, Ethics, Metaphysics); and Jurisprudence and Economics. The first President was Lord Reay, a Scottish nobleman and former Indian proconsul, who at the time was President of the Royal Asiatic Society. Three of the first Fellows 'combined political importance with scholarly eminence', namely Lord Rosebery, Arthur Balfour and John Morley, and among the academics elected were the historians F.W. Maitland and J.B. Bury, the lawyers A.V. Dicey and Sir Frederick Pollock, the anthropologist J.G. Frazer, and the economist Alfred Marshall. (Among those who would surely also have been elected as founding Fellows had they lived just a little longer were Mr Gladstone, Lord Acton, S.R. Gardiner and Henry Sidgwick.)

As these names suggest, the Academy was from the outset poised uneasily yet fruitfully between the worlds of learning and of politics, where it still remains today. But it possessed no premises, it employed no staff, it received no government grant (unlike the Royal Society), and its income from Fellows' subscriptions was exiguous. Beyond the deliberations of the Council, most of the Academy's limited administrative work was undertaken by the unpaid but energetic Secretary, Israel Gollancz, who was a Fellow and Professor of English Language and Literature at King's College, London.[7] He persuaded some of his rich friends to endow lectures in the subjects the Academy represented, thereby creating for it the beginnings of a public audience, there were two additional gifts for prizes in Greek literature and English literature, and he positioned the Academy at the heart of the national celebrations marking the tercentenary of Milton's birth in 1908.[8] From the outset, the Academy was also a very cosmopolitan organisation, serving as the 'representative of British humane scholarship among the nations of the world'. Many of the first Fellows were scholars of global interests and renown, and from the very beginning, academics based overseas, which at that time meant primarily in continental Europe, were elected into what were termed Corresponding Fellowships. The Academy also sent delegates to the international congresses of historians, orientalists and archaeologists which met with increasing regularity in the years before 1914, and hosted its share of these gatherings when they took place in London.[9] But the outbreak of the First World War dealt a severe blow to the very idea of an international republic of letters, and raised issues for the Academy which in some significant ways prefigured and anticipated those that would later come to prominence during the Blunt affair.[10]

Many of the Academy's Corresponding Fellows were based in Germany and Austria, and some were signatories to a manifesto, published in Germany during the early stages of the war, and signed by ninety-three scholars, denouncing the Allies in hostile and extravagant language. In certain quarters, as Sir Frederic Kenyon explained in his Presidential Address of 1920, such action was regarded as 'a gross crime against scholarship', on the grounds that men who had 'accepted honours and hospitality from England, and whom we believed honestly to be our friends,' had gone 'out of their way to insult the name and fame of our country', and that this constituted 'an offence against good manners and the common decencies of life which cannot be simply ignored as if it had never happened.' The result had been an agitation demanding that these scholars should be deprived of their corresponding fellowships in British learned societies. But both the British Academy and the Royal Society declined to give in to these demands, on the grounds that several German and Austrian scholars had bravely refused to sign the manifesto; that many of those who had appended their signatures had done so under duress and compulsion from the governments under which they held their posts and which paid their salaries; and that it was more prudent and dignified for the Academy and the Society to take no action, in the hope of returning to amity once the war was over.[11]

6 F.G. Kenyon, *The British Academy: The First Fifty Years* (London, 1952), pp. 5-14.

7 F.G. Kenyon, 'Sir Israel Gollancz, 1863-1930', *Proceedings of the British Academy*, 16 (1930), pp. 424-38.

8 Kenyon, *British Academy*, pp. 16-20; 'From the Archive: John Milton, 1608 to 2008 (via 1908)', *British Academy Review*, 12 (January 2009), pp. 58-9.

9 Kenyon, *British Academy*, p. 21.

10 The outbreak of the First World War also meant that Gollancz's ambitious plans for a celebration of the tercentenary of Shakespeare's death in 1616, when he had hoped that 'the world's brother-hood' would be brought together in 'common and united commemoration' of the bard, were perforce scaled back: 'From the Archive: The British Academy and the Shakespeare Tercentenary, 1916', *British Academy Review*, 28 (Summer 2016), pp. 60-1.

11 F.G. Kenyon, 'Presidential Address, 1920', *Proceedings of the British Academy*, [9] (1919-1920), pp. 24-7; Kenyon,

Relations between the Academy and German and Austrian scholars were gradually restored after 1918, and in 1935 the German and Austrian Academies were invited to join the Union Académique Internationale, which had superseded the International Association of Academies at the end of the war and was headquartered in Brussels. Neither the Union nor the Academy maintained any relations with scholars from Communist Russia, but as late as May 1939, when the British Academy hosted the annual meeting of the UAI when it took place in London, scholars from Germany were invited.[12]

In 1919, the original four subject Sections of the Academy Fellowship were re-divided into nine, and two years later, the maximum number of Fellows was increased from one hundred to one hundred and fifty. In 1924, Lord (Arthur) Balfour, a founding Fellow, and President of the Academy from 1921 to 1928, persuaded the Labour Government to provide an annual grant of £2,000, in support of research and publications but not to defray administrative costs. Three years later, on the eve of the Academy's twenty-fifth anniversary, Balfour persuaded Winston Churchill, then Chancellor of the Exchequer in Stanley Baldwin's Conservative Government, to provide the Academy with its first permanent home, namely 'free quarters' in Burlington Gardens, at the rear of Burlington House on Piccadilly, previously used by the University of London, and consisting of a large and small lecture room, a council chamber, and two rooms for (unpaid) secretarial purposes. As a result, the Academy's lecture programmes, research support and publication activities continued, but they still remained at a relatively low and under-funded level, not least because Kenyon, who had succeeded Gollancz as Secretary in 1930, was far less energetic than his predecessor.[13] In practical terms, the major issue facing the Fellows was how to respond to the threats to free intellectual inquiry represented by Communist Russia on the one hand, and Fascist Germany, Italy and Spain on the other. However different their ideologies, both creeds were deeply hostile to the values for which the British Academy stood, namely freedom of thought, evidence-based inquiry, and the unfettered and untrammelled life of the mind. Officially, the Academy took no position on these matters, but several of its Fellows, including Sir William Beveridge, John Maynard Keynes and G.M. Trevelyan were founder members of the Academic Assistance Council, which helped bring many Jewish scholars to Britain. Among them were such future Fellows of the Academy and knights of the realm as Sir Geoffrey Elton, Sir Ernst Gombrich, Sir Otto Kahn-Freund, Sir Claus Moser, Sir Nikolaus Pevsner and Sir Karl Popper.[14]

Although in straitened circumstances between 1939 and 1945, the British Academy did establish a committee to make recommendations to the Home Office 'regarding interned aliens of enemy nationality who possess special scientific or academic qualifications', one of whom was Pevsner himself.[15] At the end of hostilities, the Academy again sought to rebuild bridges with German academics, and in the autumn of 1947, the current and future Presidents, Sir Harold Bell and Sir Charles Webster, went on a mission to 'make contact with German scholars and so to help re-establish the unity of European scholarship.'[16] Thereafter, the Academy developed close links with many partners in western Europe, culminating in the European Exchange Scheme in the Humanities and Social Sciences established in 1972. By then, the Academy had also begun to establish relations with the Communist countries of eastern Europe, and by the end of the decade, it had negotiated exchange agreements with Bulgaria, Czechoslovakia, Hungary, Poland, Romania, the Council of Academies of Sciences and Arts of Yugoslavia, and the Academy of Sciences of the German Democratic Republic (East Germany). These accords enabled dozens of British scholars to travel to eastern Europe, and for many more foreign scholars to visit Britain. Relations with the Soviet Academy of Sciences were less easy, as the Russian authorities were prone to be unnecessarily bureacratic.[17] Late in 1979, Sir Alec Cairncross led an Academy delegation to China, initiating links with the Chinese Academy of Social Sciences, and the following spring, a delegation of Chinese academics visited Britain. At the time of the Blunt affair, the Academy's Deputy Secretary, Peter Brown, was preoccupied with these international matters, and just before the controversial AGM of July 1980 he had visited East Germany for another round of meetings and discussions.[18]

British Academy, p. 22. See also 'From the Archive: Canon Sanday on "International scholarship after the war", May 1918', *British Academy Review*, 33 (Summer 2018), pp. 49-51; M.D. Chapman, *Theology at War and Peace: English Theology and Germany in the First World War* (2016), ch. 6.

[12] 'From the Archive: The British Academy, and one hundred years of the Union Académique Internationale', *British Academy Review*, 36 (December 2019), pp. 51-2.

[13] Kenyon, *British Academy*, pp. 15, 31-2; M. Wheeler, *The British Academy, 1949-1968* (London, 1970), pp. 3-5.

[14] J. Seabrook, *The Refuge and the Fortress: Britain and the Flight from Tyranny* (Houndmills, 2009), pp. 28-41, 47-9, 53-6, 58-9; P. Weindling, 'From Refugee Assistance to Freedom of Learning: the Strategic Vision of A.V. Hill, 1933-1964' in S. Marks, P. Weindling and L. Wintour (eds.), *In Defence of Learning: The Plight, Persecution, and Placement of Academic Refugees, 1933-1980s* (*Proceedings of the British Academy*, 169; 2011), pp. 64, 74; A. Grenville, 'Celebrating fifty years of the Thank-Offering to Britain Fund', *British Academy Review*, 27 (February 2016), pp. 70-3; D. Cannadine, *G.M. Trevelyan: A Life in History* (London, 1992), p. 129.

[15] A. Roberts, 'The British Academy 2009-2013: reflections', *British Academy Review*, 22 (Summer 2013), p. 3, note 6.

[16] MS BA570: 'Report on a visit to Germany by Sir Harold Bell and Sir Charles Webster' [autumn 1947], p. 2.

[17] At the time of the Blunt affair, the exchange agreement with the Soviet Academy was effectively suspended: in 1979 the British Academy had proposed two visitors who were not welcomed by the Soviets (one of them, Professor Alec Nove FBA, was judged by Moscow to have been a British spy); the stand-off lasted until 1981. BA MS: Council Minutes: 17 May 1979, p. 3; 9 November 1979, p. 4; 15 February 1980, p. 3; 18 March 1980, p. 2; 16 May 1980, pp. 2-3; 7 November 1980, pp. 3-4; 17 March 1981, p. 2. E-mail correspondence, 30 March 2020, from Jane Lyddon, then the British Academy's Assistant Secretary (Overseas).

[18] *The British Academy, 1902-2002: Some Historical Documents and Notes* (London, 2002), pp. 30-34; Peter Brown,

This post-war international expansion was underpinned by a significant growth in the Academy's domestic operations. During the Second World War, its activities had virtually ceased: indeed, according to Sir Mortimer Wheeler the Academy was at 'its nadir and was nigh to death', and meant 'very little' to the Fellows or 'to anyone else'.[19] Wheeler served as Secretary from 1949 to 1968, and played a major part in the Academy's post-war resuscitation and expansion. The government grant was increased from £2,500 to £300,000, and the Academy moved from its dark and inadequate rooms in Burlington Gardens to more spacious accommodation in Burlington House on Piccadilly, including a lecture room where its Annual General Meetings were also held. New lecture series were established, the publications programme was boosted, and the Academy became the channel through which British Schools and Institutes overseas were financed. Additional funds for research awards were provided by the University Grants Committee, and the Academy increasingly began to take on the role of a *de facto* Humanities Research Council. Between 1962 and 1967, the Academy's President was Lord Robbins; it was his report on higher education, published in 1963, that prompted a major expansion in the number of British universities, and this in turn led to a further growth in the Academy, as the humanities and social sciences thrived on the new campuses that had come into being by the late 1960s. To take account of this, the maximum number of Fellows (counting only those up to the age of 72) was raised to 300 in 1965, and nine years later it was increased again to 350, while the nine subject Sections in existence at the end of the First World War had been expanded to fourteen by 1969. One of them, established in 1950, was in the history of art, and Anthony Blunt was immediately elected to it. He later served as a Vice-President, was regarded as a 'real Academy grandee', and was talked of in some quarters as a possible future President.[20]

***

Blunt had been born in a Bournemouth vicarage in 1907 to un-moneyed but devout and well-connected parents.[21] His clergyman father was a kinsman of the poet and libertine Wilfrid Scawen Blunt of Crabbet Park in West Sussex, who was a broad-acred landowner, but also a strident critic of British rule in India, Egypt and Ireland,

Burlington House was the home of the British Academy from 1969 to 1982.

interview, 18 February 2018.

[19] Wheeler, *British Academy, 1949-1968*, p. 5.

[20] Kenyon, *British Academy*, p. 34; Peter Brown, interview, 18 February 2018.

[21] P. Kidson, 'Anthony Frederick Blunt, 1907-1983', *Biographical Memoirs of Fellows of the British Academy*, xiii (2014), pp. 19-39; Carter, *Anthony Blunt*; idem, entry on Blunt in the *Oxford Dictorionary of National Biography* (*ODNB*). A. Chastel, 'Obituary: Anthony Blunt, Art Historian (1907-1983)', *Burlington Magazine*, September 1983, pp. 546-49.

and thus widely regarded as a traitor to his class and his country. His mother's family were distantly related to the Earls of Strathmore, from whom was descended the future Queen Mother, and they were friends with the Duke and Duchess of Teck, who lived close by, and whose daughter would become Queen Mary.[22] Anthony Blunt grew up in Paris, where his father became chaplain to the British embassy, and where he acquired a lasting enthusiasm for French art and architecture, and demonstrated great skill in foreign languages. He was sent to school at Marlborough College, and in 1926 won a scholarship to Trinity College, Cambridge, where he switched from mathematics to modern languages, in which he gained a double first. In 1932, he was elected a Fellow of Trinity, on the strength of a dissertation on artistic theory in France and Italy during the Renaissance and seventeenth century. Blunt remained a Fellow until 1937, and by then was also writing regularly for the *Spectator* as its art critic. His social life blossomed in Cambridge, where he was befriended by Victor, third Lord Rothschild, who in 1933 gave him £100 so he could acquire the painting *Eliezer and Rebecca* by Nicholas Poussin, the artist with whom Blunt would be most closely identified throughout his professional life.[23] While an undergraduate, he had been invited to join the Apostles, the most secretive and exclusive of all Cambridge societies, which valued freedom of thought and expression, and prized loyalty to friends above all. Like Blunt, an influential minority of Apostles were gay, which enjoined further secrecy since at that time homosexual acts in Britain were illegal.[24]

Throughout the 1930s, Blunt travelled regularly to Europe, for research and recreation, including Russia, and from early in the decade, he had taken an interest in Marxism. This was largely thanks to the influence of one of his friends, the charismatic, scandalous and outrageous Guy Burgess. A fellow Apostle, Burgess had recently converted to Communism in the belief that this was the only way of fighting Fascism, since the democracies of Britain and France were too enfeebled and infirm of purpose to do so. One result was that Blunt's art reviews became increasingly dogmatic and in thrall to social realism, including a strident attack on Picasso's *Guernica* for being insufficiently inflected by Communist theory and thought.[25] A second consequence was that in the spring of 1937, Burgess introduced Blunt to Theo Maly, a Hungarian-born agent of the Russian NKVD, which was the forerunner of the KGB. Maly asked Blunt to become a 'talent spotter', looking out for bright undergraduates who might be willing to work clandestinely for the Communist cause. Blunt duly recruited two young men, Michael Straight and Leo Long, and sized up a third, John Cairncross.[26] But in the summer of 1937, the entire London-based NKVD operation was closed down and recalled to Moscow, having been caught up in Stalin's latest purge. Like many others, Blunt was undeniably captivated by Burgess. But like Wilfrid Scawen Blunt, he also enjoyed being simultaneously an insider and a rebel, and his membership of the Apostles and his sexuality may have contributed to his liking and need for concealment and secrecy. Communism seemed to provide a way of understanding both art and the world, and he suffered no obvious pangs of conscience when, in 1939, the Soviet-Nazi pact destroyed any hopes that supporting Russia was the only way of confronting and defeating Fascism. By then, Blunt had left Cambridge, and had begun work at the recently-established Warburg Institute in London, where he encountered a generation of émigré Jewish scholars who greatly influenced his later work as an art historian.

Soon after the Second World War broke out, Blunt was recruited to MI5, like many clever academics, in his case with the help of his friend Lord Rothschild. There were some official concerns about his known left-leaning sympathies, but in the febrile wartime atmosphere, where corners had to be cut and jobs had to be rapidly filled, Blunt's appointment eventually went through.[27] He had had no connections with Moscow since 1937, having been 'dormant' thereafter, but in December 1940, by which time the NKVD was back in London, it re-established contact with him. Blunt's main task was to gather information for Russia about foreign embassies in the capital by planting agents and clandestinely opening diplomatic bags. But since he went out of his way to know every area of MI5's work, including the breaking of German military codes being undertaken at Bletchley Park, he was able to pass 1,771 documents to his Soviet spymasters before the war ended. For the first six months of 1941, Russia remained allied to Germany, and was an enemy of Britain; thereafter, Russia and Britain were on the same side, though it was scarcely an amicable alliance. Blunt's secret activities were thus initially unpatriotic and subsequently unwise, although it is still unclear whether his actions led to the deaths of British agents or allied personnel, and if so, how many.[28] The NKVD was so inefficient that many of the documents Blunt passed on were never

[22] D. Cannadine, *The Decline and Fall of the British Aristocracy* (London, 1990), pp. 382, 512, 536-38; G. Glaeys, 'The "left" and the critique of empire c.1865-1900: three roots of humanitarian foreign policy', in D. Bell (ed.), *Victorian Visions of the Global Order: Empire and International Relations in Nineteenth-Century Political Thought* (Cambridge, 2007), pp. 244-51. For Blunt's own well-developed sense of social hierarchy see A. Blunt, 'A Note on the Use of Hereditary Titles' in *Treasures from Chatsworth: The Devonshire Inheritance* (Washington DC, 1979), p. 24.

[23] K. Rose, *Elusive Rothschild: the Life of Victor, Third Baron* (London, 2003), pp. 47, 104. Lord Rothschild could not recall, many years later, whether the sum was £100 or £80. Either way, it would turn out to be an exceptionally good investment for Blunt.

[24] R. Skidelsky, *John Maynard Keynes*, vol. ii, *The Economist as Saviour, 1920-1937* (London, 1992), pp. 293, 514-17

[25] Cf. his later and very different views on the subject in A. Blunt, *Picasso's 'Guernica'* (New York, 1969).

[26] Andrew, *Defence of the Realm*, pp. 172-4.

[27] Rose, *Elusive Rothschild*, pp. 231-3; Andrew, *Defence of the Realm*, p. 269.

[28] For differing views, see Annan, *Our Age*, p. 330; R. Davenport-Hines, *Enemies Within: Communists, the Cambridge Spies and the Making of Modern Britain* (London, 2018), pp. 526-7; BM Add MS 88902/1: Blunt, unpublished handwritten memoir [c.1982], ff. 122-3.

translated, and from 1942, Russian intelligence became so suspicious of Blunt and his friends Burgess and Philby that it seriously considered having them assassinated.[29] At the end of the war, Blunt left MI5 to resume his professional avocations; but he passed on MI5 gossip to Moscow via his controller, Yuri Modin, and in 1951 he tipped off Burgess and Maclean that the British security services were closing in, which certainly precipitated their flight.[30]

Before the Second World War broke out, Blunt had already been producing articles on a wide range of art-historical subjects. In 1940 he published his revised Trinity fellowship dissertation as *Artistic Theory in Italy, 1450-1600*, dedicated to Guy Burgess, and this was followed by a book on the French architect Francois Mansart, and a catalogue of the French drawings in the Royal Collection at Windsor.[31] With the end of the war, Blunt's career took off, as he was appointed Surveyor of the King's Pictures in 1945, and two years later he became Director of the Courtauld Institute.[32] At Windsor and Buckingham Palace, he professionalised the care of the Royal Collection, bringing in restorers and academics, and oversaw the opening of the Queen's Gallery in 1962. At the Courtauld, he was a brilliant and inspirational teacher, numbering among his students such luminaries as Nicholas Serota, Oliver Millar, Anita Brookner, Alan Bowness, John Shearman and Neil MacGregor, and he did more than anyone else to establish art history as a serious academic discipline in post-war British universities. Among Blunt's many books was a masterly survey of *Art and Architecture in France, 1500-1700* (1953), he curated a Poussin exhibition at the Louvre in 1960, and seven years later published his landmark – if controversial – monograph on the artist.[33] By then, Blunt was at the height of his powers and renown, acknowledged by the presentation of a *Festschrift*, edited by his friend Ellis Waterhouse, entitled *Studies in Renaissance and Baroque Art presented to Anthony Blunt on his sixtieth birthday* (1967). He was the first picture adviser to the National Trust, curated exhibitions at the Royal Academy, sat on almost every influential national art committee, and lectured widely in Europe and America. Accordingly, when Blunt retired from his Surveyor-ship of the Queen's Pictures in 1972, and from the Courtauld in 1974, he did so full of years and, apparently, full of honours, too.

[29] Andrew, *Defence of the Realm*, pp. 270-2, 289-92, 420.
[30] Y. Modin, *My Five Cambridge Friends* (London, 1994), pp.79-93, 270-86.
[31] A. Blunt, *Artistic Theory in Italy, 1450-1600* (Oxford, 1940); idem, *Francois Mansart and the Origins of French Classical Architecture* (London, 1941); idem, *The French Drawings in the Collection of His Majesty the King at Windsor Castle* (Oxford, 1945).
[32] A. Blunt, 'Samuel Courtauld as Collector and Benefactor', in D. Cooper (ed.), *The Courtauld Collection: a catalogue and introduction* (London, 1954), pp. 1-76.
[33] A. Blunt, *Nicholas Poussin* (London, 1967). For the protracted and acrimonious disagreements between Blunt and Denis Mahon, see Carter, *Anthony Blunt*, pp. 421-35.

Yet throughout this time, Blunt was under constant strain since he was always at risk of exposure as a former spy. In the aftermath of the defection of Burgess and Maclean, he was regularly but vainly interrogated by the British security services, even though there was much gossip at the Courtauld and beyond, speculating that he was hiding many guilty secrets. This may explain why the energetic socialite and charming party giver of the 1930s had metamorphosed into the cold, aloof, distant, arrogant professor of the 1950s and 1960s, and why Blunt refused most invitations to bring art history to a broader public audience in the way that Kenneth Clark would do with such panache and success. He drank heavily, was on deep medication, was hospitalised with exhaustion in 1945, and suffered an attack of Bell's palsy in 1953. Eleven years later, Michael Straight, who had been offered a top job in Washington DC, admitted to the FBI that he had been recruited to the Communist cause by Blunt before the Second World War, and was prepared to testify against him. Although this would still be only the word of one person against another, Straight's admission, which the FBI eventually passed on, gave MI5 the ammunition it had so long lacked. Confronted with this evidence, Blunt finally confessed, having been guaranteed immunity from prosecution in exchange for telling everything he knew (which did not turn out to be much).[34] The higher echelons of the security services were aware of this deal, as were the law officers of the government, successive Home Secretaries, the monarch's private secretary, and Queen Elizabeth II herself, which no doubt explains why, on his retirement as the surveyor of the sovereign's pictures, Blunt had not been advanced from KCVO to GCVO, and nor had he been recognised by the state when he relinquished the Directorship of the Courtauld, as might in both cases have otherwise been expected.[35]

***

One person who knew nothing of these matters was the pre-eminent Greek scholar Sir Kenneth Dover, who had succeeded Sir Isaiah Berlin as President of the British Academy in 1978, the year before Thatcher's bombshell revelations.[36] Like Blunt, Dover was precociously clever, but his background and upbringing had been very different. He was born in suburban London in 1920, his father was a minor civil servant in the Ministry of Transport, and his mother was the daughter of two schoolteachers. From an early

[34] Andrew, *Defence of the Realm*, pp. 436-7.
[35] D.R. Thorpe (ed.), *Who Loses, Who Wins: The Journals of Kenneth Rose*, vol. ii, *1979-2014* (London, 2019), pp. 222, 339; Carter, *Anthony Blunt*, pp. 448-9.
[36] D.A. Russell and F.S. Halliwell, 'Kenneth James Dover, 1920-2010', *Biographical Memoirs of Fellows of the British Academy*, xi (2012), pp. 153-75; P.G.Adamson, entry on Dover in *ODNB*; K. Dover, *Marginal Comment: A Memoir* (London, 1994).

age Dover was a tireless reader, and in 1932 he won a scholarship to St Paul's School, which Berlin had failed to garner several years earlier. The classics teaching was of the highest quality, and Dover soon demonstrated exceptional talents in ancient Greek literature and history (though he was never much interested in Greek philosophy).[37] He was also exploring the grammar of western Pacific languages, he became fascinated by issues of belief and morality, he discovered a powerfully rationalistic need to subject his own experiences and those of others to critical scrutiny, and he began to cultivate a Stoic reserve about his own emotions. He already distrusted feelings, was committed to reason and truth, was limited in his imaginative insights into others, and was inclined to priggishness.[38] In October 1938 Dover won an open scholarship to Balliol College, Oxford, where he enjoyed a glittering academic career, taking firsts in mods and greats, and winning numerous university prizes. His studies were interrupted by war service, which was very different from Blunt's, in the Royal Artillery in the western desert and in Italy, where he was mentioned in dispatches. Dover married in the same year he eventually graduated, and was elected a tutorial fellow of Balliol in 1948, where he stayed for seven years, publishing articles of distinctive precision and inimitable finesse on Greek literary and historical topics.

But Dover was not wholly happy as a Fellow of Balliol, and against the advice of several colleagues, he accepted the chair of Greek at the University of St Andrews in 1955, where he remained until 1976, declining the offer of the Regius Professorship of Greek at Oxford in 1969, and later being turned down for the same chair in Cambridge. Dover's lengthy stay at St Andrews was both personally congenial and academically creative. He soon became captivated by the beauty of the surrounding Scottish countryside, where he and his wife set up what they came to regard as their permanent home, and Dover established an international reputation as the outstanding Hellenist of his generation, bringing to successful fruition several projects on which he had begun work while at Oxford. Among his many publications were the highly technical *Greek Word Order* (1960), testimony to his interest in language and syntax; an edition of Aristophanes's *Clouds* (1968), whose earthy realism and intricate poetic virtuosity Dover greatly admired; *Lysias and the Corpus Lysiacum* (1968), exploring the role of speechwriters in the system of forensic oratory in classical Athens; a co-authored volume of the *Historical Commentary on Thucydides* (1970), a writer with whose fastidious rationality and austere intelligence Dover undoubtedly felt a close affinity; and *Greek Popular Morality* (1974), a pioneering attempt to discover the mentality of ordinary Greeks, as (perhaps) revealed in the canonical texts of oratory and comedy. Yet even as he was pursuing this intense schedule of research and publication, Dover was a conscientious teacher, who built up the Greek Department at St Andrews, and he was an active figure in the senior administration of the university, twice serving as dean of arts, in 1960-63 and 1973-75. He also played a wider part in the affairs of his subject, co-editing the *Classical Quarterly* (1962-68), and serving as President of the Hellenic Society (1971-74) and of the Classical Association (1975).

Sir Kenneth Dover, President of the British Academy at the time of the Blunt affair.

[37] M. Ignatieff, *Isaiah Berlin: A Life* (New York, 1999), p. 40.

[38] Dover, *Marginal Comment*, pp. 1-4; Keith Thomas interview, 4 November 2019.

Dover had been elected a Fellow of the British Academy in 1966, and ten years later, he returned to Oxford as president of Corpus Christi College, where he was a clear-headed administrator, naively expecting all Fellows to be as rational and reasonable as he was in the conduct of business. He oversaw the admission of the first female undergraduates, was the only head of an Oxford college to vote against the proposal to confer an honorary degree on Margaret Thatcher, and chaired a university committee which in 1983 would propose major reforms of the Oxford admissions system, including the abolition of entrance scholarships. Dover's main academic work during these years was a study of homosexuality in the ancient Greek world, initially sparked by his appreciation of the homoerotic sensibility of the *Symposium*, the only work of Plato's for which he felt much sympathy, and of which he produced an edition in 1980. Two years earlier, Dover had published the book for which he became best known, and which reached his largest audience, namely *Greek Homosexuality*. The times were propitious: in 1967, homosexual acts between consenting adults in private who were over the age of twenty-one had been de-criminalised in the United Kingdom; two years later the Gay Liberation Front was established in the United States, which began to sponsor Gay Pride marches in American cities. These developments stimulated academic research into the history of same-sex relationships, and Dover's book was both pioneering and controversial. Drawing on the explicit images in Hellenic vase-painting, and the vulgar humour of classical Athenian comedy, he wrote of Greek homosexuality with a clinical explicitness and a direct candour, especially concerning the significance and meaning of anal penetration, which was the very antithesis of the euphemisms and evasions that had characterised earlier writings on the subject.[39]

In 1977, Dover was knighted for services to scholarship, and the following year he was elected President of the British Academy. He had been an active Fellow in his own Section, and had chaired a committee to 'watch over the possibilities of exploiting computers to contribute to the solution of literary problems,' but he accepted the Presidency reluctantly: 'Oh, *why* do people think I can do that sort of thing?', he wondered at the time. He disliked formal occasions, did not enjoy dressing up, and witty after-dinner speeches were not his forte. Dover's Presidential Addresses to the Annual General Meetings of the Academy were Olympian in tone and austere in language, and full of classical allusions which must have baffled many Fellows whose areas of expertise were very different from his own. 'If', he remarked in one of them, 'I seem to be speaking didactically, even reprovingly, please attribute this to the spirit of the *parabasis* which I have imbibed from Attic Old Comedy.'[40] During Dover's Presidency, the Academy fended off the cuts in public funding to which other institutions were subjected in the early years of Thatcher's governments, its research support activities were enlarged, and its international programmes were expanded in volume and geographical range. Dover also led the search to find new premises for the Academy, which had outgrown its cramped accommodation in Burlington House; this eventually resulted in the acquisition of a Decimus Burton villa on the outer circle of Regent's Park, set back from the end of a Nash terrace, which became the Academy's home and headquarters from 1982 to 1998.

But inevitably, the defining episode of Dover's presidency turned out to be the Blunt affair, and it took him completely by surprise. For many years, Blunt's spying activities had been well known, not only at Buckingham Palace and in some parts of Whitehall and Westminster, but also in some parts of Oxford University.[41] This was certainly the case at All Souls College, in part thanks to the writings and indiscretions of Goronwy Rees, a former Fellow, who had worked for MI6 in the aftermath of the Second World War, and who subsequently became Principal of the University College of Wales at Aberystwyth. In serious need of money by 1956, he wrote several articles in the *Sunday People* newspaper in March and April, for which he was paid £4,000, and which offered some teasing allusions to the identity of 'the Fourth Man'.[42] In 1972, Rees produced a memoir, *A Chapter of Accidents*, which featured Blunt in the guise of several different but unnamed individuals, and five years later he told *The Times* that the Fourth Man had been based in Cambridge and that his name began with B and had five letters.[43] But such knowledge had not seeped across the Oxford High Street as far as Corpus, which meant that Dover had no prior knowledge of the issue that would soon engulf the Academy in the greatest crisis of its existence. He had known Blunt since 1972, when he joined the Research Awards Committee of the Leverhulme Trust, although they were never more than acquaintances. Blunt was a cold fish, and Dover was priggish, so it is difficult to imagine that they would ever have got on. This may help explain why, when Thatcher unmasked Blunt, Dover was 'totally surprised'. But to begin with, he was not remotely concerned. 'The news', he later recalled, 'of his treachery, closely followed by the revocation of his knighthood, did not raise in my mind any question at all about the maintenance of his status as a Fellow of the British Academy.'[44]

***

[39] F.S. Halliwell, 'Foreword: The Book and its Author', in K.J. Dover, *Greek Homosexuality* (London, 2016 edn), pp. ix-xiv; Russell and Halliwell, 'Kenneth James Dover', pp. 161-4; Dover, *Marginal Comment*, pp. 111-18.

[40] Russell and Halliwell, 'Kenneth James Dover', pp. 168 and note 18; Dover, *Marginal Comment*, pp. 167-8.

[41] Thorpe, *Who Loses, Who Wins*, p. 222; Keith Thomas interview, 4 November 2019.

[42] Annan MS 5/1/180: R. Cobb to Lord Annan, Ides of March 1983. Keith Thomas interview, 4 November 2019.

[43] Annan, *Our Age*, pp. 308-9; Carter, *Anthony Blunt*, p. 469.

[44] Dover, *Marginal Comment*, p, 212.

Kenneth Dover (front row, first on the left) first came to know Anthony Blunt (back row, third from the right) in the early 1970s, when they served together on this Research Awards Advisory Committee of the Leverhulme Trust. Also pictured is Dame Helen Gardner FBA, who would have her own role in 'the Blunt affair'.

Yet beyond the confines of the British Academy and Corpus Christi College, Oxford, the public mood, and media interest, both immediately before and after Blunt's unmasking, was increasingly febrile, and Dover did not do (or understand) febrile. In September and October 1979, the serialisation of John Le Carré's novel, *Tinker, Tailor, Soldier, Spy* had been broadcast on television, vividly depicting a British secret service undergoing a collective crisis of identity and self-doubt, and riddled by moles and traitors, one of whom, Bill Haydon, appreciated fine art, had a homosexual side, and as played by Ian Richardson even exhibited some of Blunt's hauteur.[45] The following month, the journalist Andrew Boyle published *The Climate of Treason: Five Who Spied For Russia*, a deeply flawed book, full of inaccuracies and innuendos, which depended heavily on interviews with Goronwy Rees, but which attracted a great deal of attention.[46] In it, Boyle described the career of the 'Fourth Man', naming him as 'Maurice', a revealing pseudonym for those already in the know. Boyle was alluding to the novel of the same title by E.M. Forster, another Cambridge Apostle, who was also gay, and believed that loyalty to friends was more important than loyalty to country. On 8 November, *Private Eye* named Blunt as 'Maurice', and also outed him as gay, and seven days later, Thatcher made the first of her parliamentary announcements on the matter, officially confirming

[45] A. Sisman, *John Le Carré: The Biography* (London, 2015), p. 413.

[46] Davenport-Hines, *Enemies Within*, pp. 525-27. For one especially perceptive review of *The Climate of Treason*, see Noel Annan, 'All honourable men', *TLS*, 7 December 1979, pp. 83-5. See also Annan MS 5/1/873: Lord (Victor) Rothschild to Annan, 12 December 1979; 5/1/984, Hugh Trevor-Roper to Annan, 13 December 1979.

what *Private Eye* had claimed. Blunt went into hiding, but on 20 November, he held a press conference in the offices of *The Times*, before a deliberately restricted group of journalists, having been served a lunch of smoked trout, fruit salad, white wine, coffee and cigars, at which he claimed he 'bitterly regretted' what he had done, insisted he had 'acted according to my conscience', but realised he had been 'totally wrong.' The opulence of the meal, combined with what many regarded as his shifty and evasive answers, meant the occasion was a public relations disaster for Blunt.[47]

As a story that would both captivate and enrage the media, this could scarcely be surpassed (could even Le Carré have made *this* up?). For Blunt had not only been outed as the 'Fourth Man', but he had also been the most privileged and professionally successful of the 'Cambridge spies': well-educated, well-connected, honoured and esteemed, equally at ease in the groves of academe, the corridors of power, and the palaces of royalty, and the beneficiary of an immunity deal that to his critics had all the hallmarks of an establishment cover-up. And in addition to being a man who had betrayed his country, yet been exceptionally well treated and rewarded by it, Blunt was also gay (and while same-sex sex was no longer illegal in Britain by then, it was still widely regarded as being deviant, abnormal and perverted behaviour). 'Traitor at the Queen's Right Hand', thundered a headline in the *Daily Mail*; 'Treacherous Communist Poof', declared John Junor in the *Daily Express*; a 'pansy aesthete', sneered Malcolm Muggeridge in the *Evening Standard*.[48] Here, ironically, was a link to Dover of which neither he nor Blunt could have been aware. For in *Greek Homosexuality*, Dover had rightly noted that 'in modern popular humour, despite much of the evidence furnished by our everyday acquaintance with homosexual men, the homosexual stereotype is extremely persistent: a man of delicate features and slight physique, imitating women in his stance, gestures, movements and voice, and therefore appropriately denoted by such terms as "fairy" and "pansy".' But Dover's perceptive insight was scarcely to the point, in the light of such a media barrage, for immediately after Thatcher's un-masking of Blunt, he had endured his second Presidential 'surprise', in the form of a brief and determined letter from Professor J.H. ('Jack') Plumb FBA, the eminent historian and Master of Christ's College, Cambridge.[49] It was the beginning of what would soon become known, in the Academy and far beyond, as 'the Blunt affair'.

Professor Anthony Blunt outlining his role in the spy scandal, at a press conference at the offices of 'The Times', on 20 November 1979.
(Photo © Hulton-Deutsch Collection/Corbis via Getty Images.)

[47] Carter, *Anthony Blunt*, p. 481. For press reactions to Blunt's press conference, see *Sun*, *Daily Mirror*, *Daily Mail*, *Guardian*, *Daily Telegraph* and *The Times* itself, all 21 November 1979. A fellow art historian, Roy Strong, was equally censorious: 'Suave, condescending deviousness, no single word of regret, no expression of sorrow for having conceivably exposed the Queen to any embarrassment': *The Roy Strong Diaries, 1967-1987* (London, 1997), p. 246, entry for 28 November 1979.

[48] Andrew, *Defence of the Realm*, p. 706; Carter, *Anthony Blunt*, p. 475.

[49] Dover, *Greek Homosexuality*, p. 68; idem, *Marginal Comment*, p. 212.

Documentary narrative

On 15 November 1979, Prime Minister Margaret Thatcher revealed in the House of Commons that Anthony Blunt FBA had been a Soviet spy;[1] and it was announced that he would be stripped of his knighthood. The very next day, the historian J.H. ('Jack') Plumb FBA wrote to the President of the British Academy, Kenneth Dover, demanding that the Academy take 'immediate action' to remove Blunt from its Fellowship **[1]**.[2]

Professor J. H. Plumb FBA

1: J.H. Plumb to Kenneth Dover, 16 November 1979.

PROFESSOR J.H.PLUMB, F.B.A.

The Master's Lodge, Christ's College, Cambridge, CB2 3BU Telephone 67641

PRIVATE

16 November 1979

Dear Dover,

I hope that immediate action will be taken to expel Anthony Blunt from the Academy. I do not think we should harbour traitors.

Yours sincerely,

J. H. Plumb

Sir Kenneth Dover, PBA,
Corpus Christi College,
OXFORD OX1 4JF

By permission of the Trustees of the Estate of Sir John Plumb

[1] In 'Materials' (see above 'Note on the documents and sources', p. x), Dover admits that he was 'greatly surprised' by the revelation that Blunt had been a Soviet agent: he knew that Blunt's preferred aperitif was vodka, 'but I don't normally draw conclusions about people's politics from their taste in liquor'.

[2] Like Blunt, many Fellows of the Academy had worked in the the intelligence services during the Second World War, among them Plumb, who had been at Bletchley Park: see D. Cannadine, 'John Harold Plumb, 1911-2001', *Proceedings of the British Academy*, 124 (2004), p. 277.

Dover reveals in 'Materials' that he was taken aback by Plumb's letter, because the news of Blunt's treachery had not raised in his own mind any question about Blunt's Fellowship of the British Academy. He replied to Plumb **[2]**. Although he shared Plumb's sentiments about 'traitors', he had to point out that no 'immediate' action was possible: the Academy's Council could not, 'for *any* reason', expel a Fellow without referring the matter to the Annual General Meeting; and he also speculated that not all Fellows might be equally damning of Blunt's betrayal of his country. But in a postscript, he indicated that he would treat Plumb's note as a request to put the expulsion of Blunt on the agenda for the next meeting of the Academy's Council – of which Plumb was a member. On that same day, Dover wrote to the Academy's Secretary, John Carswell: 'I have been asked to put the expulsion of Blunt from the Academy (Stat.11(1)) on the agenda for the next Council meeting, and I think I must comply with this request, which is not an unreasonable one.'[3]

Plumb was not alone in raising the question of Blunt's continued Fellowship of the British Academy. On 21 November 1979, David Walker FBA, a professor of law, wrote to Carswell suggesting that the Council consider the case of Blunt: 'My personal view is that a person who is a self-confessed traitor to this country is not a fit and proper person to belong to a society which must seek to uphold and promote the standing and honour of the United Kingdom.' At a meeting of the Institute of Classical Studies on 23 November 1979, the archaeologist Grahame Clark FBA hinted to Carswell 'the possibility of proceeding against his fellowship of the Academy'. And at a Royal Society dinner on 30 November, Dover was approached by a group of scientists who 'in a jocular mood' asked him whether the Academy was going to expel Blunt. In December, Blunt was told that the Fellows of Trinity College, Cambridge, had voted to remove his Honorary Fellowship of the college if he did not resign voluntarily – which he did.

[3] 'Stat.11 (1)' refers to the Academy's Bye-Law 11 (1), under which the Blunt case would be taken forward.

2: Kenneth Dover to J.H. Plumb, 19 November 1979.

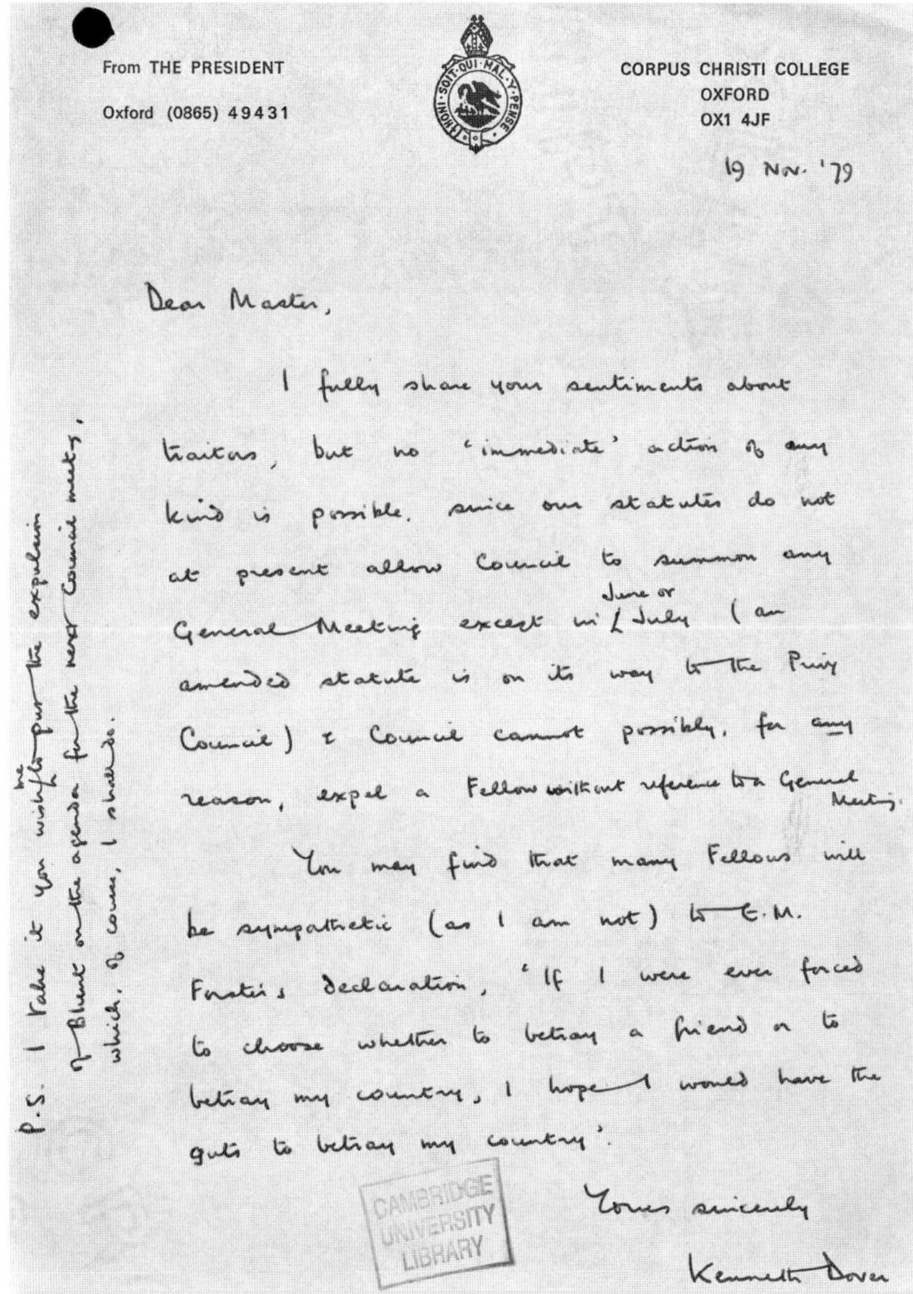
From THE PRESIDENT
Oxford (0865) 49431

CORPUS CHRISTI COLLEGE
OXFORD
OX1 4JF

19 Nov. '79

Dear Master,

I fully share your sentiments about traitors, but no 'immediate' action of any kind is possible, since our statutes do not at present allow Council to summon any General Meeting except in June or July (an amended statute is on its way to the Privy Council) & Council cannot possibly, for any reason, expel a Fellow without reference to a General Meeting.

You may find that many Fellows will be sympathetic (as I am not) to E.M. Forster's declaration, 'If I were ever forced to choose whether to betray a friend or to betray my country, I hope I would have the guts to betray my country'.

Yours sincerely

Kenneth Dover

P.S. I take it you wish to have the expulsion of Blunt on the agenda for the next Council meeting, which, of course, I shall do.

3: Hugh Trevor-Roper to Kenneth Dover, 9 January 1980.

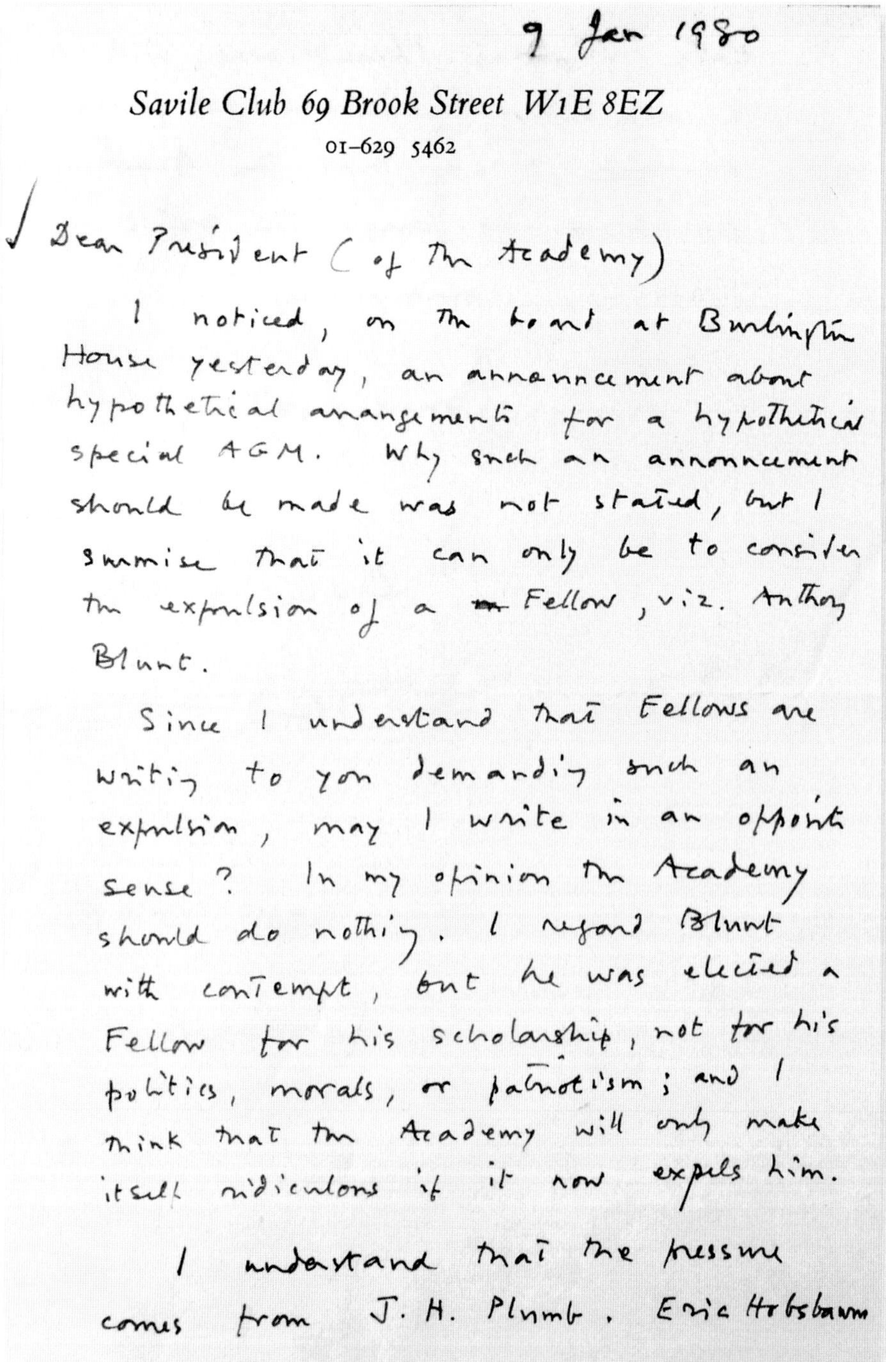

9 Jan 1980

Savile Club 69 Brook Street W1E 8EZ

01–629 5462

Dear President (of the Academy)

I noticed, on the board at Burlington House yesterday, an announcement about hypothetical arrangements for a hypothetical special AGM. Why such an announcement should be made was not stated, but I surmise that it can only be to consider the expulsion of a Fellow, viz. Anthony Blunt.

Since I understand that Fellows are writing to you demanding such an expulsion, may I write in an opposite sense? In my opinion the Academy should do nothing. I regard Blunt with contempt, but he was elected a Fellow for his scholarship, not for his politics, morals, or patriotism; and I think that the Academy will only make itself ridiculous if it now expels him.

I understand that the pressure comes from J. H. Plumb. Eric Hobsbawm

However, opinions on the Blunt affair were far from uniform. In January 1980, Dover received a letter from the historian Hugh Trevor-Roper FBA (recently ennobled as Lord Dacre of Glanton) **[3]**.[4] Trevor-Roper said he regarded Blunt 'with contempt'; but Blunt had been 'elected a Fellow for his scholarship, not for his politics, morals, or patriotism', and the Academy would make itself 'ridiculous' if it now expelled him. He was also caustic about the motivations of Plumb, one of the 'old Cambridge communists', for pursuing Blunt. As further evidence that views were varied, Carswell reported a rumour that the classicist Roger Mynors FBA might resign from the Academy if Blunt were expelled.

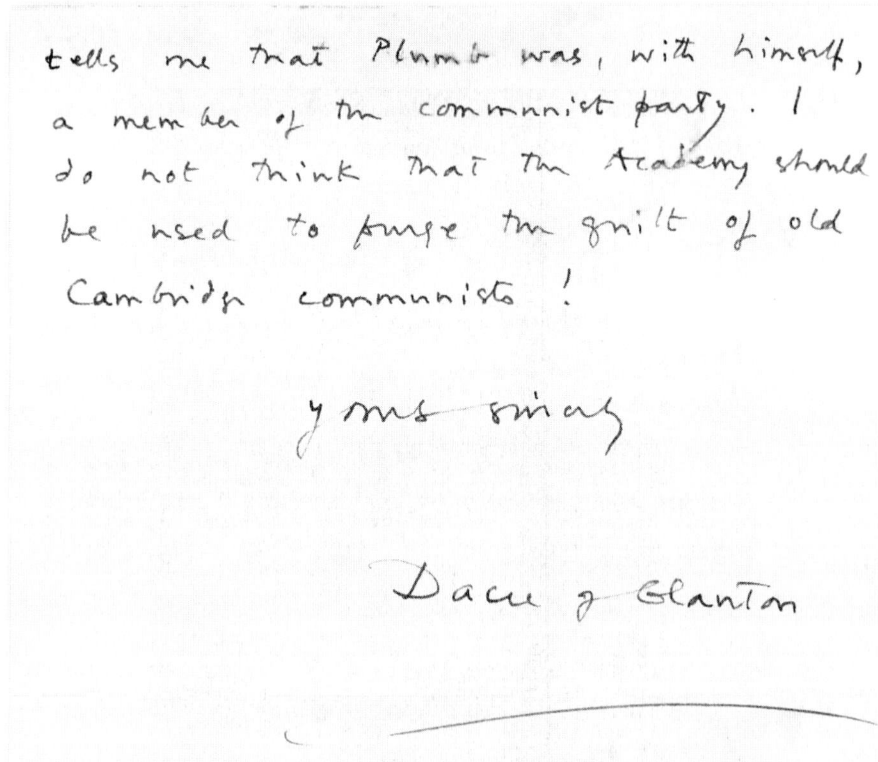

tells me that Plumb was, with himself, a member of the communist party. I do not think that the Academy should be used to purge the guilt of old Cambridge communists!

Yours sincerely

Dacre of Glanton

By permission of Peters Fraser & Dunlop on behalf of the Estate of Lord Dacre of Glanton

[4] At the start of his letter, Trevor-Roper refers to a notice he had seen about the calling of a special General Meeting. In fact, this meeting had been called in order to approve proposed changes to the Academy's Charter and Bye-laws. So he was wrong to surmise that it was about the Blunt affair. Trevor-Roper had his own experience of intelligence work during the war: see B. Worden, 'Hugh Redwald Trevor-Roper, 1914-2003', *Proceedings of the British Academy*, 150 (2008), p. 252.

In January 1980, the Academy held its customary meetings of 'Sections' (the subject groupings of Fellows). A letter to Dover from the art historian William Watson FBA reported opinions on the Blunt affair that had been expressed informally by a number of Fellows in Section 11, the Section for the History of Art – of which Blunt was a member **[4]**.[5] Watson had not raised the issue in the meeting itself in his capacity as chair of the Section, but Fellows had volunteered their thoughts to him both before and afterwards. The predominant view was that the Academy should not 'act outside its brief' to expel Blunt or place him in a position where he would feel obliged to resign: 'the award of our Fellowship is made for contribution to knowledge', and 'this character of it must be clearly preserved'.

Professor William Watson FBA

[5] During the Second World War, Watson served in the Intelligence Corps in North Africa (intercepting German messages for Bletchley), Italy, and India: see R. Scott, 'William Watson, 1917-2007', *Proceedings of the British Academy*, 161 (2009), p. 365.

4: William Watson to Kenneth Dover, 7 February 1980.

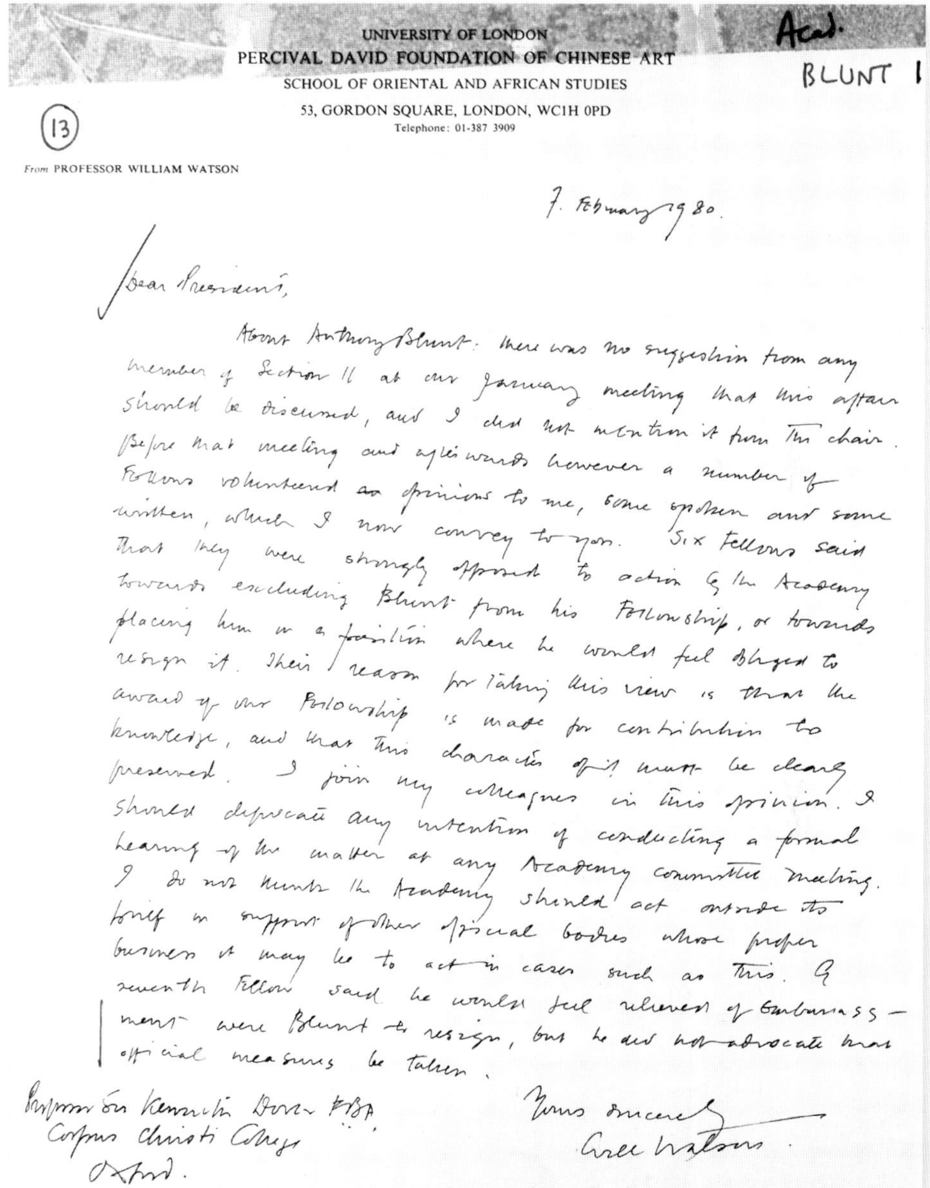

UNIVERSITY OF LONDON
PERCIVAL DAVID FOUNDATION OF CHINESE ART
SCHOOL OF ORIENTAL AND AFRICAN STUDIES
53, GORDON SQUARE, LONDON, WC1H 0PD
Telephone: 01-387 3909

Acad.
BLUNT I

(13)

From PROFESSOR WILLIAM WATSON

7. February 1980.

Dear President,

About Anthony Blunt: there was no suggestion from any member of Section 11 at our January meeting that this affair should be discussed, and I did not mention it from the chair. Before that meeting and afterwards however a number of Fellows volunteered opinions to me, some spoken and some written, which I now convey to you. Six Fellows said that they were strongly opposed to action by the Academy towards excluding Blunt from his Fellowship, or towards placing him in a position where he would feel obliged to resign it. Their reason for taking this view is that the award of our Fellowship is made for contribution to knowledge, and that this character of it must be clearly preserved. I join my colleagues in this opinion. I should deprecate any intention of conducting a formal hearing of the matter at any Academy committee meeting. I do not think the Academy should act outside its brief in support of other official bodies whose proper business it may be to act in cases such as this. A seventh Fellow said he would feel relieved of embarrassment were Blunt to resign, but he did not advocate that official measures be taken.

Yours sincerely
W. Watson.

Professor Sir Kenneth Dover FBA
Corpus Christi College
Oxford.

The first opportunity the Academy's Council had to discuss the Blunt affair was at its meeting on 15 February 1980. These gatherings took place in the Secretary's room, around what had once been Mortimer Wheeler's dining table. Peter Brown, then the Academy's Deputy Secretary, describes the setting as 'a very tight squeeze, very intimate and highly charged; you really were in somebody's face when you spoke.'[6] But he also recalls that all of Council's discussions of the Blunt case were 'the most impressive piece of intellectual firepower I've ever experienced … everybody spoke and the reasons given for the lines that they took were very powerful … nearly everyone had a different slant.'

At the Council meeting, the agenda included Plumb's proposal that Blunt should be expelled under Bye-Law 11. British Academy Bye-Law 11 (1) stated that 'If the Council so recommends the Fellows at an Annual General Meeting may remove the name of a person from the list of Fellows on the ground that he or she is not a fit and proper person to be a Fellow, and thereupon he or she will cease to be a Fellow'. Paragraph (2) stipulated that 'A Fellow liable to expulsion shall have the right to be heard before the Council in his or her own defence.'

In 'Materials', Dover describes the mood of the meeting as calm: 'everyone spoke deliberately … There was no rhetoric and no heat; Peter Brown told me afterwards that he thought the issue had shown Council at its best.' Carswell recalled that, during the discussion, it soon became clear that Council was almost evenly divided between those who thought Blunt should be expelled and those who didn't.[7] Of the members who were against expulsion, there were two main camps: 'those who showed some tender-heartedness towards Blunt personally (e.g. arguing that his offences were committed many years ago, that he was an old man, that he had suffered enough) and those who condemned his behaviour and character, but nevertheless did not consider expulsion was a proper step for a non-scholarly offence.' When everyone had had their say and the discussion came to a natural close, Dover put Plumb's motion to the vote.

Other than Dover (who did not vote), there were 16 members present who were eligible to vote.[8] The Council Minutes **[5]** note that eight members voted for Blunt's expulsion and seven voted against it – making a total of 15 votes cast. In 'Materials', Dover states that 'Nine members of Council voted for a recommendation to expel Blunt, and eight against' – making a total of 17 votes cast. Although this discrepancy is not accounted for, the result was not in doubt.

[6] Peter Brown interview, 12 February 2018. Mortimer Wheeler had been the Academy's Secretary 1949-1968.

[7] John Carswell, as the Academy's Secretary, is listed in the Minutes as attending the Council meetings; but as an Academy employee rather than a Fellow, he was not a member of Council, and though he certainly had views about Blunt, he was not himself able to vote on the issue.

[8] At that time, the Academy's Publications Secretary – then the historian J. Michael Wallace-Hadrill – was invited to Council meetings, but was not a full member entitled to vote; Wallace-Hadrill had in fact served in MI6 during the war, working at one point under Kim Philby: see I. Wood, 'John Michael Wallace-Hadrill, 1916-1985', *Proceedings of the British Academy*, 124 (2004), pp. 334-5. It may be noted that other Council members round that table had their own experiences of intelligence work in the war: like Plumb, the archaeologist John Evans had also served at Bletchley Park: see C. Renfrew, 'John Davies Evans, 1925-2011', *Biographical Memoirs of Fellows of the British Academy*, xiv (2015), p. 142.

Expulsion **11.** (*1*) **If the Council so recommends the Fellows at an Annual General Meeting may remove the name of a person from the list of Fellows on the ground that he or she is not a fit and proper person to be a Fellow, and thereupon he or she will cease to be a Fellow.**

(*2*) **A Fellow liable to expulsion shall have the right to be heard before the Council in his or her own defence.**

Bye-Law 11 from 'The British Academy Directory' (July 1979)

Professor J. Michael Wallace-Hadrill FBA

5: Minutes of the meeting of Council, 15 February 1980 [extracts]

Council Minutes 1/80

THE BRITISH ACADEMY

MEETING OF COUNCIL

Friday 15 February 1980

PRESENT
Sir Kenneth Dover (President)
Professor L.J. Austin
Professor A.J. Brown
The Revd. Professor G.B. Caird
The Revd. Professor W.O. Chadwick
Professor J.A. Crook
Professor R.H.C. Davis
Professor J.D. Evans
Professor M.B. Hesse
Professor M.E. Howard
Professor S. Körner
Professor F.S.L. Lyons
Professor J.H. Plumb
Professor C.R. Quirk
Professor E. Ullendorff
Mr. J.P. Carswell (Secretary)
Professor E.W. Handley (Foreign Secretary)
Professor P. Mathias (Treasurer)
Professor J.M. Wallace-Hadrill (Publications Secretary)

APOLOGIES
Professor T.B. Smith

7. PROPOSAL FOR COUNCIL ACTION UNDER BYE-LAW 11

The President explained the procedure laid down in the Bye-laws if the question of removing a Fellow on grounds of unsuitability were raised. At the present meeting discussion had to be limited to any proposal that proceedings should be initiated and no specific recommendation could be made until the Fellow who might be the subject of it had been/ heard by Council. Professor J.H. Plumb then moved that Council should proceed under the Bye-law against Professor Anthony Blunt. After discussion, in which most members of the Council spoke, Professor Plumb's motion was put to the vote. 8 members voted for it and 7 against. The President did not vote. The President declared the motion carried and said that he would write to Professor Blunt in accordance with the Bye-law inviting him to be present when Council met in March.

/ given the opportunity of being

After the meeting, the two Vice-Presidents, the historians Michael Howard FBA and Owen Chadwick FBA, asked Dover which way he would have voted; 'I told them I would have voted for expulsion'. However, Dover believed that the arguments put forward at the meeting in favour of expulsion were poor, and he was surprised that what he called 'the real charge' against Blunt was not mentioned. For Dover, the fact that Blunt had gone against the objects of the Academy should have been the real charge against him: 'he had worked for the victory of a totalitarian government profoundly hostile to the spirit of free enquiry necessary for scholarship'.

Professor Michael Howard CBE MC FBA

The Revd Professor Owen Chadwick FBA

The fact that the Blunt question had been discussed at the Council meeting was leaked to the *Sunday Telegraph*. Dover was approached for a comment but offered none, although he did his best to keep the conversation reasonable and friendly: 'Unwise to antagonise journalists *praeter necessitatem*'. On reading the piece when it appeared on 17 February **[6]**, Dover thought that the last two paragraphs – about the Academy being a body in receipt of government funding, and about parallel events within the University of London where a few days earlier Blunt had *not* been stripped of his Emeritus Professorship – were 'off the point'. He commented: 'the "duty to the public" line played a much smaller role than the line of moral revulsion at the meeting, and no time was spent on discussion of the London University decision.'

Dover wrote to Blunt to inform him that the Academy's Council had discussed a proposal that his name 'be removed from the list of Fellows', and to give him the opportunity to exercise his right 'to be heard in your own defence' at the next meeting of the Council, in March. Though at least one member of Council suspected Plumb as the source of the *Sunday Telegraph* article,[9] Dover added a postscript asserting that the story could not have derived from anyone who had attended the Council meeting **[7]**.

In his reply **[8]**, Blunt said that he didn't think any purpose would be served by attending the Council meeting to speak in his own defence, 'as I have nothing to add to what I have already said' (at the press conference held in the offices of *The Times*), other than to restate his regrets – 'which I am frequently accused of not having expressed'.

[9] A.J.P. Taylor MS 1/3: Michael Howard to A.J.P. Taylor FBA, 18 February 1980, presumed that the source of the leak was J.H. Plumb.

6: *Sunday Telegraph* article, 17 February 1980.

Blunt may be stripped of Academy honour

3903

By CHARLES LAURENCE

THE Council of the British Academy, the academic body for arts and humanities, has raised the possibility of stripping Professor Anthony Blunt, the traitor, of his fellowship of the Academy, a prized honour.

Sir Kenneth Dover

The Council discussed the matter at a meeting at its headquarters at Burlington House, Piccadilly, on Friday.

In the chair was Sir Kenneth Dover, President of the Academy, who is also President of Corpus Christi College, [illegible]

It is now expected that the Academy members will be asked at their annual meeting in July either to call for Professor Blunt's resignation or to expel him.

The Council has no powers itself to expel Professor Blunt, only to make a recommendation to the annual meeting. It is understood that the prevailing attitude on Friday was that Professor Blunt should have resigned his fellowship after he was exposed by Mrs Thatcher as the "fourth man" in the Burgess-Maclean-Philby spy ring.

Grants given

The British Academy performs the same function for the arts and humanities as the better-known Royal Society does for the sciences. It is made up of senior academics.

The Academy distributes about £1,000,000 a year in Government grants for advanced research and bestows fellowships on academics who have made a major contribution in their field.

Sir Kenneth Dover refused to comment on Friday's meeting.

It is understood that the council members took the attitude that as a national body, supported by the Government and distributing public money for research, they had a duty to the public where Professor Blunt was concerned.

They dismissed the precedent set last week by London University, which decided against stripping Professor Blunt of his Emeritus Professorship, conferred on him in 1974

7: Kenneth Dover to Anthony Blunt, 16-17 February 1980.

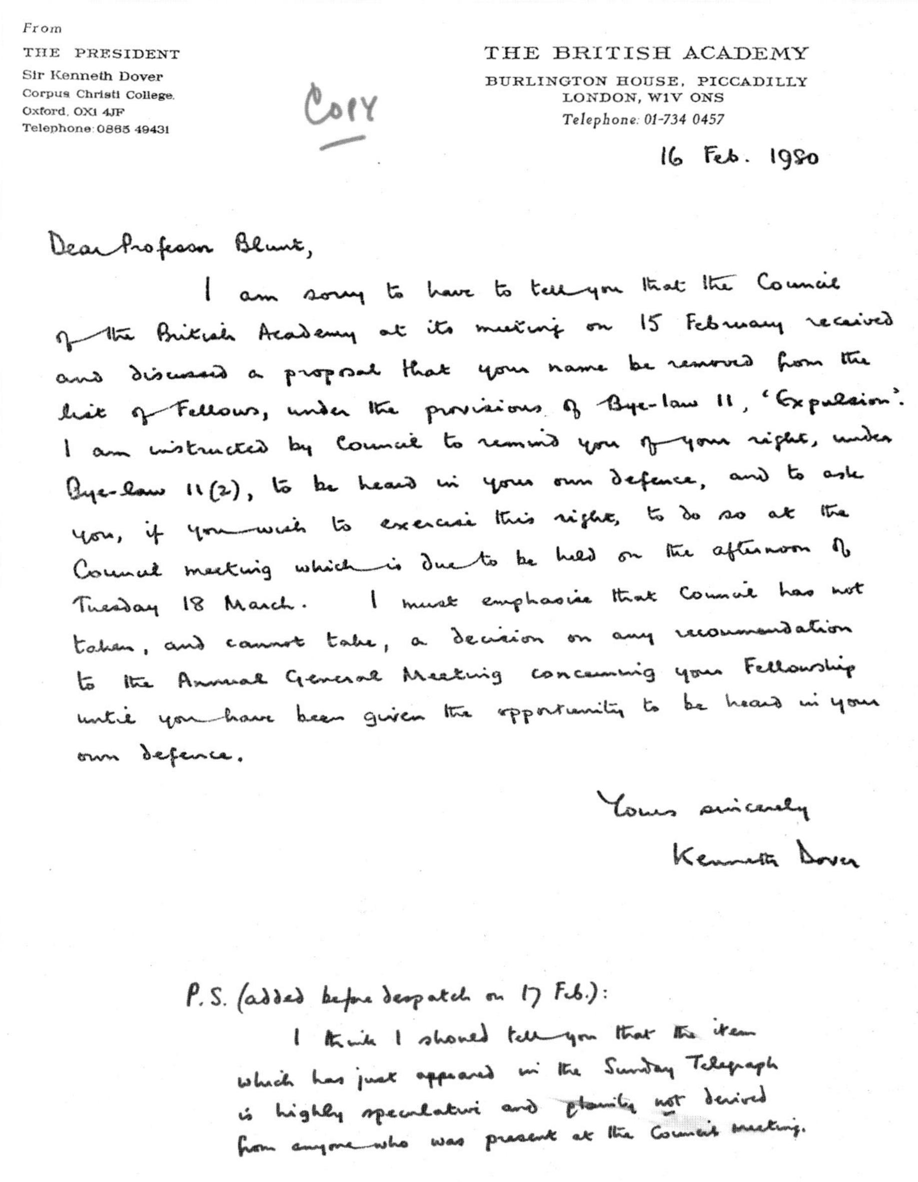

From
THE PRESIDENT
Sir Kenneth Dover
Corpus Christi College,
Oxford, OX1 4JF
Telephone: 0865 49431

COPY

THE BRITISH ACADEMY
BURLINGTON HOUSE, PICCADILLY
LONDON, W1V ONS
Telephone: 01-734 0457

16 Feb. 1980

Dear Professor Blunt,

I am sorry to have to tell you that the Council of the British Academy at its meeting on 15 February received and discussed a proposal that your name be removed from the list of Fellows, under the provisions of Bye-law 11, 'Expulsion'. I am instructed by Council to remind you of your right, under Bye-law 11(2), to be heard in your own defence, and to ask you, if you wish to exercise this right, to do so at the Council meeting which is due to be held on the afternoon of Tuesday 18 March. I must emphasise that Council has not taken, and cannot take, a decision on any recommendation to the Annual General Meeting concerning your Fellowship until you have been given the opportunity to be heard in your own defence.

Yours sincerely

Kenneth Dover

P.S. (added before despatch on 17 Feb.):

I think I should tell you that the item which has just appeared in the Sunday Telegraph is highly speculative and ~~plainly~~ not derived from anyone who was present at the Council meeting.

8: Anthony Blunt to Kenneth Dover, 25 February 1980.

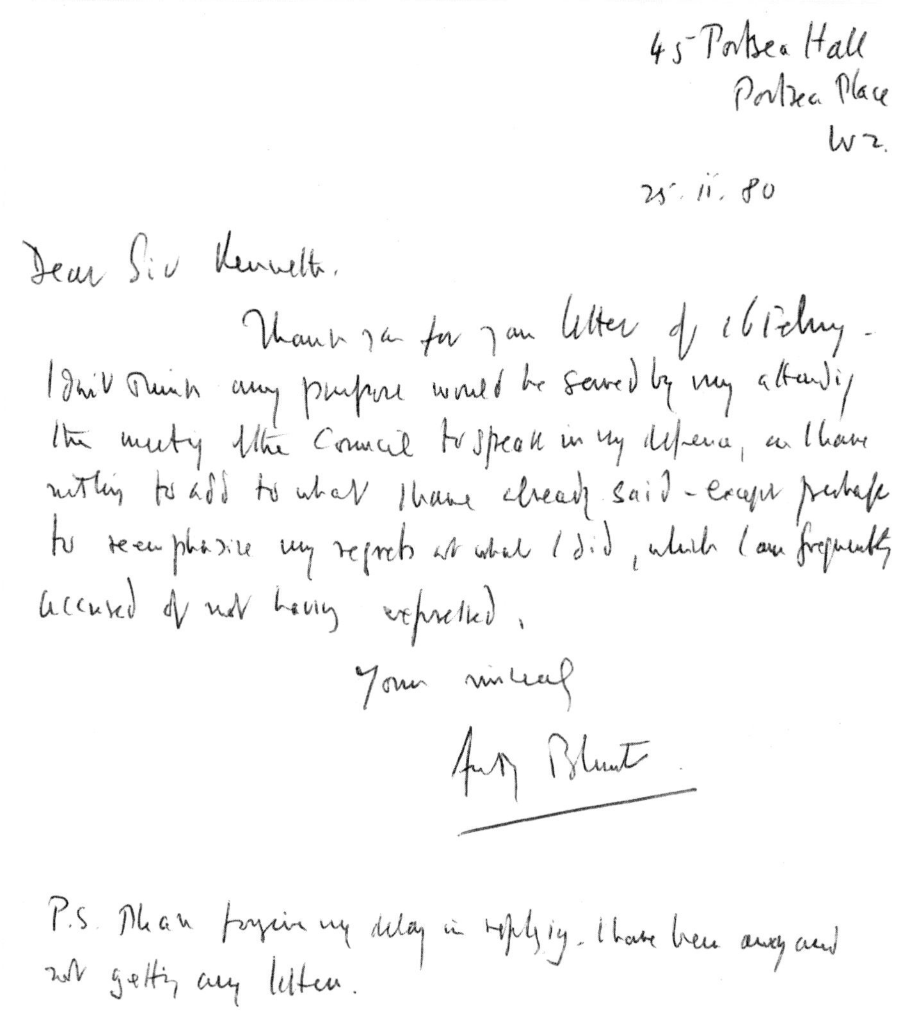

45 Portsea Hall
Portsea Place
W2.

25. ii. 80

Dear Sir Kenneth,

Thank you for your letter of 16 Feby. I don't think any purpose would be served by my attending the meeting of the Council to speak in my defence, as I have nothing to add to what I have already said – except perhaps to re-emphasize my regrets at what I did, which I am frequently accused of not having expressed.

Yours sincerely

Anthony Blunt

P.S. Please forgive my delay in replying. I have been away and not getting any letters.

After the February meeting of Council, Fellows of the Academy began writing to Dover, expressing disquiet at how the Blunt affair was developing. The philosopher Richard Wollheim **[9]** warned that 'the issue is bound to be enormously divisive.' If Blunt were expelled, or even if he were pressured to resign, a number of Fellows 'would be sufficiently upset by this result to be in grave doubt whether they would want still to be associated with Academy' – and he included himself among them. Dover scribbled on the letter that this was clearly 'A threat!' Similarly, the historian A.J.P. Taylor **[10]** warned that pressing the question of Blunt's Fellowship would 'provoke dissension and acrimony such as the Academy has never known', and that he himself would 'of course resign' if any motion to expel were carried.[10]

The historian Eric Hobsbawm **[11]** expressed the hope that 'a majority of Fellows consider it a matter of principle that, as people are honoured by election exclusively on academic grounds, they should only be removed as "not fit and proper persons" on such grounds'. He argued that reaching a consensus on academic distinction was not too hard to achieve. 'Consensus on private and public behaviour is a different matter, especially when emotions are strongly engaged, as they usually are.' In his opinion, 'the reputation of our Academy and of this country for civilised behaviour would suffer if we expelled Blunt, whatever our views of his conduct.'

Professor Richard Wollheim FBA

Professor Eric Hobsbawm FBA

[10] In 'Materials', Dover commented that there was a 'cheering side' to Taylor's letter: if Blunt were expelled, 'at least the Academy would simultaneously rid itself of a man who was such a fool as to say "of course" in this context.'

9: Richard Wollheim to Kenneth Dover, 21 February 1980.

DEPARTMENT OF PHILOSOPHY
UNIVERSITY COLLEGE LONDON
GOWER STREET LONDON WC1E 6BT
Telephone 01-387 7050

Professor Richard Wollheim 21st February, 1980.

CONFIDENTIAL

answered

Dear Kenneth,

I am sure that the last thing that you want is another letter on the issue of Anthony Blunt. However, I do feel compelled to write to you about it. I fully recognise that the matter has its own momentum and that the rules of the Academy do not give you very much room for manoeuvre, but I should like to point out that the issue is bound to be enormously divisive. If expulsion goes through there certainly will be quite a number of people, including myself, who would have to consider very seriously their Fellowships and whether they would remain content to hold them. If, however, the matter stopped short of this and Blunt is made to resign his Fellowship there still would be a number of people, again including myself, who would be sufficiently upset by this result to be in grave doubt whether they would want still to be associated with the Academy. As I say, I do not know if anything can now be done about this, but I do feel that it is a consideration which should be very much in the forefront of people's minds.

A threat!

I am sorry to inflict this on you.

Yours,

Richard

Sir Kenneth Dover,
President,
The British Academy,
Burlington House,
Piccadilly,
London,
W1V 0NS

10: A.J.P. Taylor to Kenneth Dover, 22 February 1980.

32 TWISDEN ROAD
LONDON
NW5 1LD
01-485 1507

22 February 1980

Dear S.r Kenneth Dover,

I learn with deep regret that Council proposes to refer the question of Professor Blunt's Fellowship to a General Meeting. This step will, I fear, provoke dissension and acrimony such as the Academy has never known before. However my purpose is not to protest now. I wish only to ensure that, if the question is raised, I shall be given an opportunity to speak against the motion. I hope you can set my mind at rest over this. I shall of course resign my Fellowship if the motion is carried.

Yours sincerely,

A J P Taylor

A J P Taylor

11: Eric Hobsbawm to Kenneth Dover, 28 February 1980.

23

BIRKBECK COLLEGE
University of London

Department of History
01-580 6622

Malet Street
London, WC1E 7HX

28 Feb 80

Dear Dover,

I was startled to hear that the Council of the British Academy is considering whether to recommend to a General Meeting of the Fellows the expulsion from the Academy of Prof. A.Blunt. Since the initiative in such a matter must, if I read the Bye-Laws rightly, come from Council and a General Meeting cannot take this decision against the recommendation of Council, I write to you in the first instance, as you are our and its President.

To expel a Fellow in any circumstances - has it ever happened before in our Academy? - is a serious step. To consider expelling him for reasons which have nothing to do with the criteria which determined his election, is an even more serious step and requires much heartsearching. There are fortunately not many Academies which have expelled members on non-academic grounds, and those which have are not commonly admired for having done so. One might add that, to what most of us would regard as their honour, some such academies have resisted the temptation (or the pressure) to do so.

I hope that a majority of Fellows consider it a matter of principle that, as people are honoured by election exclusively on academic grounds, they should only be removed as 'not fit and proper persons' on such grounds. If Bentley were alive today, we should judge him by his eminence as a classical scholar and not by his extracurricular behaviour, however controversial. On the other hand it is always possible to envisage cases of behaviour so shocking that one might be willing to swallow one's principles. Yet the basic difficulty is, that the decision as to what constitutes such behaviour must be highly subjective, even when it is not subject to the variable judgment of history. The criteria of academic distinction are such that, given time, consensus about such distinction is significant and not too hard to achieve. Consensus on private and public behaviour is a different matter, especially when emotions are strongly engaged, as they usually are. There may be times when strong public passions produce such a consensus - though it is certain that in the present instance opinion in the Academy is divided - but what is its significance?

Would we, if Jacques Soustelle had been a member of our Academy, have ceased to regard him as a 'fit and proper person' when this acknowledged expert on Aztec society attempted the overthrow of the government of his nation, was tried for treason and fled abroad for several years in the 1960s? Probably most of us would have at least been tempted to do so. Many of us, including myself and almost certainly the vast majority of his academic colleagues, continue to abominate his conduct and his opinions. Would we have been right to expel him? Was the Ecole des Hautes Etudes wrong in refusing to deprive him of his post and in reintegrating him on his return after he had been amnestied? I think on reflection one would conclude that the reputation of the French academic community and of French civilisation stands higher, because of this refusal. I cite this case because it is both clear and extreme. It is not, in principle, irrelevant to our decision. I think that the reputation of our Academy and of this country for civilised behaviour would suffer if we expelled Blunt, whatever our views of his conduct. Nor do I think I am alone in this view.

Yours sincerely

E.J. Hobsbawm

E.J.Hobsbawm

The next meeting of the Academy's Council was to be held on 18 March 1980. Ahead of it, the legal scholar Thomas B. Smith FBA – the only member who had not been present at the February meeting – wrote to Carswell to express his regret that he had not then been able to attend: 'Had I done so, I should have given strong support to Professor Plumb's motion. … I had a certain personal concern with events when Blunt and his associates were active.' He therefore asked whether it would be possible to have his own turn to 'speak briefly' at the forthcoming meeting, 'or to direct a few questions to Blunt'.[11] But Blunt had declined the invitation to appear. Dover had to inform members of Council of Blunt's decision, and to set out some guidelines for how the meeting should proceed.

Dover believed that he had a good idea of how each member would vote on the Blunt question, and who would be absent from the meeting. He was therefore aware that, as President, he might end up in the position of having the casting vote. He had made up his mind that, if this proved to be the case, he would feel compelled to use his casting vote in Blunt's favour. Dover was convinced that this might come as a shock to some Council members, so he decided to draft a memorandum to explain his position. In this draft, Dover outlined what he regarded as 'the real charge' against Blunt: 'that he freely and deliberately transferred his loyalty to a totalitarian government whose conception of the relation between power and scholarship is not only irreconcilable with ours but is calculated to frustrate the purposes for which our Academy exists'. He concluded: 'For that reason my personal opinion is that Blunt is not a fit and proper person to be a Fellow'. Yet Dover went on to say that if he was required to give a casting vote, it would be for acquittal, despite his own views. As a classicist, he drew on ancient Greek precedents to explain his reasoning: 'The vote of Athena was imagined as being cast for the defendant when the voting was equal on the Areopagus, and as a lifelong student and lover of the *Oresteia* I cannot now bring myself to give a casting vote against a defendant'.

Dover would explain in 'Materials' that he was grateful that his two Vice-Presidents, Howard and Chadwick, 'were not only sensible and cool-headed men but were also opposed to expulsion'. He decided to send his draft to them in advance, knowing that they would give 'good advice on the appropriateness of sending it out to all members of Council'. Both Vice-Presidents supported the idea of sending such a briefing note. But Chadwick thought it was too long, observing: 'You sound at times almost as though you need to write an apologia for your own conduct.' Both men advised Dover to send 'a shorter and more impersonal' communication. Dover took this advice, and circulated to Council (on 11 March) an amended memorandum **[12]**. It alerted members to the fact that Blunt had declined the invitation to attend, and it suggested three questions that Council would have to ask itself, together with lines of reasoning to test whether Blunt was 'a fit and proper person to be a Fellow'. He also declared that 'it is extremely important that I should be able to defend our decision without any hesitation or equivocation.'

Professor Thomas B. Smith QC FBA

[11] T.B. Smith to John Carswell, 4 March 1980. In a later letter to Carswell, 12 March 1980, Smith hinted further at his own past in intelligence matters: 'I am not free to travel in the Soviet Union without risking embarrassment to myself and the Government', and he was 'taking advice' as to what he might be allowed to say at the forthcoming Council meeting 'regarding past events'. According to Lord Hunter's memoir of him, during 1946 and 1947 Smith was 'attached in one of the Intelligence Services to the Foreign Office': J. Hunter, 'Thomas Broun Smith, 1915-1998', *Proceedings of the British Academy*, 82 (1993), p. 459.

12: Memorandum from Kenneth Dover for the meeting of Council on 18 March 1980.

re agenda item 6

Strictly Confidential

THE BRITISH ACADEMY

Members of Council

Council Meeting 18 March 1980

Professor Blunt has declined my invitation to attend the Council meeting on 18 March. He considers that 'no purpose would be served' by his attendance. I have told him that if he remains of that opinion up to 18 March I shall report to Council accordingly.

I hope that it may be helpful if I propose some guide-lines for our discussion of this issue. I found that our discussion on 15 Feb. started many trains of thought, and some aspects of the issue have become clearer to me after a fortnight's reflection. Other members of Council have no doubt had the same experience.

Our decision on 15 Feb. was to inform Professor Blunt that we had received and discussed a proposal that we should recommend his expulsion, and that he had a right to be heard in his own defence. That decision having now been implemented, three decisions remain:

(1) Is Professor Blunt a fit and proper person to be a Fellow?

If our answer to this question is to be 'No', it is of the highest importance that our reasons for it be such that I can defend them, if called upon to do so, with conviction and vigour.

In my submission, it is not enough to say that integrity is indivisible or that moral delinquency justifies expulsion. Some may say that the proposition that integrity is indivisible has already been refuted by Professor Blunt's academic career, to say nothing of other careers in many countries and many periods. Others may point out that there are various kinds of moral delinquency, and may ask when Council will turn its attention to (e.g.) adulterers.

I suggest therefore that we address ourselves to three questions in particular (without prejudice to discussion of any other questions which any member of Council regards as specially important):

(a) Is treason sui generis? Everyone is free to choose his own ultimate moral priorities, and we can choose to treat treason as sui generis whether or not we think that a majority of Fellows will agree.

(b) Ought Professor Blunt to have realised that in transferring his allegiance to the government of the Soviet Union he was transferring it to a totalitarian government whose conception of the relation between power and historical and literary studies is necessarily inimical to the furtherance of the purposes for which the Academy exists?

(c) If in 1950 we had had very strong reason to believe that Professor Blunt had transferred his allegiance to a totalitarian government and was working as its agent, would his sponsors, his Section and Council have regarded him as a fit and proper person to be elected (Bye-law 27 (1)b)?

If we decide that Professor Blunt is not a fit and proper person to be a Fellow, our next decision must be:

(2) Shall we decide forthwith whether or not to recommend his expulsion, or shall we defer our decision until the Council meeting of 16 May?

If we do not wish to defer decision, we must then decide:

(3) Shall we recommend his expulsion at the Annual General Meeting?

It is perfectly open to us to decide both that Professor Blunt is not a fit and proper person and that we will nevertheless refrain from recommending his expulsion (Bye-law 11 says 'may', not 'shall').

Members of Council have probably become aware, as I have, that there are Fellows who say that they would feel impelled to vote for expulsion if it were proposed but nonetheless hope that it will not be proposed and regret that the issue has been raised. There are also Fellows whose decision whether or not to remain Fellows themselves will turn upon the outcome of the issue.

We are free to give our answers to questions (2) and (3) in the light of what we conceive to be the probable consequences to the Academy. Here again, it is extremely important that I should be able to defend our decision without any hesitation or equivocation.

K.J. Dover

Almost immediately, Dover received another letter from Plumb **[13]**, expressing his astonishment at the content of the briefing document Dover had sent out. According to Plumb, a *British* Academy – a body supported out of government funds, and one that would be expected 'to be upholders of British traditions and attitudes' – should have a clear stance on treason. And he warned that if the question of Blunt's expulsion were not put to the Annual General Meeting, 'a number of Fellows, including myself, will resign and make our position clear in the public press as to why we are doing so … the honour of the Academy is at stake.'

Dover replied to Plumb **[14]**. While noting the threat of Plumb and others to resign, he pointed out that Fellows who were supporters of Blunt were also threatening to resign. He bemoaned: 'I find it profoundly depressing that neither set of potential resigners understands very readily the intelligent & honourable thinking which has led the other set to the conclusion it has reached.'

13: J.H. Plumb to Kenneth Dover, 12 March 1980.

PROFESSOR J.H.PLUMB, F.B.A.

The Master's Lodge, Christ's College, Cambridge, CB2 3BU Telephone 67641

12 March 1980

STRICTLY CONFIDENTIAL

Dear President,

I was rather astonished to get your further brief about Blunt as I thought the Council had taken a decision to send this to the AGM if Blunt declined to appear before the Council.

My position is quite clear and I hope that of the others who voted for the motion is too. We are not a society for the study of the history of art. If we were I should not have been pressing this matter. We are a British Academy, supported out of Government funds and surely we are expected to be upholders of British traditions and attitudes both in this country and abroad. It seems to me that for the British Academy, treason is sui generis and we should so treat it.

With regard to your second question, certainly any man of modest judgment by 1940, whatever his intellectual confusion in the early thirties, should have realised the nature of Soviet Society. I cannot believe for one moment that, had we known or even had a strong reason to believe, that Blunt had transferred his allegiance to a totalitarian government and was working as their agent, we should have regarded him as a fit and proper person to continue as an Academician in 1950. I shall press for recommending his expulsion at the AGM.

I think it is only fair that you should warn members of the Council, particularly those who seem to have no strong feelings in this matter, that, if the question of expulsion is not brought before the general meeting, a number of Fellows, including myself, will resign and make our position quite clear in the public press as to why we are doing so. Naturally we shall take this step with regret but it seems to me that the honour of the Academy is at stake.

Am I right in thinking that you are going to bring this matter up at the meeting on 18 March? It is exceedingly difficult for me to get to that meeting but naturally I will cancel everything else in order to do so if this matter is an the agenda.

Yours sincerely,

J.H.P.

14: Kenneth Dover to J.H. Plumb, 14 March 1980.

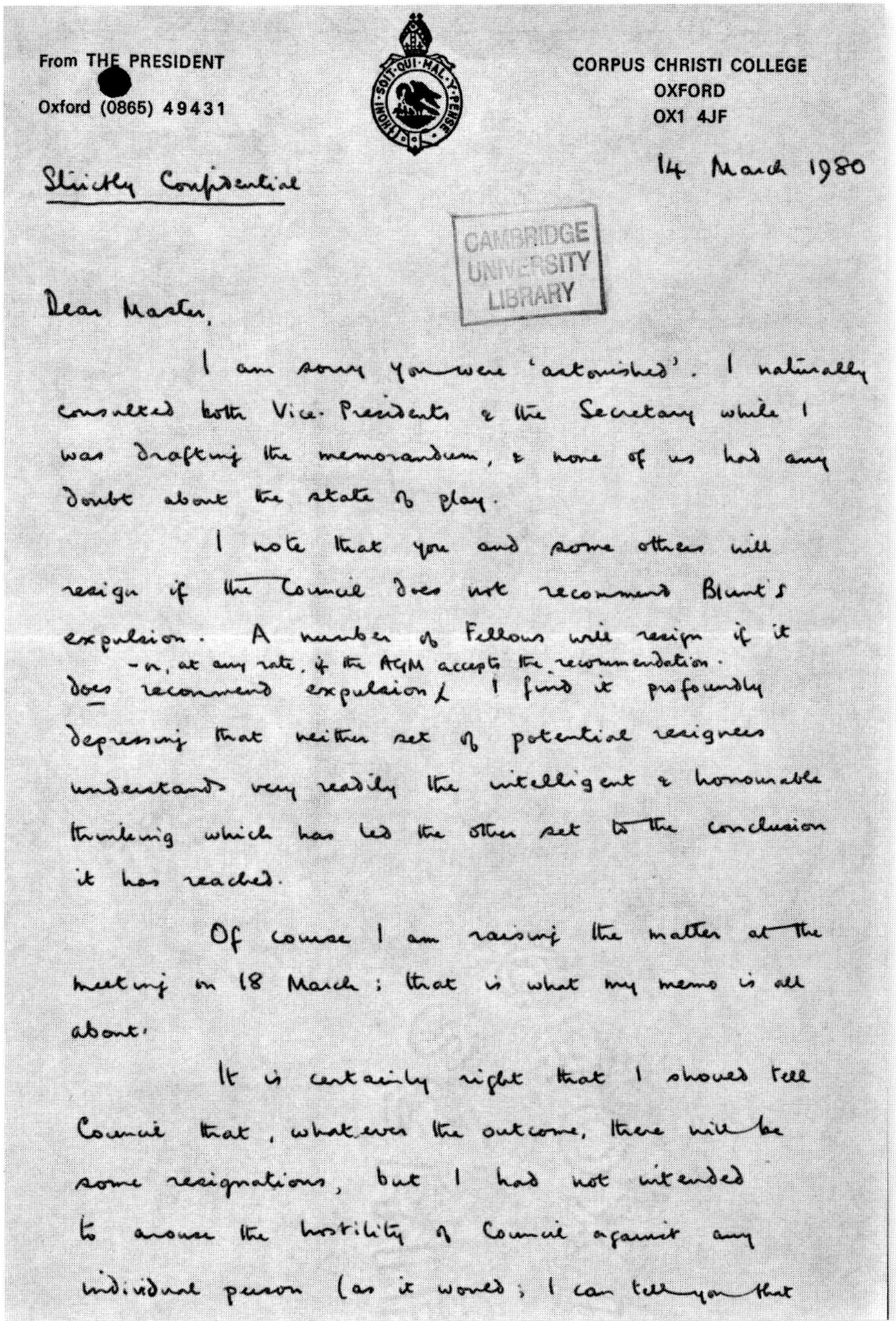

From THE PRESIDENT

Oxford (0865) 49431

CORPUS CHRISTI COLLEGE
OXFORD
OX1 4JF

14 March 1980

Strictly Confidential

Dear Master,

I am sorry you were 'astonished'. I naturally consulted both Vice-Presidents & the Secretary while I was drafting the memorandum, & none of us had any doubt about the state of play.

I note that you and some others will resign if the Council does not recommend Blunt's expulsion. A number of Fellows will resign if it does recommend expulsion – or, at any rate, if the AGM accepts the recommendation. I find it profoundly depressing that neither set of potential resignees understands very readily the intelligent & honourable thinking which has led the other set to the conclusion it has reached.

Of course I am raising the matter at the meeting on 18 March: that is what my memo is all about.

It is certainly right that I should tell Council that, whatever the outcome, there will be some resignations, but I had not intended to arouse the hostility of Council against any individual person (as it would; I can tell you that

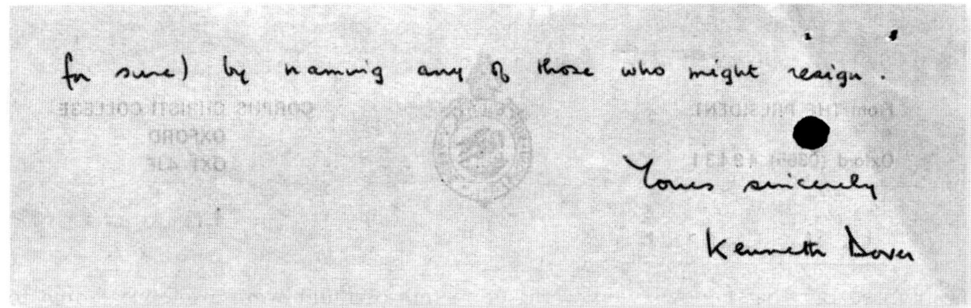

for sure) by naming any of those who might resign.

Yours sincerely

Kenneth Dover

I shall of course resign my Fellowship if the motion [to expel Blunt] is carried.

A.J.P. Taylor, 22 February 1980

... if the question of Blunt's expulsion is not brought before the general meeting, a number of Fellows, including myself, will resign and make our position clear in the public press as to why we are doing so.

J.H. Plumb, 12 March 1980

I find it profoundly depressing that neither set of potential resigners understands very readily the intelligent & honourable thinking which has led the other set to the conclusion it has reached.

Kenneth Dover, 14 March 1980

That feeling was strong among Blunt's supporters had been revealed to Dover in a letter he had recently received from the historian Richard Cobb FBA **[15]**. Cobb said he was in correspondence with A.J.P. Taylor, and went on: 'One would not like to remain in an institution that took it upon itself publicly to harry one of its members in such a disgraceful manner. And I am assured by Professor Blunt that he is not going to resign. He has had many letters from Fellows begging him not to do so. Let us hope the wretched suggestion will be quietly buried.'[12]

Professor Richard Cobb CBE FBA

15: Richard Cobb to Kenneth Dover, 12 March 1980.

From the Professor of Modern History — *Worcester College Oxford OX1 2HB*

12 March 1980

(36)

Dear Sir Kenneth,

I have been most distressed to learn that there have been various suggestions proposing the expulsion of Anthony Blunt from the Academy. I do hope such a proposal is not taken up formally; it could only do the Academy the greatest harm. And I know that a number of historians feel the same way. I have written to Alan Taylor to express my full support for any move that he may suggest. One would not like to remain in an institution that took upon itself publicly to harry one of its members in such a disgraceful manner. And I am assured by Professor Blunt that he is not going to resign. He has had many letters from Fellows begging him not to do so. Let us hope the wretched suggestion will be quietly buried.

Yours sincerely

Richard Cobb.

(Richard Cobb)

[12] Another historian, Gerald Aylmer FBA, wrote to Dover on 15 March 1980, to say that he was 'disturbed' to hear that Council was to consider expelling a Fellow. 'My personal opinion is that Council would be better advised to take no action at all in this matter'.

The Academy's Council met again on 18 March 1980. As records of this decisive meeting, there are the formal minutes **[16]**, and also the handwritten notes taken at the time by John Carswell as Secretary and Peter Brown as Deputy Secretary **[17]** – which combine to provide an indication of how the discussion flowed. In 'Materials', Dover describes the meeting as being conducted in a 'grave and leisurely way, without excitement or extravagant language'. Brown recalls that T.B. Smith, the one member who had missed the opportunity to express an opinion at the February meeting, gave a long speech ('he was not a person who was concise'). He defined the technical difference between treason and treachery, but concluded that, although treachery was not as bad as treason, it was still pretty bad and therefore Blunt should go.[13] When Michael Howard had originally commented on Dover's draft memorandum, he had added his opinion that 'Blunt's treachery was a youthful folly committed out of ignorance and arrogance ... but it should not be allowed to outweigh thirty years of scholarly achievements.' Now in the meeting, Howard pursued this 'statute of limitations' argument. Brown also recalls that the other Vice-President, Owen Chadwick, 'suddenly exploded', saying that he loathed witch hunts: 'he was emotionally very powerful indeed; I think his moral authority shone more than that of perhaps anybody else round that table.'

When Council voted on the question: 'Is Professor Blunt a fit and proper person to be a Fellow?', three voted in favour of Blunt, nine against, and three abstained. There was then unanimous agreement that they should decide there and then whether or not to recommend expulsion to the Annual General Meeting, rather than defer the issue. On the key third question before them – whether they should indeed recommend expulsion – the vote was closer, with eight voting in favour and seven against. In 'Materials', Dover notes that there was an odd thing about this final vote which only struck him later: 'The vote was 8:7, but the number of people present and entitled to vote (excluding me) was 16. So, someone abstained; but I don't know who it was. If Caird had been present, the vote would have been 8:8,[14] and I would have given my casting vote in Blunt's favour. If the abstainer had voted also, I might not even have needed to give a casting vote.'

As an observer of that vote, Brown has suggested that passing the question to the rest of the Fellowship at the Annual General Meeting was really just a means of resolving an impasse. If it had been a matter for Council alone, 'I don't think Dover could have extracted a resolution out of Council to expel Blunt.' Of Dover's chairing of the meeting, Brown has commented that it was 'absolutely masterly': 'I said to him that by the end of the whole process I couldn't believe that anybody could have known what his personal view was. He was scrupulously detached and unprejudiced.'

[13] Peter Brown interview, 12 February 2018.

[14] The biblical studies scholar George Caird FBA had indicated his views to Dover in a letter of 12 March 1980. He argued that treason 'has much the same umbra and penumbra of ambiguity as a good many other moral terms'. He concluded 'I am one of those who regret that the question has been raised.'

16: Minutes of the meeting of Council, 18 March 1980 [extracts]

PRIVATE AND
CONFIDENTIAL

COUNCIL MINUTES 2/80

THE BRITISH ACADEMY

MEETING OF COUNCIL

Tuesday 18 March 1980

PRESENT
Sir Kenneth Dover (President)
Professor L.J. Austin
Professor A.J. Brown
The Revd. Professor W.O. Chadwick
Professor J A. Crook
Professor R.H.C. Davis
Professor J.D. Evans
Professor M.B. Hesse
Professor M.E. Howard
Professor S. Körner
Professor F.S.L. Lyons
Professor J.H. Plumb
Professor C.R. Quirk
Professor T.B. Smith
Professor E. Ullendorff
Mr. J.P. Carswell (Secretary)
Professor E.W. Handley (Foreign Secretary)
Professor P. Mathias (Treasurer)

APOLOGIES
The Revd. Professor G.B. Caird, Professor J.M. Wallace-Hadrill

1. MINUTES

The minutes, subject to a drafting change to paragraph 7 inserting the words "given the opportunity of being" before "heard" in line 6, were approved and signed.

6. PROPOSAL FOR COUNCIL ACTION UNDER BYE-LAW 11

Council resumed the question of the position of Professor Blunt under Bye-law 11. The President said he had written to Professor Blunt as decided at the last meeting, and had received the following reply, dated 25 February 1980:

" Dear Sir Kenneth,

Thank you for your letter of 16 February. I don't think any purpose would be served by my attending the meeting of the Council to speak in my defence, as I have nothing to add to what I have already said - except perhaps to re-emphasise my regrets at what I did, which I am frequently accused of not having expressed.

Yours sincerely,

Anthony Blunt "

The President suggested that the discussion should follow the pattern proposed in the memorandum he had circulated. Council should not, he considered, be influenced by suggestions of possible resignations, some of which had been reported to him, or by the prospect of publicity, since both these were risks whichever way Council decided to proceed. Nevertheless, Council's proceedings were confidential, and he hoped it would be agreed by all those present that no disclosures should be made to anybody by them individually, unless or until authorised by Council. If personally approached he would say that he had no statement whatever to make on the matter. Council agreed with the President's statement.

In discussion, the following points were made:

(1) What Professor Blunt admitted to having done, though doubtfully treason in the technical sense, was a grave breach of trust and could be characterised as treachery. This conduct had continued in an important respect after his election as a Fellow.

(2) Fitness for election was not necessarily the same as fitness to continue in the Fellowship.

(3) There was no doubt about the distinction of Professor Blunt's contribution to scholarship, and scholarly values could, and in the case of the Academy should, be distinguished from other values. On the other hand, the Academy was a public institution to which it could be said offences such as those committed by Professor Blunt were relevant.

(4) The course of conduct objected to had ended many years ago, and had been followed by a long career of undoubted scholarly distinction. On the other hand, there was no rule of law setting a time limit for responsibility for offences of this kind, especially when they had been concealed.

(5) The holding or propagation of particular opinions did not render a person unfit to be a Fellow; nor did the commission of a criminal offence necessarily do so.

Council then voted on the question "whether Professor Blunt was a fit and proper person to be a Fellow". Yes : 3; No : 9. The President did not vote.

Council then decided unanimously to proceed to the question whether Council should recommend to the Annual General Meeting that Professor Blunt should cease to be a Fellow.

It was then proposed, and unanimously agreed, that if such a motion was carried it should be subject to authority being given to the President, using his discretion as to the means, to invite Professor Blunt to resign; and that the decision should not be acted upon until the President reported the result.

Council then voted on the question whether Council should recommend that Professor Blunt should cease to be a Fellow, if, at the time Council announced the business for the Annual General Meeting, he had not resigned. In Favour : 8; Against : 7. The President did not vote.

Mr John Carswell CB

Mr Peter Brown

17: Notes of the meeting of Council, 18 March 1980, taken by the Secretary, John Carswell, and the Deputy Secretary, Peter Brown [transcribed and collated]

	Notes taken by John Carswell	**Notes taken by Peter Brown**
	Blunt's letter read by President.	Blunt's letter
[Dover]	PBA's memo. (1) There will be resignations, whatever we do. (2) There will be publicity, whatever we do.	Resignations whatever happens, & reasons will be made public
	Treason sui generis means. There are some offences of a specially academic kind. But among ordinary general offences is treason special, and as such justify expulsion.	
	Whatever we do can be defended publicly – not worried about that.	
	Sunday Times.[15] Contains many inaccuracies. But points to a source within Council. PBA & I need directions on what we should say.	
Plumb	Treason a special category within the law.	Under law, treason is in a special category
Smith	If B has committed treason, he only has protection in England. But has the greatest difficulty in perceiving Blunt has committed treason 'by adhering to the King's enemies', rather than the technical term treason. What Prof B has done is breach of trust, which is surely an offence raising the question of expulsion. Political opinion not a ground for expulsion. A few months after his election he connived at the escape of Maclean. Blood on Philby's hands.	Cld be prosecuted in Scotland. Diff in seeing how B has committed treason. Cannot press too much on category of treason. Rather, treachery. Abuse of trust, betrayal. How much blood? Within a few months of election, B was engaged in these activities.
Chadwick	Fitness to [be] elected not quite the same as fitness to be a continuing member.	Not proposing to elect, but to diselect. Diff? Whether expedient to strip

[15] The fact that Council was dicussing Blunt's Fellowship featured in a gossip column in the *Sunday Times* on 16 March 1980. The columnist predicted that Blunt would 'quietly resign, and the tiny earthquake which might just have struck Piccadilly be averted.'

Howard	Possible informal 'statute of limitations'. Out of contact with Soviets for 25 years. A great scholar. Should we punish a man for what he did 25 years ago	Statute of limitations? 25 years ago. Like a disease gone dormant & resurfacing. Since then highly respected member of society. Hasn't purged offence. But do we judge him in same way
Crook	Our responsibility as a public Academy. Treachery specially relevant to us.	How we wld behave if a private club & a public body has to be dist. National duty to promote & speak in name of scholarship
Chadwick		Not fit & proper when elected. Loathe Nazi hunters chasing after 40 years.
Ullendorff		In narrow sense not fit & proper.
Hesse	In no doubt he is unfit now & was unfit then.	? of expediency the more diff. Not fit & proper. Not youthful indiscretion
Quirk		Worrying ambiguities about Q1 – fitness, propriety. In one respect has increased – achievement for which he was elected. If confessed & punished in 1950, might have been fit & proper in 1970s
Austin	Massive contribution, but massive blot on his copy book. Must look at the man as a whole. Not fit in 1950. Doubts whether could be said not fit now	Label of traitor fitted in 1950. If consider man as whole & take into account exceptional services to sch, not clear whether not now fit & proper
Plumb		If society of art-historians, Austin's point better. But we are a national society with responsibilities
A.J. Brown	Defence of scholarly, as distinct from other values. The two should not be mixed.	Stand for defence of scholarly values, & acad. Integrity.
Smith	No limitation of time in crime. Resumed his contacts after election to Academy. Has in no way purged his offence.	Time factor: there is no limitation. Had he been punished, he might have purged his offence. But within few months of election, resuming contacts with KGB.
Q.1. vote	Is he a fit & proper person. 3 yes 9 no 3 abstentions	Yes 3 No 9 Abstentions 3
		A number of Fellows have urged B not to resign. Why shld a man consult the convenience of his executioners?
		A recommendation by Council required. Cld be raised at AGM & Council told to think again.
	Agreed that these proceedings are strictly confidential	Confidentiality – not allowed to discuss. Confidentiality is indivisible

Austin		Astounded to think that confid. can be breached when considering a ? of ethics.
Chadwick		Don't defer – fairer to Blunt
Carswell		Action now puts pressures on confid.
Q.2. vote	To proceed now unanimous	Now – unanimous
Smith		Positive request shld be put to him to resign
Dover		How great is diff between expulsion & invitation to resign
Plumb		Infinitely prefer him to resign. Honourable.
		(Antiquaries asked him to resign)
Ullendorff		Wld request to resign go beyond moral & legal powers of C[ouncil]?
Howard		Formal letter + informal invitation to resign? Spare Ac. much agony & himself much pain
Handley		Council is disposed to rec … to be confirmed at next meeting. Wld he care to resign first
Dover		Wld prefer to do this thro' an intermediary
Ullendorff		Wld vote in favour of 3 to give AGM chance to discuss
Handley		How representative is the AGM
Chadwick		Doesn't approve of E U[llendorff]'s democracy. Responsibility is ours.
Ullendorff		PBA [President of the British Academy] to explain that only way to bring it about
Dover		News will get out. Looks bad to rec something we don't believe in
		Suggestion that shld conduct a ballot of F[ellow]s
Smith		No opportunity for 'jury' to be heard, only
Q.3.		If 'yes', shld endeavour to cause to resign.

Quirk		Cld not try & bring it about by communicating result of Q1?
Plumb		If yes, help to make B's mind up.
Howard		? : might he not stick his toes in.
Handley		What would PBA prefer?
Dover		Q3 now
Q.3. [vote]	Should we recommend his expulsion?	✓ 8 : X 7
		∴ K J D[over] will try to achieve resignation.
		The fact of communication breaches confidentiality.
		Matters in suspense: C[ouncil] is considering the matter still
		C[ouncil] reaffirmed that proceedings entirely confid. & cannot even reveal what was on the agenda

The handwritten notes of the meeting reveal that several members felt that Blunt should be invited to resign, before they confirmed their recommendation to the AGM. A precedent had recently been set by the Society of Antiquaries, where Blunt's resignation had been secured by giving him plain notice that if he did not do so he was likely to be expelled. Dover objected to this scheme; as he put it in 'Materials': 'I would have felt ashamed of asking a man if he would be so good as to consult the convenience of his executioners'. And because there were many Fellows of the Academy who thought Blunt should remain a Fellow, Dover reasoned that 'it would be surprising if he [Blunt] disagreed with them'. Despite his reluctance, Dover agreed to ascertain Blunt's thinking but only through an intermediary. In the aftermath of Council's meeting he wrote to another art historian, Peter Lasko FBA (who had succeeded Blunt as Director of the Courtauld Institute) **[18]**. Dover concluded by inviting Lasko – if he judged it to be in the best interests of everyone – 'to try to persuade him to resign'.

Lasko replied on 23 March **[19]**, having had the opportunity to speak to Blunt the day before. When Blunt had been told of the substance of Dover's letter, 'His response was immediate and quite positive – he felt most strongly that he did not wish to resign.' So, as Dover put it in 'Materials', 'there was going to be no easy way out for Council'.

Professor Peter Lasko FBA

18: Kenneth Dover to Peter Lasko, 18 March 1980.

FROM THE PRESIDENT

OXFORD 49431

CORPUS CHRISTI COLLEGE
OXFORD
OX1 4JF

18 March 1980

Personal and Confidential

Dear Peter,

I would be very grateful for your advice – and, if you feel able to give it, your help – in the matter of Anthony Blunt.

Although accounts which appeared in the press were mistaken on some points of detail, no amount of tight-lipped confidentiality can conceal the obvious fact that many members of Council are disposed to get Anthony out of the Academy. But to the best of my belief every one of those who are so disposed would be relieved if he resigned first. Equally, no one of them will be deterred from recommending his expulsion if he does not resign, because they think he ought to be out.

My prediction is that if he doesn't resign Council will in the end recommend his expulsion; that the AGM will probably (but not certainly) reject the recommendation – which doesn't matter in the least; and that a fair amount of sensational and inaccurate publicity will descend on the Academy – which matters a great deal. If he does resign, some of his strongest supporters will still resign in sympathy, regarding his resignation as forced upon him, but the acrimony and consequent publicity will be less.

I don't feel I can suggest resignation to him myself. Though I have known him since about 1970, I can't pretend at the moment that I am not the Chairman of Council and official spokesman of the Academy. Also, I would feel a fool in asking any man to be so kind as to consult the convenience of his executioners and put them in a better light.

This is where you might come in. Can you tell me your impression of his thinking on the subject of resignation? And if you can, do you feel inclined to do so? If not, a simple NO suffices as an answer, and I will respect that for good and all. If you are among those who think he should dig in his heels and defy the Academy to do its worst, you are not alone. By now I have heard enough intelligent and honourable arguments from people on <u>both</u> sides to understand how they have arrived at irreconcilable views.

But <u>if</u> you yourself think it would be better for Anthony to resign, in his own interests and/or in the interests of the Academy, then, in that case – <u>and only in that case</u> – I am asking you to try to persuade him to resign.

I propose to maintain silence on my own opinion until after I have ceased to be President, but I can say that if I were ever required <u>ex officio</u> to give a casting vote it would of course be the 'vote of Athena' for acquittal, in the traditions of the Areopagus.

Yours sincerely

Kenneth

19: Peter Lasko to Kenneth Dover, 23 March 1980.

UNIVERSITY OF LONDON
COURTAULD INSTITUTE OF ART
20 PORTMAN SQUARE LONDON W1H OBE
TELEPHONE: 01-935 9292-5
01-486 5913-4

23. 3. 80.

Dear Kenneth

I spoke to Anthony yesterday – and I was happy to do so. I can assure you it wasn't at all difficult – mainly because I took my queue from your beautifully balanced letter – and simply asked him how he felt about the Academy. I offered to drop the subject if he preferred not to discuss it!

His response was immediate and quite positive – he felt most strongly that he did not wish to resign. I certainly made no attempt to persuade him – and I am quite sure I would not have succeeded had I tried. Others might, of course. Especially those who feel far more strongly than I do that the best interests of the Academy might be served if he did.

I do hope that this news doesn't make life in the immediate future too unpleasant for you personally!

Yours ever

Peter.

That the Blunt question was the subject of informal discussion during the March 1980 round of Section meetings is revealed in a letter to Dover from the art historian John Beckwith FBA **[20]**. He was sad and alarmed to hear at the meeting of Section 11 that 'there is a proposal to ask my friend Anthony Blunt to resign because of all this "Fourth Man" business.' Beckwith thought that Blunt had suffered enough and that 'to expel him, or force him to resign from the Academy which is surely not concerned with political matters, would be shameful.'

Mr John Beckwith FBA

20: John Beckwith to Kenneth Dover, 26 March 1980

FLAT 12,
77, LADBROKE GROVE,
W. 11

01-727 7277

26th March 1980.

Dear President,

At the meeting of Section 11 of the Academy yesterday I heard with sadness and alarm that there is a proposal to ask my friend Anthony Blunt to resign because of all this "Fourth Man" business. It is all such past history, Anthony has confessed, and his service to the Queen, to the Courtauld Institute and to art-historical scholarship far outweighs in my opinion his past work with the Russians. I am a practising Roman Catholic and have always viewed with distaste Marxist philosophy and the goings-on in "iron curtain" countries; nor could I have given information to any foreign power. But the climate of opinion in the 1930s was so different. The enemy was Fascism and few of us knew the full horrors of either régime.

I had friends who fought in the Spanish Civil War on both the left and the right fronts. No one thought the worse of them for it. Think of the Mitford family - so divided politically.

My view is that Anthony Blunt has suffered enough, that he should no longer be harassed, and to expel him, or force him to resign from the Academy which is surely not concerned with political matters, would be shameful.

Yours sincerely,

John Beckwith

John Beckwith.

The final meeting of Council before the AGM in July, took place on 16 May 1980. The meeting confirmed the decision made on 18 March without further discussion **[21]**. Owen Chadwick subsequently objected to the word 'unanimously' in item 3 of the minutes, on the grounds that, had a vote taken place, he would have voted against it. The minute was later amended at to read '*nem. con.*'[16]

[16] After the meeting of Council, there was a reception for a delegation from the Chinese Academy of Social Sciences, at which a formal exchange agreement between the two academies was signed.

21: Minutes of the meeting of Council, 16 May 1980 [extracts]

Private and Confidential   COUNCIL MINUTES 3/80

THE BRITISH ACADEMY

MEETING OF COUNCIL

Friday 16 May 1980

PRESENT
Sir Kenneth Dover (President)
Professor L.J. Austin
Professor A.J. Brown
The Revd. Professor G.B. Caird
The Revd. Professor W.O. Chadwick
Professor J.A. Crook
Professor R.H.C. Davis
Professor J.D. Evans
Professor M.B. Hesse
Professor M.E. Howard
Professor J.H. Plumb
Professor T.B. Smith
Professor E. Ullendorff
Mr. J.P. Carswell (Secretary)
Professor E.W. Handley (Foreign Secretary)
Professor P. Mathias (Treasurer)
Professor J.M. Wallace-Hadrill (Publications Secretary)

APOLOGIES
Professor S. Körner, Professor F.S.L. Lyons, Professor C.R. Quirk

1. MINUTES

The minutes of the meeting held on 18 March 1980 were approved and signed.

7. BUSINESS FOR THE ANNUAL GENERAL MEETING

(3) Recommendation under Bye-law 11. The President reported that in accordance with the instructions of Council at its last meeting (Minutes 2/80 (6)) he had established Professor Blunt's attitude to possible resignation, which was that he would not resign. Council ~~unanimously~~ nem. con. agreed that it must proceed in accordance with its decision. Decision at the Annual General Meeting should be reached by majority of those present and voting, by secret ballot.

Ahead of the Annual General Meeting in early July, two former Presidents of the British Academy sought to intervene. Lionel Robbins had been President from 1962 to 1967; Isaiah Berlin had been Dover's predecessor as President, from 1974 to 1978. As an amendment to Council's recommendation that Blunt be expelled from the Fellowship, they devised a motion that invited the AGM to 'deplore' Blunt's conduct but take no further action. According to 'Materials', it was their hope that this new proposal 'might command general assent and generate less bitterness'.[17]

In a letter written on 14 March to the philosopher Bernard Williams FBA, Berlin had regretted how affairs at the Academy were already then unfolding: 'It now looks as if, whichever way the thing goes, there will be some effusion of blood, and I cannot help feeling that this could have been avoided.'[18] His own view was that Blunt should not be expelled, but he feared that view was not based 'on any general principle about which I can speak with clear passion … it is just a question of where one draws the line'.

On 5 June Berlin wrote to Robbins **[22]** to report a recent conversation with two other Fellows of the Academy, the economist Basil Yamey and the historian John Hale. They had suggested that if the alternative motion was in the name of both Robbins and Berlin (i.e. two former Presidents), 'this would weight it too far towards the "establishment", and might be counter-productive'. Berlin argued that it would be better if the name of the literary critic Helen Gardner FBA was attached to the motion rather than his – perhaps with the addition of another 'non-establishment' name, such as that of Trevor-Roper. And he reiterated that his view about Blunt was not based on 'a firm principle', because he could imagine 'circumstances in which I should be inclined to vote for deprivation of a person who had committed a particularly heinous act even if he were a scholar and genius' – and so if he were questioned, 'it would sound weak'.

Sir Isaiah Berlin OM CBE FBA

22: Isaiah Berlin to Lionel Robbins, 5 June 1980.

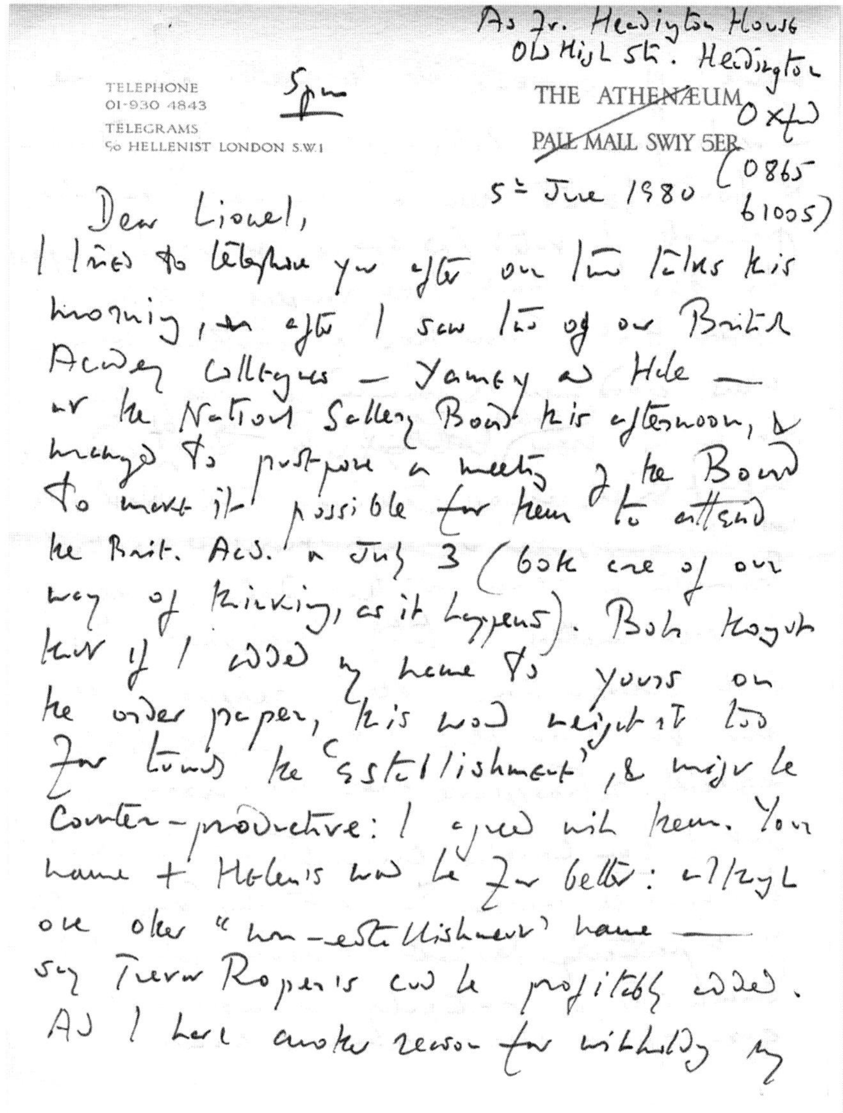

As fr. Headington House
Old High St. Headington
Oxford
(0865 61005)

TELEPHONE
01-930 4843
TELEGRAMS
So HELLENIST LONDON S.W.1

5pm

THE ATHENÆUM
PALL MALL SW1Y 5ER

5th June 1980

Dear Lionel,

I tried to telephone you after our talk this morning, & after I saw two of our British Academy colleagues – Yamey & Hale – at the National Gallery Board this afternoon, & managed to postpone a meeting of the Board to make it possible for them to attend the Brit. Acad. on July 3 (both are of our way of thinking, as it happens). Both thought that if I added my name to yours on the order paper, this would weight it too far towards the "establishment", & might be counter-productive: I agreed with them. Your name + Helen's would be far better: although one other "non-establishment" name – say Trevor Roper's could be profitably added. And I have another reason for withholding my

[17] It is also explained in 'Materials' that the motion originally spoke of 'not in any way condoning the conduct of Professor Anthony Blunt', and may have been changed purely for stylistic reasons.

[18] I. Berlin to B. Williams, 14 March 1980, in H. Hardy and M. Pottle (eds), *Affirming: Isaiah Berlin letters, 1975-1997* (London, 2015), p. 126.

name: if someone at the meeting asks me — or the press do later (someone — e.g. Plumb — is bound to tell them all that passes) on what principle I voted (or spoke) ~~&c~~ as I propose to do, I cannot, like yourself, & Helen, & Herbert Hart & Trevor Roper & doubtless many others, good men (& women) & true, say that in my view ~~[illegible]~~ public recognition of ~~the~~ academic merit ~~with the recognition is totally independent~~ is nothing to do with moral or political character or behaviour; that folly or wickedness in such matters is totally irrelevant to such recognition: I deeply respect those who do think this: I think loyalty tests especially retrospective ones are horrifying: but I can conceive circumstances in which I should be inclined to vote for deprivation if a particularly ~~heinous~~ person who had committed a particularly heinous act even if he were a scholar of genius:

TELEPHONE
01-930 4843
TELEGRAMS
So HELLENIST LONDON S.W.1

THE ATHENÆUM
PALL MALL SW1Y 5ER

it seems to me a question of where one draws the line: I know very clearly where I draw it in this case, & propose to come, support you by a few words, & vote: but I cannot, in all conscience, found my behaviour on a firm principle: & if I admit that (if questioned) it would sound weak, & weaken the case. Hence I'll ask Carswell to omit my name: & add T-Roper's and/or Wallace-Hadrill's if I manage to see them, or someone else's of that kind: if I fail to do this, I'll add my name, a little à contre coeur, to strengthen the ticket even by a tiny bit.

Yours ever

Isaiah.

When the agenda for the AGM was sent out in June 1980 **[23]**, item 10 was 'Conduct of a Fellow (Professor Anthony Blunt)'. It included both Council's recommendation that Blunt's name 'be removed from the list of Fellows on the ground that he is not a fit and proper person to be a Fellow', and also the motion from Lionel Robbins – seconded by Helen Gardner – that the Meeting should 'deplore' Blunt's conduct but decide 'not to proceed further in the matter'.

23: Agenda for the Annual General Meeting of 3 July 1980.

Private and Confidential

THE BRITISH ACADEMY

THE SEVENTY-EIGHTH ORDINARY ANNUAL GENERAL MEETING
will be held in the Rooms of the British Academy,
on Thursday 3 July 1980 at 2.30 pm

A G E N D A

1. Minutes of the Seventy-Seventh Annual General Meeting held on 28 June 1979 and the General Meeting held on 26 March 1980 (circulated herewith for confirmation).
2. The Secretary's Report for the year 1979-80
3. Presentation and Adoption of the Annual Accounts 1979-80 (circulated herewith)
4. Election of Auditors for 1980-81 and approval of Audit Fee for 1980-81
5. Election of (a) Ordinary Fellows (Enclosure A)
   (b) Corresponding Fellows (Enclosure B)
   (c) Honorary Fellows (Note: Council has proposed the names of Mrs. M.A. Cotton, Sir William Deakin, Sir Geoffrey Keynes)
6. Election of President, Treasurer, Foreign Secretary, and Publications Secretary
   (Note: The Council has nominated as President, Sir Kenneth Dover; as Treasurer, Professor P. Mathias; as Foreign Secretary, Professor E.W. Handley; as Publications Secretary, Professor J.M. Wallace-Hadrill)*
7. Election of new Members of Council
   (Note: The Council has nominated Professor R. Dahrendorf, Professor J.R. Hale, Professor J.K.S. St. Joseph, Dr. A.W. Tyson, and Professor J.M. Wallace-Hadrill in place of Professor L.J. Austin, Professor A.J. Brown, Professor J.D. Evans, Professor F.S.L. Lyons, and Professor J.H. Plumb (whose term of service on the Council has expired).)*
8. Awards of Medals and Prizes
9. Deaths of Fellows
10. Conduct of a Fellow (Professor Anthony Blunt)

    To consider a recommendation by Council and a motion concerning Professor Anthony Blunt.

    Council gives notice of the following recommendation under Bye-Law 11**.

    > That the name of Professor Anthony Blunt be removed from the list of Fellows on the ground that he is not a fit and proper person to be a Fellow.

    Lord Robbins has given notice of the following motion:

    > This Meeting deplores the conduct of Professor Anthony Blunt and decides not to proceed further in the matter.

    Seconded by Dame Helen Gardner

The President intends to introduce this part of the Agenda and then to call on Lord Robbins to move his motion. The decision on this motion, reached after any necessary debate, will be the decision by the meeting whether or not to proceed with the recommendation by Council.

11. Address by the President

12. Any other business

*Any alternative nominations should reach the Secretary at least seven days before the meeting; the names of the proposer and seconder should be given in each case and the candidate's written consent to stand for election be furnished; the proposed should be present at the meeting to support the nomination.

**The wording of this Bye-Law is given in the attached Notice, which Fellows are particularly requested to read.

Tea will be served after the meeting

The Twenty-Fifth Annual Dinner will be held in the Middle Temple Hall, 7 pm for 7.30 pm

Notice

1. Only Fellows, including Corresponding and Honorary Fellows, and officers of the Secretariat are admitted to the Meeting. Fellows are asked to bring this agenda with them, and identify themselves to the member of the Secretariat at the entrance to the Academy. They will then be recorded as having been present.

2. Corresponding and Honorary Fellows, though entitled to be present, are excluded by the Charter from voting or speaking.

3. The Charter and Bye-Laws require that all decisions taken at a General Meeting should be taken by Ordinary Fellows present. In the absence of other guidance from the Bye-Laws, Council considers this must be interpreted as meaning that any vote is to be decided by a majority of Ordinary Fellows present and voting, and that abstentions should not be recorded.

4. Council has directed that in case of a vote on this occasion it should be secret, and facilities are being provided accordingly.

5. Fellows are reminded that the Meeting is a private occasion. If the Press requires a public statement on any decision reached, one will be made officially as soon after the Meeting as possible.

Bye-Law 11

(1) If the Council so recommends the Fellows at an Annual General Meeting may remove the name of a person from the list of Fellows on the ground that he or she is not a fit and proper person to be a Fellow, and thereupon he or she will cease to be a Fellow.

(2) A Fellow liable to expulsion shall have the right to be heard before the Council in his or her own defence.

The agenda stimulated considerable comment. The legal scholar F.A. Mann FBA wrote to Carswell stressing his unqualified support for Council's recommendation that Blunt be expelled. He added that 'Byelaw 11 compels us as a matter of law to remove his name, for no objective person can deny that the conditions of Byelaw 11 are fulfilled. In other words, we have no discretion in the matter at all. The terms of the Byelaw are plain and must be observed.' Dover replied that the word 'may' in Bye-Law 11 (1) afforded the AGM complete freedom to either accept or reject Council's recommendation. He also warned Mann that many Fellows – 'perhaps a majority; perhaps even a very large majority' – considered crimes and sins to be irrelevant to a person's fitness to be a Fellow.

The strength of Mann's feeling on the subject can be seen in his response to Dover's letter **[24]**. And in respect of Robbins' motion to 'deplore' Blunt's conduct but do no more, Mann asked: 'Would Lord Robbins be prepared to sit next to him at dinner?' Mann's interpretation of the word 'may' in Bye-Law 11 prompted Dover to consult the legal scholar Robert Megarry FBA. Megarry reassured Dover that 'both the language of the bye-law and the relationship between the Council and the A.G.M. seem to me to point strongly against "may" having any sense of obligation about it'.

Dr F.A. Mann CBE FBA

24: F.A. Mann to Kenneth Dover, 19 June 1980.

FROM DR. F. A. MANN, F. B.A.

TELEPHONE:
01-236 3070

WATLING HOUSE,
35-37, CANNON STREET,
LONDON, EC4M 5SD

19th June 1980

Sir Kenneth Dover,
President,
The British Academy,
Corpus Christi College,
OXFORD, OX1 4JF.

Dear President,

Thank you very much for your letter of the 12th June.

If before 1950 Blunt had been convicted of treason or had confessed to have committed treason, surely no Fellow would have proposed his election, and if any such proposal had been made it would have been rejected on the ground that Blunt was not a fit and proper person to be a Fellow. This would have been so however eminent his academic position would have been. I suggest that up to this point there cannot be any room for controversy.

In fact Blunt confessed 30 years after his election. How can it be suggested that nonetheless he remains a fit and proper person to be a Fellow? His academic eminence is as irrelevant now as it would have been in 1950. His criminality is as clear now as it was in 1950 had the facts then been known.

To "deplore" his conduct is simply not good enough. Would Lord Robbins be prepared to sit next to him at dinner?

Yours sincerely,

F. A. Mann

Dr. F. A. Mann

Dover received several other letters regarding the Blunt affair. The classicist Reginald Winnington-Ingram FBA wrote to say that he would be unable to attend the AGM but, if he were there, he would support Robbins' motion: 'Blunt was betrayed by a fatal combination of naivety and arrogance'.[19] Members of the public also wrote in to express their view: a Mrs Crombie, for example, hoped that the Academy would 'stop the hunting of Professor Blunt'.

Letters even started appearing in the press, including one from A.J.P. Taylor who declared in *The Times* that he would resign from the Academy if Blunt were expelled. Two days later another letter appeared in *The Times* suggesting that Taylor's stance had given Fellows a strong reason to expel Blunt. Although this letter purported to be from Max Beloff FBA, it was in fact a fake; the real author continues to be a mystery.

One of those writing in support of Blunt's expulsion was the historian Robert Blake FBA **[25]**. The only way to exclude Blunt from the life of the Academy, he argued, was to remove him from the list of Fellows; 'promises about him not turning up or participating' were not good enough – 'Promises can be broken', as Blunt's life had already exemplified.[20]

Lord (Robert) Blake FBA

[19] Reginald Winnington-Ingram to Kenneth Dover, 17 June 1980.

[20] Blake had his own experience of intelligence work. At the end of the war he was serving in MI6, where he apparently found Kim Philby to be an agreeable colleague: see R. Shannon, 'Robert Norman William Blake, 1916-2003', *Proceedings of the British Academy*, 153 (2008), p. 71.

25: Robert Blake to Kenneth Dover, 19 June 1980.

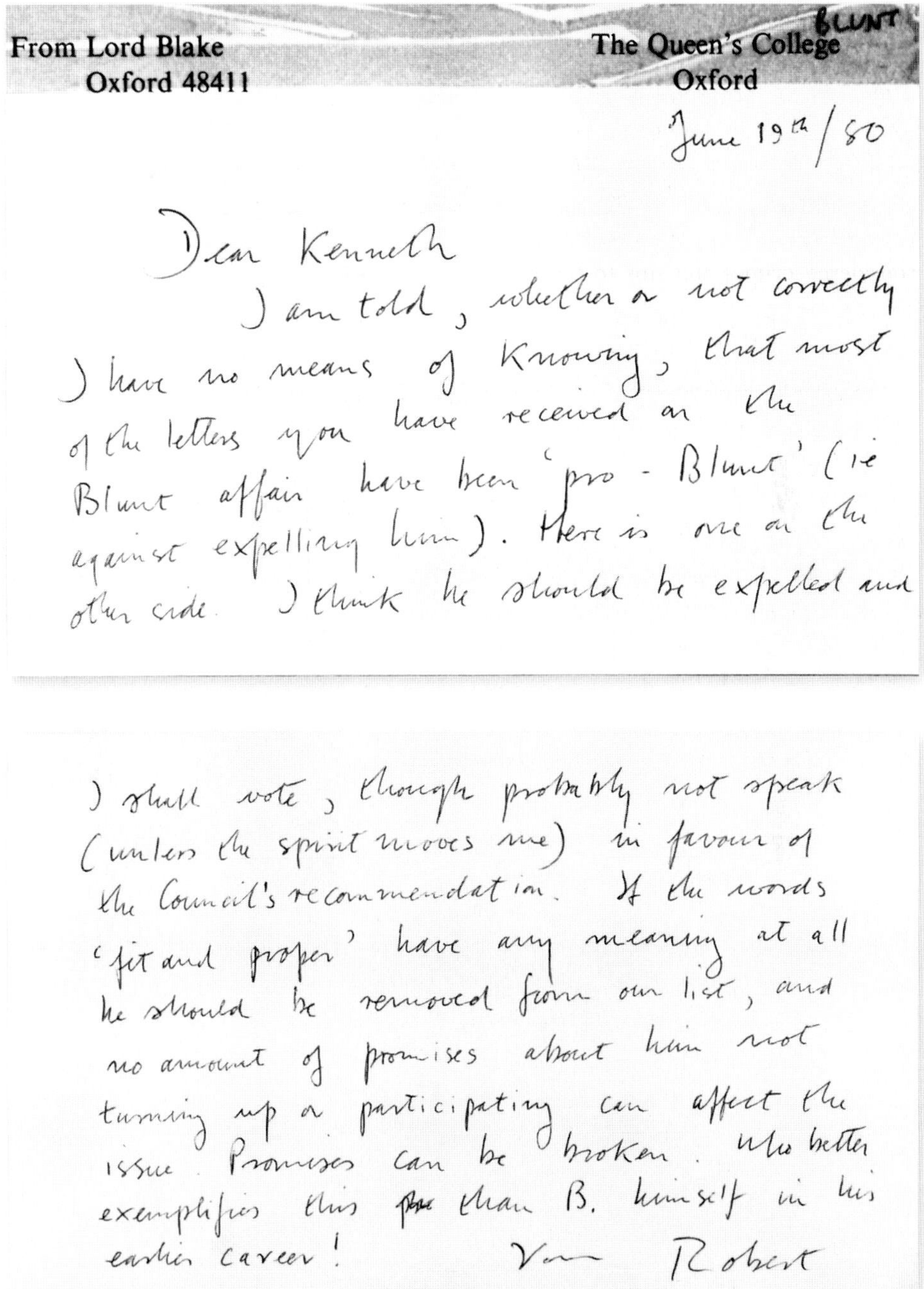

BLUNT

From Lord Blake
Oxford 48411

The Queen's College
Oxford

June 19th/80

Dear Kenneth

I am told, whether or not correctly I have no means of knowing, that most of the letters you have received on the Blunt affair have been 'pro-Blunt' (ie against expelling him). Here is one on the other side. I think he should be expelled and

I shall vote, though probably not speak (unless the spirit moves me) in favour of the Council's recommendation. If the words 'fit and proper' have any meaning at all he should be removed from our list, and no amount of promises about him not turning up or participating can affect the issue. Promises can be broken. Who better exemplifies this than B. himself in his earlier career!

Yours Robert

The 78th Ordinary Annual General Meeting of the British Academy was held at 2.30pm on 3 July 1980. During the afternoon, a steady stream of journalists began to assemble in the courtyard outside the Academy's offices at Burlington House. To protect the meeting's privacy, the blinds of the ground-floor lecture room had been drawn, and staff were stationed at the doors to ensure that only Fellows were admitted. Peter Brown recalls that it was a very hot day and the room was packed, so 'it got rather oppressive, quite apart from the emotional atmosphere'.[21]

In 1980 there were 409 Fellows, 188 of whom attended the meeting.[22] This remains the most attended AGM in the Academy's history. Even before it reached item 10 on the agenda, the meeting had witnessed a most unusual moment of controversy, when there was an (unsuccessful) objection to one of the candidates being recommended for election to the Academy's Fellowship.

When the penultimate item on 'Conduct of a Fellow (Professor Anthony Blunt)' was reached, Dover made some introductory remarks, and added: 'there is one assurance I would like to give every individual Fellow who votes on this matter. Whichever way you vote, you will find yourself in the company of people just as intelligent and just as honourable as you would have found on the other side'.

Lord (Lionel) Robbins CH CB FBA

Notes by Carswell, the Secretary, provide some indication of what followed. Lionel Robbins was the first to speak **[26]**. He acknowledged the gravity of Blunt's misconduct. But he argued that the Academy's function was to advance learning and to give public recognition to scholarly excellence, and that there would be 'grave difficulties of principle' if it based its approach to disciplinary action on wider considerations. 'The community we live in is pluralistic rather than totalitarian', he said. He concluded that the Academy was not called upon to do anything more than dissociate itself from Blunt's actions 'falling outside our own terms of reference'. Helen Gardner then spoke to second the motion, associating herself entirely with Robbins' remarks, and hoping very much that the matter would not be taken further.

[21] Peter Brown interview, 12 February 2018.

[22] The minutes (document 27) record the attendance as 187; in 'Materials', Dover gives the attendance as '187 Fellows (not counting me)'. Peter Brown suggests the official figure 'is almost certainly an underestimate, taking no account of those that the attendance book being circulated didn't reach or late-comers' (interview, 12 February 2018).

26: Speech of Lionel Robbins at Annual General Meeting, 3 July 1980.

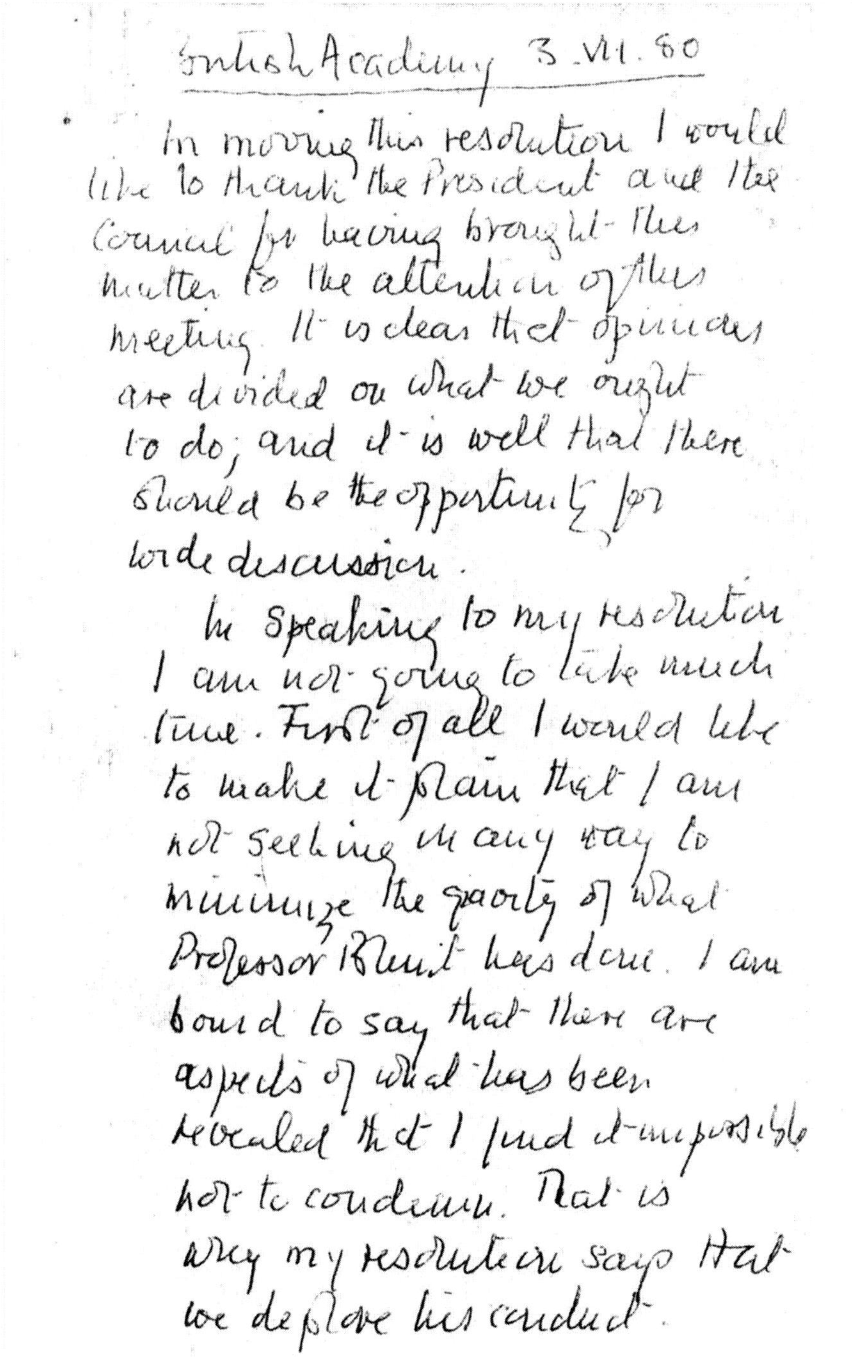

British Academy 3.VII.80

In moving this resolution I would like to thank the President and the Council for having brought this matter to the attention of this meeting. It is clear that opinions are divided on what we ought to do, and it is well that there should be the opportunity for wide discussion.

In speaking to my resolution I am not going to take much time. First of all I would like to make it plain that I am not seeking in any way to minimize the gravity of what Professor Blunt has done. I am bound to say that there are aspects of what has been revealed that I find it impossible not to condemn. That is why my resolution says that we deplore his conduct.

Secondly I come the point where my resolution says that we decide not to proceed further in the matter.

This arises specifically from my understanding of the role of the Academy in our society. I am far from the belief that such a decision would be appropriate for all societies. If Professor Blunt were <u>now</u> responsible for teaching the young and attracting recruits for a university society. I confess that consideration of his position in that respect would seem to me to be incumbent on those in authority.

But the Academy is not such an institution. In my judgement at least, the function of the Academy is to advance learning and to give public recognition to academic excellence. and I see grave difficulties of principle if we go beyond that function and base our discipline on wider considerations. The ~~society~~ community we live in is pluralistic rather than totalitarian.

Thus, confronted with this truly depressing situation, I do not think that we are called upon to do anything more than make it quite clear that we dissociated ourselves from Professor Blunt's actions falling outside our own terms of reference

T.B. Smith spoke to oppose the motion,[23] arguing that Blunt would not have been elected if Fellows had known about his subversive activities. He also claimed that Blunt had continued these activities since becoming a Fellow, when he was neither particularly young nor inexperienced. Smith continued by insisting that Blunt had done real harm and yet had shown no real regret. A.J.P. Taylor told the meeting that he would vote for Robbins' motion but wished to disassociate himself from the 'deplore' part of it. Taylor maintained that Blunt's conduct beyond the field of art history had nothing to do with the Academy. Other Fellows who spoke included the philosopher Michael Dummett, Plumb, and the historian Richard Southern.[24] According to 'Materials', Southern said that he was in a quandary because he didn't want to vote on such a matter at all as it seemed to be entirely outside the Academy's province. Throughout the discussion, the numismatist Christopher Blunt FBA – Anthony Blunt's older brother – 'sat with his eyes to the ground, unmoving but looking grim'.

After 40 minutes of debate, the legal scholar L.C.B. ('Jim') Gower proposed that the meeting should move on to the next item on the agenda.[25] Several Fellows were keen to second the motion. Somewhat taken aback by the way things were going, Dover was unsure what to do. Carswell, seated on the platform next to him, said that procedurally they ought to vote on the Robbins motion, but Dover thought that the meeting had a perfect right not to vote on an item if it didn't want to. The matter was resolved when Robbins withdrew his motion, and so a vote on Gower's proposal took place instead. The minutes of the meeting **[27]** show that it was supported by 120 votes to 42. The AGM therefore avoided making a decision either on Council's recommendation to expel Blunt, or on Robbins' suggestion that members, whilst deploring Blunt's conduct, would take no further action in the matter.[26]

[23] According to Trevor-Roper's letter to Hugh Lloyd-Jones FBA, 27 July 1980, 'The case for expulsion was put (not very well) by T.B. Smith, the oracle of Scotch law' (*One Hundred Letters from Hugh Trevor-Roper*, 2013, pp. 249-50). John Carswell's handwritten notes identify the first person to speak against the Robbins motion as 'J.C. Smith' (who, like T.B. Smith, was both FBA and QC), but this is clearly a slip.

[24] According to Trevor-Roper's letter to Lloyd-Jones, Plumb spoke against the motion 'very weakly'. Like Plumb, Dummett and Southern had their own experiences of intelligence work in the war. Dummett served in a Bletchley Park outpost in India, translating intercepted Japanese messages: see D. Isaacson and I. Rumfitt, 'Michael Anthony Eardley Dummett, 1925-2011', *Biographical Memoirs of Fellows of the British Academy*, xvii (2018), p. 194. Southern served in the Political Intelligence Department at the War Office: see A. Murray, 'Richard William Southern, 1912-2001', *Proceedings of the British Academy*, 120 (2003), p. 428.

[25] In his letter to Plumb of 14 August 1980 (document 48), Dover recalled 'the extraordinary wave of relief and relaxation that went through the rows of faces when he proposed it'.

[26] The Gower motion was passed on a simple show of hands. Ahead of the AGM, Carswell had specially acquired a set of black and white balls, so that Fellows would be able to vote in secret on the two main Blunt motions. Whether these could actually have been used, given the large attendance, is questionable. Jane Lyddon e-mail correspondence, 30 March 2020.

27: Minutes of the Annual General Meeting, 3 July 1980 [extracts]

PRIVATE AND
CONFIDENTIAL

THE BRITISH ACADEMY

Minutes of the Seventy-Eighth Ordinary Annual General Meeting held in the Rooms of the British Academy at Burlington House on 3 July 1980 at 2.30 pm

1. PRESENT

There was an attendance of 187 Fellows. The President, Sir Kenneth Dover, was in the Chair.

12. CONDUCT OF A FELLOW

The meeting considered the motion shown on the Agenda (Item 10), namely that "This meeting deplores the conduct of Professor Anthony Blunt and decides not to proceed further in this matter" and, after debate, decided not to pass judgement on a matter not appertaining to scholarship, and voted by 120 to 42 to proceed to the next business on the Agenda.

Sir Richard Southern FBA, who spoke at the AGM

After the vote on Gower's motion had been taken, Robert Blake asked whether the result meant that Blunt was entitled to go on being invited to Academy functions. When Dover replied that it did, Peter Brown recalls that the ever-florid Blake turned 'a red I've never seen before' and hurried out of the room[27] just as the meeting moved on to its final piece of business, Dover's Presidential Address.[28] After the meeting, A.J.P. Taylor and the sociologist Ralf Dahrendorf spoke to the journalists gathered in the courtyard outside the Academy's rooms. Taylor told them that he was proud that the Academy had shown itself able to 'tolerate the intolerable'. Dahrendorf said the outcome of the meeting demonstrated that the Academy was 'about scholarship'.[29]

Dover had prepared three different press statements prior to the AGM in the hope that they would cover all eventualities: the rejection of Robbins' motion and the acceptance of expulsion; the rejection of both Robbins' motion and expulsion; or the acceptance of Robbins' motion. Now that the meeting had taken another turn, Dover was compelled to compose a new statement **[28]**. It briefly reports how the Blunt discussion had gone (with no mention that Council's original recommendation had been on the agenda), then goes on to stress the sincerity and integrity of all the Fellows engaged in the debate, on whichever side of the argument. It offers some after-the-event justification for why a body with the character of the British Academy should place greater emphasis on Blunt's academic distinction as an art historian, a distinction 'which cannot be unmade by any other facts'. The notice concludes: 'The implication of the decision is that the Academy is an inappropriate body to pass judgement on conduct in matters other than scholarship.'

[27] Peter Brown interview, 12 February 2018: Brown says that several people thought that Blake's intervention had lowered the tone. According to Richard Shannon's 'Biographical Memoir', Blake was shocked 'at the contingency of being expected to sit next to the odious Blunt at table' (Shannon, 'Robert Norman William Blake', pp. 101-2). In his letter to Lloyd-Jones, Trevor-Roper revealed that he and Blake had lunched together before the meeting at the Beefsteak Club, and therefore when Blake delivered his 'pompous declaration' to the AGM, he was 'inflamed with claret and port' (*One Hundred Letters*, p. 250).

[28] The text of Dover's Presidential Address is published in *Proceedings of the British Academy*, 66 (1980), pp. 79-84.

[29] Reported in *The Times*, 4 July 1980. The *Daily Mail*, 4 July, quoted A.J.P. Taylor as saying: 'I don't know whether Professor Blunt will dance a jig or regard our decision as a nonsense, the silly old goat. But this was a victory for decency.'

28: British Academy press release issued after the Annual General Meeting, 3 July 1980.

The Annual General Meeting of the British Academy on July 3rd 1980 debated a motion which said: 'This Meeting deplores the conduct of Professor Anthony Blunt and decides not to proceed further in the matter'.

After long discussion it was decided by a large majority to pass on to the next item of the agenda. No vote, therefore, was taken on Lord Robbins' motion, and the meeting was not called upon to take a decision on the continuance of Professor Blunt as a Fellow.

This is the first time that the Academy has considered such a matter, and it has had no guiding precedent. Every Fellow votes as an individual; we have no party lines or party whips. I know the views of Fellows who expressed their views at the meeting or had previously expressed them to me; about the views of others I can only speculate. Many of those who voted may well have had more than one good reason for voting as they did.

The fact that the Academy has the character of a national institution, administers public funds made available for research in the humanities, and is treated by the academies of other countries as representative of the humanities in this country, is held by many to be a relevant consideration in a case which involved a hidden transference of loyalty in matters affecting national security. However, the Charter of the Academy lays down as the purpose of the Academy the furtherance of historical, philosophical and philological studies, and it lays down as a criterion for election distinction in some branch of those studies. The scale and distinction of Professor Blunt's contributions, as scholar and teacher, to the history of art are a fact which cannot be unmade by any other facts.

The implication of the decision is that the Academy is an inappropriate body to pass judgement on conduct in matters other than scholarship.

3 July 1980 Sir Kenneth Dover, PBA

The next day Anthony Blunt wrote to Lionel Robbins **[29]** to thank him for his support. 'My first moment of delight was when I received the agenda and read your motion, but my delight was greatly increased when I heard reports of what you had actually said at the meeting, and, of course, when I knew the result of the vote.' Blunt regretted the distress he had caused. 'I think you must know what my motives were, even if – like myself now – you heartily disapprove.'

29: Anthony Blunt to Lionel Robbins, 4 July 1980.

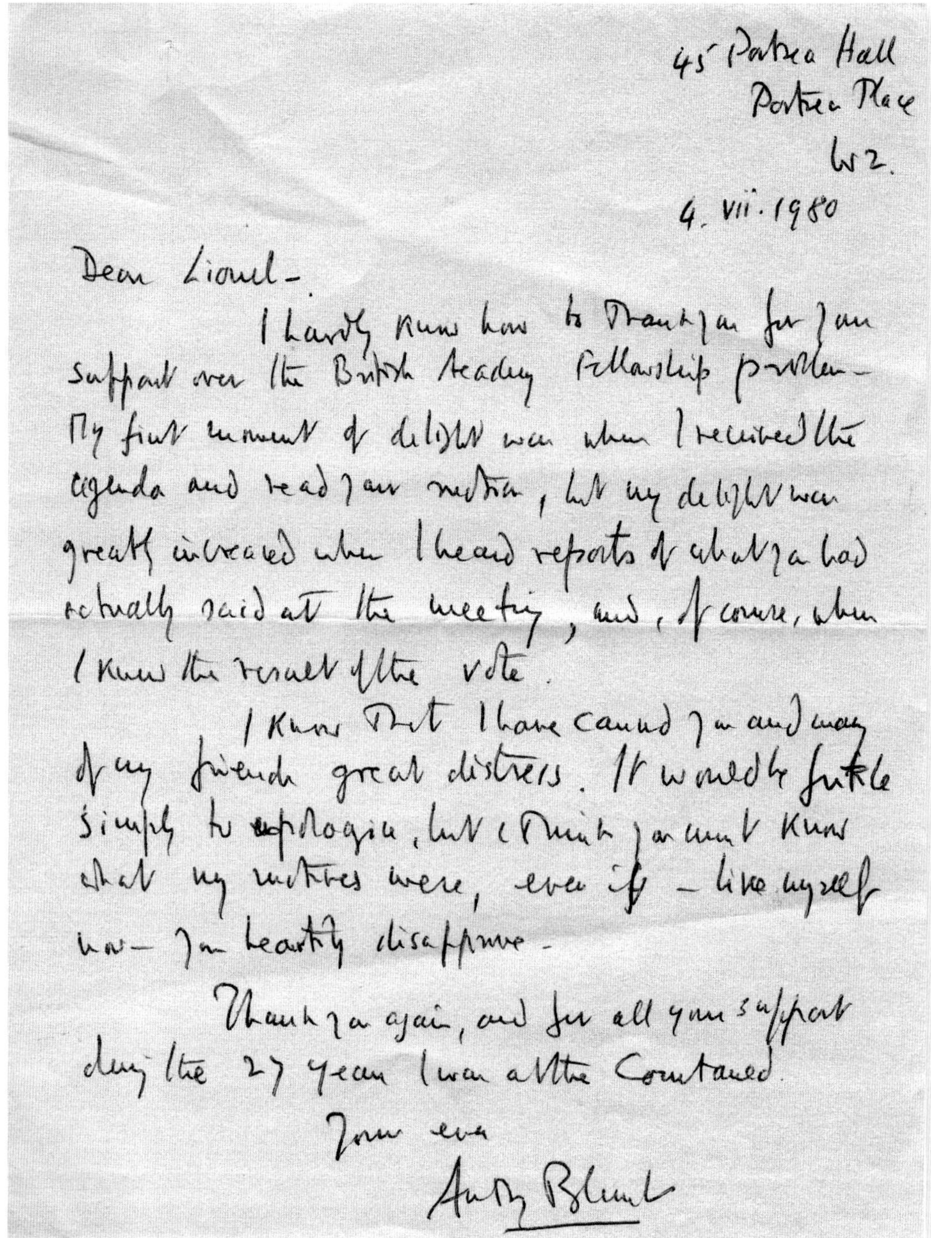

45 Portsea Hall
Portsea Place
W2.

4. vii. 1980

Dear Lionel –

I hardly know how to thank you for your support over the British Academy Fellowship problem – My first moment of delight was when I received the agenda and read your motion, but my delight was greatly increased when I heard reports of what you had actually said at the meeting, and, of course, when I knew the result of the vote.

I know that I have caused you and many of my friends great distress. It would be futile simply to apologize, but I think you must know what my motives were, even if – like myself now – you heartily disapprove.

Thank you again, and for all your support during the 27 years I was at the Courtauld.

Yours ever

Anthony Blunt

On that same day, 4 July, Dover wrote to Blunt to correct a BBC television news report stating that the AGM had 'deplored' his conduct. Blunt replied **[30]** to say that he hadn't in fact been aware of the report, but he took the opportunity to say how he was 'greatly relieved' by the decision of the Annual General Meeting: 'I may not be a good attendant at Academy functions, but I value my Fellowship very deeply.'

30: Anthony Blunt to Kenneth Dover, [undated, July 1980].

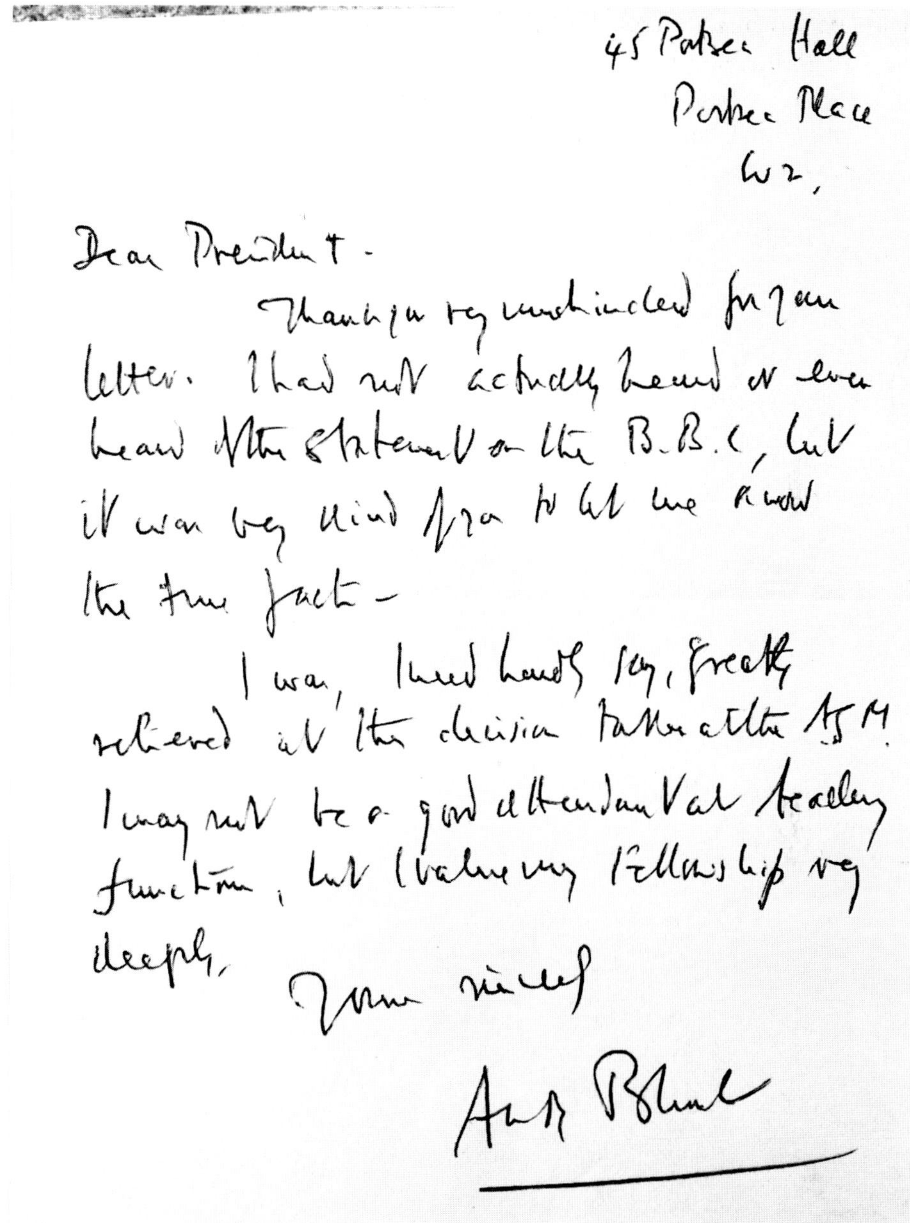
45 Portsea Hall
Portsea Place
W2,

Dear President -

Thank you very much indeed for your letter. I had not actually heard or even heard of the statement on the B.B.C., but it was very kind of you to let me know the true facts -

I was, I need hardly say, greatly relieved at the decision taken at the AGM. I may not be a good attendant at Academy functions, but I value my Fellowship very deeply.

Yours sincerely

Anthony Blunt

But while Anthony Blunt was pleased at the outcome of the Annual General Meeting, others definitely were not. The day after it, Robert Blake wrote to Dover **[31]** to offer an explanation for his hasty departure – that he had to get to an important vote in the House of Lords. Blake went on to say that he didn't mind in the least if his exit had seemed 'discourteous to our wrong-headed colleagues who voted in the majority'. The fact that the AGM couldn't even bring itself to 'deplore' Blunt's conduct was 'disgraceful and discreditable. Most people outside the academic cloisters are astounded.'

31: Robert Blake to Kenneth Dover, 4 July 1980.

Telephone 48411
Provost: Lord Blake, F.B.A., J.P.

The Queen's College
Oxford

4 July 1980

Dear Kenneth,

I hope you did not think I was being personally discourteous to you when I walked out at the beginning of your address yesterday. If I was being discourteous to our wrong-headed colleagues who voted in the majority I don't mind in the least. I had promised to obey a Conservative two-line Whip in the Lords (the House scarcely ever has three-line whips and so this is a fairly cogent command) on the Committee stage of the Housing Bill as soon as I could get away. In fact I just made it for the most important division of the day.

I think the Academy's decision was disgraceful and discreditable. Most people outside the academic cloisters are astounded. It will have done our image nothing but harm. Lord Robbins's motion would have been just tolerable but to refuse even to 'deplore' the conduct of a traitor seems to me insufferable. I would have voted for expulsion without the slightest hesitation.

Yours ever,

Robert

Sir Kenneth Dover, FRSE, FBA,
President of The British Academy,
Burlington House,
Piccadilly,
London.

Three other Fellows of the British Academy took their dissatisfaction at the turn of events further, and wrote to Dover to resign their Fellowships. Theodore Skeat and Colin Roberts were both scholars whose area of expertise was the study of ancient papyri. Skeat **[32]** believed that, as a body established by Royal Charter, the Academy should not keep within its number 'someone whom the Sovereign has publicly degraded from the order of knighthood'. He had decided that he could no longer remain a Fellow of 'a body in which personal integrity is regarded by the majority of members as an irrelevancy'.

Mr Theodore Skeat FBA

32: Theodore Skeat to Kenneth Dover, 4 July 1980.

63 Ashbourne Road,
London W 5 3 D H.

4 July 1980

My dear Dover,

I have been thinking over the proceedings at the Annual General Meeting yesterday with regard to the Council's recommendation "that the name of Professor Anthony Blunt be removed from the list of Fellows on the ground that he is not a fit and proper person to be a Fellow." For me the question at issue is a simple one. Since the Academy was founded by Royal Charter, I do not see how we can retain among our members someone whom the Sovereign has publicly degraded from the order of knighthood. That yesterday's meeting should have failed to follow the clear lead given by Her Majesty the Queen seems to me wholly deplorable, and I have been compelled to consider my further membership of the Academy.

I have now decided that I can no longer retain membership of a body in which personal integrity is regarded by the majority of members as an irrelevancy, and have resolved to resign forthwith my Fellowship of the Academy and also to resign from the two Academy Committees of which I am currently a member, the Computer Committee and the Oxyrhynchus Papyri Committee.

I am sure that my grandfather, Professor W.W. Skeat, who was one of the First Fellows, and who was both a scholar and a patriot, would have approved the action I am taking.

I take leave of the Academy with the utmost regret and with no hard feelings, since this is a clash of opinions and attitudes to life. I wish also to record my deep gratitude for the honour which the Academy paid me by electing me a Fellow in 1963, and for the many kindnesses I have received both from the Academy and its staff over the last seventeen years.

Yours very sincerely,
Theodore Skeat

Roberts [33], who had not been present at the AGM, wrote a few days later. He found the outcome of that meeting 'deeply disturbing', because it implied that scholarship could be 'carried on in a vacuum' – an attitude that was 'dangerous as well as distasteful'.[30]

Dr Colin Roberts CBE FBA

[30] Colin Roberts had his own experience of intelligence work during the war, in the Foreign Office – including service at Bletchley Park: see D. Russell and P. Parsons, 'Colin Henderson Roberts, 1909-1990', *Proceedings of the British Academy*, 84 (1994), p. 480. Roberts and Skeat would not remain in a permanent state of breach with the British Academy. In 1983, the Academy published a very successful book jointly authored by the two of them, on *The Birth of the Codex*.

33: Colin Roberts to Kenneth Dover, 10 July 1980.

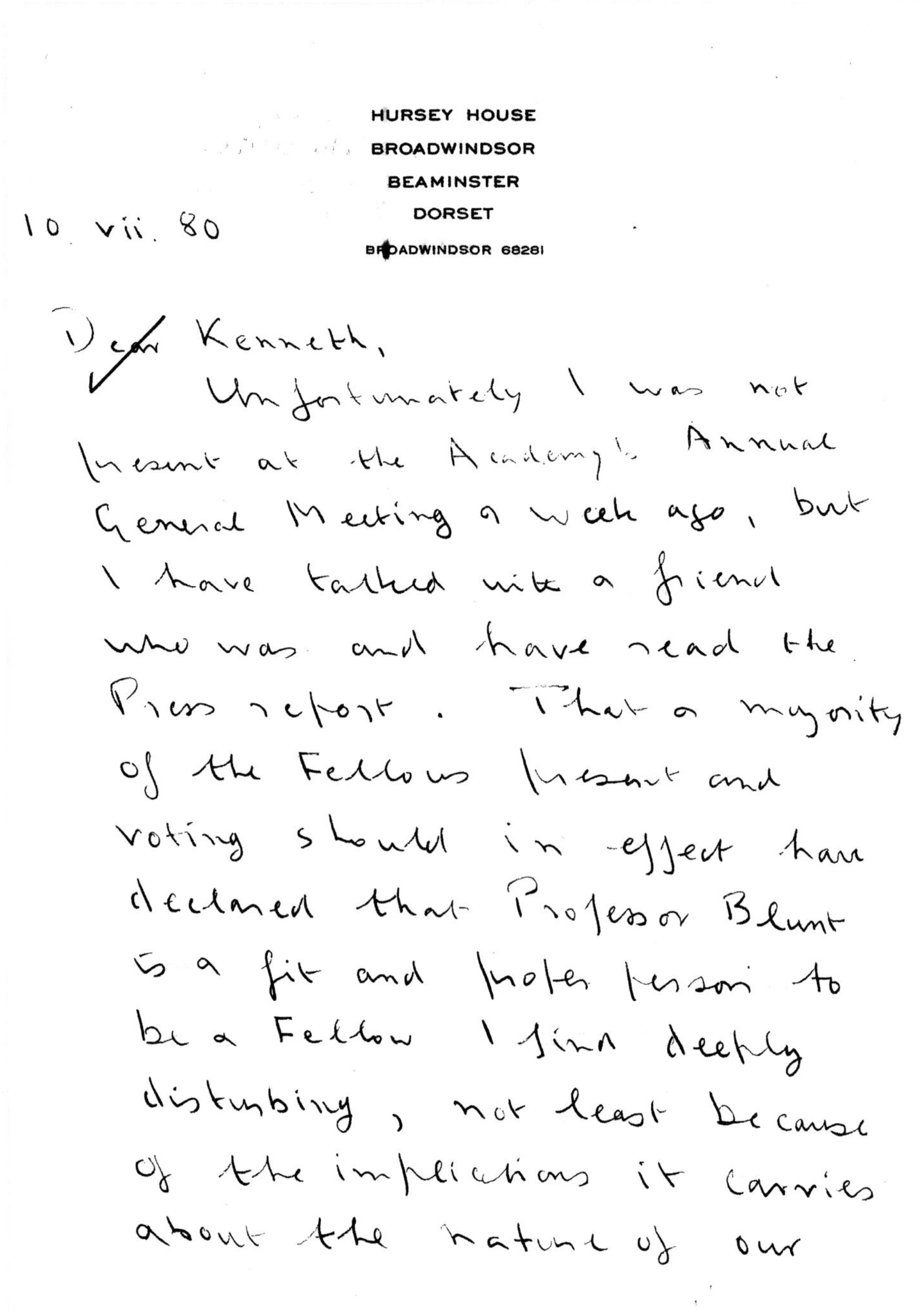

HURSEY HOUSE
BROADWINDSOR
BEAMINSTER
DORSET

BROADWINDSOR 68281

10 vii. 80

Dear Kenneth,

Unfortunately I was not present at the Academy's Annual General Meeting a week ago, but I have talked with a friend who was and have read the Press report. That a majority of the Fellows present and voting should in effect have declared that Professor Blunt is a fit and proper person to be a Fellow I find deeply disturbing, not least because of the implications it carries about the nature of our

Society; it would seem to follow that matters of conduct are totally irrelevant to membership and that the pursuit of scholarship should, or at any rate can, be carried on in a vacuum.

I find this attitude so dangerous as well as distasteful that I have decided with great reluctance that I must resign my Fellowship and membership of any Academy Committees. Membership of the Academy is an honour of which I have been very conscious and which for many years has given me enjoyment and interest; my regret at leaving it is proportionate. And I should not wish to go without expressing my appreciation of those with whom I have been associated, not least the Staff of the Academy.

Yours ever

Colin Roberts

The third Fellow to resign was the ancient historian John Crook **[34]**. He was a member of Council and had voted to recommend Blunt's expulsion – a view that at the AGM had been 'so overwhelmingly thrust aside … as not to be voted on at all'. He was 'deeply dismayed at the evident size of the majority' who held what seemed to him 'an untenable view' of the Academy's nature and 'its necessary relationship to the life of the nation in general'. The Academy could not be 'an ivory tower of nothing but scholarship', and he feared 'the danger of scholars just standing aside'. He conceded that his resignation might be an emotional reaction: 'the personal truth is that I don't possess that long a spoon'.[31]

Professor John Crook FBA

[31] Crook's resignation is discussed in P.D.A. Garnsey, 'John Anthony Crook, 1921-2007', *Proceedings of the British Academy*, 161 (2009), pp. 124-5.

34: John Crook to Kenneth Dover, 6 July 1980.

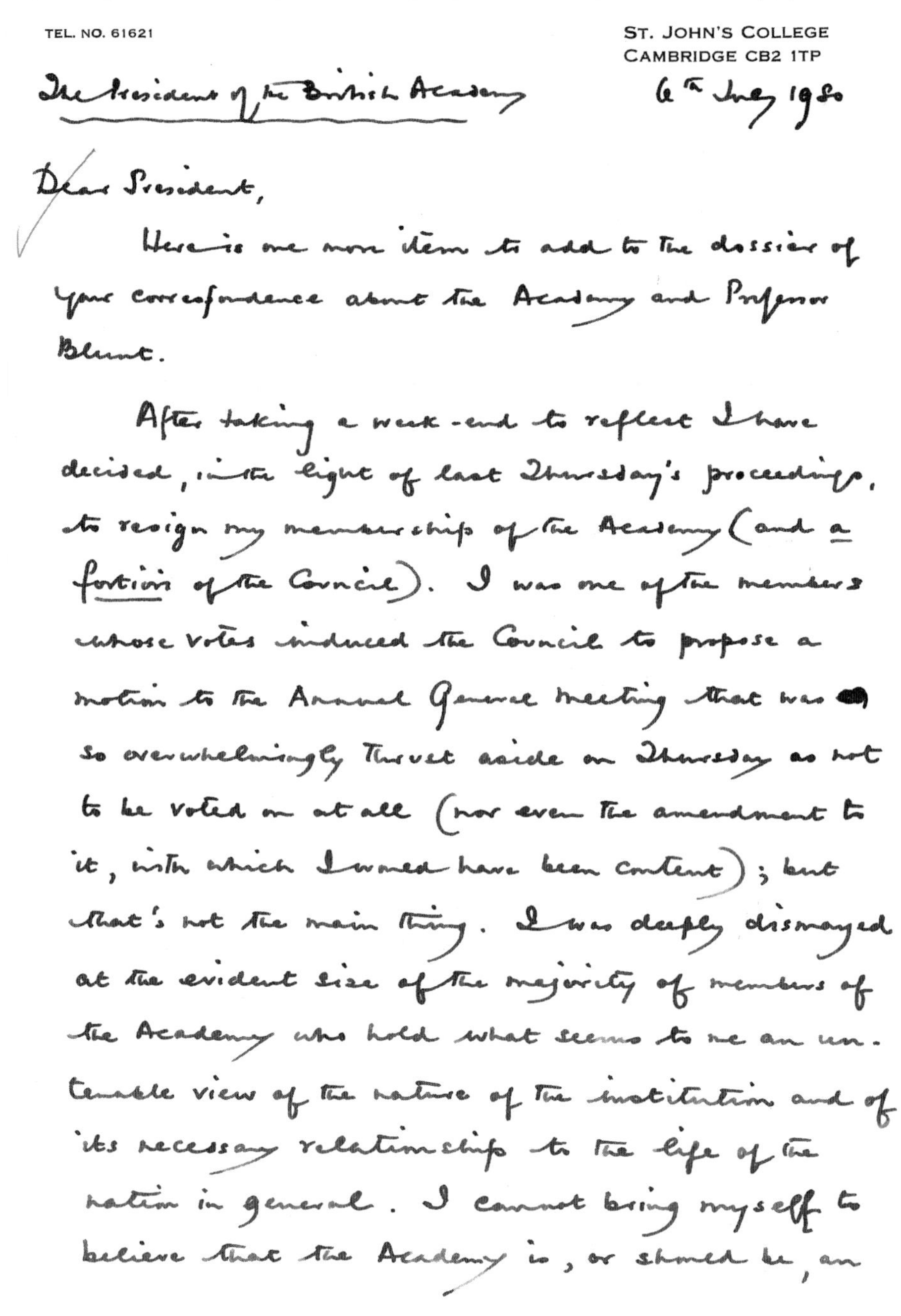

TEL. NO. 61621

ST. JOHN'S COLLEGE
CAMBRIDGE CB2 1TP

The President of the British Academy

6th July 1980

Dear President,

Here is one more item to add to the dossier of your correspondence about the Academy and Professor Blunt.

After taking a week-end to reflect I have decided, in the light of last Thursday's proceedings, to resign my membership of the Academy (and a fortiori of the Council). I was one of the members whose votes induced the Council to propose a motion to the Annual General Meeting that was so overwhelmingly thrust aside on Thursday as not to be voted on at all (nor even the amendment to it, with which I would have been content); but that's not the main thing. I was deeply dismayed at the evident size of the majority of members of the Academy who hold what seems to me an untenable view of the nature of the institution and of its necessary relationship to the life of the nation in general. I cannot bring myself to believe that the Academy is, or should be, an

TEL. NO. 61621 2 ST. JOHN'S COLLEGE
CAMBRIDGE CB2 1TP

ivory tower of nothing but scholarships. I re-cognize the intensity with which people fear the consequences of allowing politics to touch scholarship, but for my own part I fear more intensely the danger of scholars just standing aside. I further believe that, while open expression of political opposition is honourable and necessary and ought not to be persecuted in any nation or by any body, secret gnawing at the foundations of the state damages the whole of society, including, ultimately, its scholarship. Of an institution that has so signally and decisively rejected these beliefs of mine I cannot endure any longer to be a part.

Your words to the meeting were generous and wise, and I accept that those with whom I so profoundly disagree are not only the large majority but also no less sensitive and earnest in their convictions than I hope I am. I do believe that a wrong (a tiny one) was done to the national interest last Thursday;

TEL. NO. 61621 3 ST. JOHN'S COLLEGE
CAMBRIDGE CB2 1TP

but it may well be that what I have written above is no more than a rationalization of emotion, and that the simple, personal truth is that I don't possess that long a spoon.

Anyhow, I hereby give notice of my resignation from the British Academy as from the date when you receive this letter, or from whatever other date may be least inconvenient for you and the officers of the Academy.

Yours sincerely

J M Crook

[John Crook]

By permission of St John's College, Cambridge

Since the Academy's main business had been completed for the academic year, Dover moved up to his house in St Andrews at the end of July for the rest of the summer. But unknown to him – and undocumented in the British Academy's own archives – a determined group of malcontents within the Academy's Fellowship (or 'the nasties', to use the terminology of the ancient historian Geoffrey de Ste. Croix FBA)[32] had begun plotting to overturn the result of the AGM.

On 7 July, the historian Ian Christie FBA wrote to Plumb to say how 'livid' he still felt. He copied to Plumb a letter he had sent to *The Times*, criticising the Academy's 'monstrous error of judgement' – a letter which the newspaper had not printed. Christie said he had also written to Blake: 'if historians of Oxford, Cambridge and London all join forces on the issue', it might lead to 'sufficient unpleasantness' to induce Blunt to resign. He sought to 'sap the liberal-intellectual argument' that had prevailed at the AGM. Historians, he argued, could not adopt such an 'ivory towers' mentality: 'History is at the sharp end of any conflict with totalitarianism'. Plumb replied on 14 July – he had been in New York since 'that wretched meeting'. He reported that Blake, the historian John Ehrman FBA, and himself were all considering resignation, but felt that if they did 'this would be one more victory for Blunt.' Christie wrote back the next day. He said he had no intention of resigning and 'running away from our responsibilities'. He also reported his understanding that Blake too would not resign, 'although he was prepared to boycott any social gathering at which he might encounter Blunt'.

The Times did not publish Christie's letter, but on 26 July the *Daily Telegraph* published one from George Huxley, a Professor of Greek at Queen's University, Belfast. Though not himself a Fellow of the British Academy, Huxley had exchanged letters with Dover about the need to expel Blunt back in December 1979 and January 1980 – indeed, he had been one of the earliest correspondents on the subject. Now he felt compelled to protest publicly about the Academy's 'shameful failure'. The Academy enjoyed royal patronage, it represented British scholarship internationally, and in the absence of a Humanities Research Council it disbursed public money. Taxpayers, Huxley argued, might now question 'whether the Academy should continue to perform its present public functions'. And individual Fellows might bear in mind that 'those who tolerate traitors … are themselves in danger of acting treasonably.'

From that moment, correspondence and comments about the Blunt business began to appear in the *Telegraph* on an almost daily basis. Christie published a letter there on 1 August (incorporating much of his unpublished missive to *The Times*); the next day he wrote to Plumb inviting him to follow it up by 'bowling a swift over-arm' of his own. On 2 August, a letter in the *Daily Telegraph* from Skeat made public that he had resigned over the issue – which prompted articles in the *Sunday Telegraph*, the *Daily Telegraph* and *The Times* over the next two days about those who had resigned and those who might yet do so. And, through a letter in the *Telegraph* on 4 August, a new voice entered the fray to condemn the AGM decision, that of Norman Gash FBA, a historian at the University of St Andrews, who had been unable to attend the meeting.

Professor Ian Christie FBA

[32] In his letter of 5 July 1980 to Dover, de Ste. Croix commended him on his conduct of the AGM 'in a situation of great difficulty and unpleasantness'. He went on: 'If only some of the nasties had threatened to resign unless …!'

The press coverage had the effect of stirring other Fellows who were unhappy at the AGM's decision. On 3 August, the scholar of Hittite studies, Oliver Gurney FBA, wrote to Dover **[35]** to explore how the decision might be rescinded. If all those who disapproved of it simply resigned, he said, the Academy would be weakened. Confessing that most of the Fellows he knew were on the other side of the argument, Gurney said he had heard a news report that there was 'a movement among the Fellows to fight the decision from the inside', and he wished to support that.

Professor Oliver Gurney FBA

35: Oliver Gurney to Kenneth Dover, 3 August 1980.

3rd August 1980

Dear President,

I was disturbed to hear and read this morning that Colin Roberts and Mr. Skeat and a third Fellow (Lord Blake?) have resigned from the Academy over the Blunt affair and am wondering what is the right course of action, as I agree particularly with Mr. Skeat that a society with a royal charter cannot tolerate in its midst a member who has shown himself disloyal to the Crown, and I was one of those who voted with the minority at the A.G.M. I feel, however, that the Academy is much more important than Mr. Blunt and that if all those who disapprove of that decision were to resign, the Academy would merely be weakened and be so much less able to discharge its functions. What is wanted is somehow to get that decision rescinded, in order to restore the Academy's good name. I thought therefore that I would write to you to ask whether you have had other letters to the same effect and whether, if a large number of signatures could be obtained to some sort of manifesto, there would be any possibility of overturning the decision of the A.G.M. Unfortunately almost all the Fellows I have talked to have supported the decision and I do not know anyone personally who is on this side of the fence. But the news-reader said this morning that there was a movement among the Fellows to fight the decision from the inside. Do you know anything of this? If so, I would gladly support it.

Yours sincerely,

O R Gurney

O. R. GURNEY

While some were determined to contest the AGM's decision from within the Academy's ranks, a fourth Fellow now decided that it was time to resign. Explaining his reasons in his letter of 4 August **[36]**, Charles Bawden said that, during the time Blunt had been associated with the 'Stalinist régime', many scholars 'were killed or allowed to die in prisons and concentration camps': that was the philosophy that Blunt had served. In notes he later wrote about his life, Bawden – a scholar of Mongolian studies – expanded on this: 'I knew little of happenings in the USSR, but I did know something of what had happened in the dreadful years of the 1930s in her satellite Mongolia. There, too, the truth and decency had been suppressed, individuals and families destroyed, and, worst of all from an academic point of view, honest scholars killed or imprisoned. Men whom I later knew and counted as colleagues and friends had been persecuted. Others, whose work I knew and respected, had been murdered.'[33]

Professor Charles Bawden FBA

[33] Quoted in V. Veit, 'Charles Bawden', *Biographical Memoirs of Fellows of the British Academy*, xviii (2019), pp. 465-6. Bawden had himself undertaken intelligence work during the war, including some time at Bletchley (Veit, pp. 452-3).

36: Charles Bawden to Kenneth Dover, 4 August 1980.

19 Richings Way,
Iver,
Bucks.
4 August 1980.

Dear Sir Kenneth,

After much anxious thought I have come to the conclusion that I can no longer remain a Fellow of the British Academy. This letter constitutes my formal resignation of my Fellowship.

My resignation is of course connected with the case of Professor A. Blunt, FBA. I am not concerned here with the political aspects of Professor Blunt's activities, but with their implications for the cause of scholarship. The Stalinist régime which, secretly and from the security of this country, Professor Blunt chose voluntarily to serve, subordinated scholarship to political control. Worse than that, during the time when Professor Blunt was associated with that régime, many Russian and other scholars, who were within the borders of the USSR, were killed or allowed to die in prisons and concentration camps. Names spring to mind even in the small sector of orientalism with which I am connected. This was the philosophy which Professor Blunt served, and presumably wished to promote.

I cannot accept the majority decision of the Fellows that such activities and views are not matters of which the Academy should take cognizance. The gap which separates me from that decision is too wide to admit compromise, and as my view is evidently a minority one, I feel it right that I should submit my resignation. I do this with the utmost regret, as I have valued my Fellowship more than anything else in my academic career, and had looked forward to belonging to, and serving, the Academy for many years to come.

Yours sincerely,

C.R. Bawden.

The President of the British Academy,
Sir Kenneth Dover, FBA.

Copy to Professor O.R. Gurney, FBA,
Chairman of Section 4.

With Dover now in Scotland, Peter Brown kept him informed of events. His letter of 5 August **[37]** revealed the rising level of press and public interest to which the British Academy was now being subjected. He also referred to a visit from a *Daily Mail* journalist, an episode on which he has subsequently elaborated: 'He wanted to see the rooms of the Academy, because he believed that the British Academy was a homosexual club for the establishment, at which regular orgies, led by Blunt, took place.'[34] Brown managed to persuade him that nothing of the kind took place there, and no more was heard about it. That this journalist was not alone in his preconceived notion of the Academy is confirmed by an anonymous piece of correspondence mentioned in Brown's letter. An article in the *Daily Telegraph* on 4 August had quoted Dover as saying that he did not believe the Academy's reputation had been lowered in the eyes of the public. A reader of that article sent Dover a brief note **[38]**, presuming that the Academy was 'largely homosexual'.

38: Anonymous letter to Kenneth Dover, 4 August 1980.

Sir Kenneth Dover -

"Sir Kenneth said he did not believe that the Academy's reputation had been lowered in the eyes of the public."

Many have come to the conclusion that the Academy is largely homosexual hence the retention of Blunt.

DT READER

37: Peter Brown to Kenneth Dover, 5 August 1980.

From
P. W. H. BROWN
DEPUTY SECRETARY

THE BRITISH ACADEMY
BURLINGTON HOUSE, PICCADILLY
LONDON, W1V ONS
Telephone 01-734 0457

5 August 1980.

Dear Kenneth,

I enclose a letter of resignation from Professor Charles Bawden which grieves me. He's an old friend and I particularly take to heart his last sentence. I wrote to Mr Skeat, Dr Roberts and Professor Crook (who replies that he rather enjoys being cast in the role of 'third man').

Press enquiries continue to flow in, and we had a visit from the Daily Mail yesterday afternoon. More lightheartedly, I may say that we received this morning a quintessentially 'Daily Telegraph' letter from a retired Lt.-Col. denoucing liars, thieves, swindlers, poltroons (yes, truly) and traitors; an anonymous letter from 'DT Reader' who concludes that the Academy is largely homosexual; and a letter from a Friend of the Royal Academy saying that he will never visit an exhibition there again. In between these various excitements we do a little work.

Yours,

Peter

Sir Kenneth Dover P.B.A.,
49 Hepburn Gardens,
St Andrews,
Fife. KY16 9LS.

[34] Peter Brown interview, 12 February 2018.

On 8 August, Blunt wrote to Dover **[39]** to say how distressed he was at the way the *Daily Telegraph* was 'using me as a stick with which to beat the Academy'. He now realised that it had been foolish to assume that, after the AGM's vote, 'the matter would be dropped'. In 'Materials', Dover confides that he was uncertain how to reply – 'Though I would have been quite willing to execute Blunt, I had no desire to be rude to him' – so he put off doing so.

39: Anthony Blunt to Kenneth Dover, 8 August 1980.

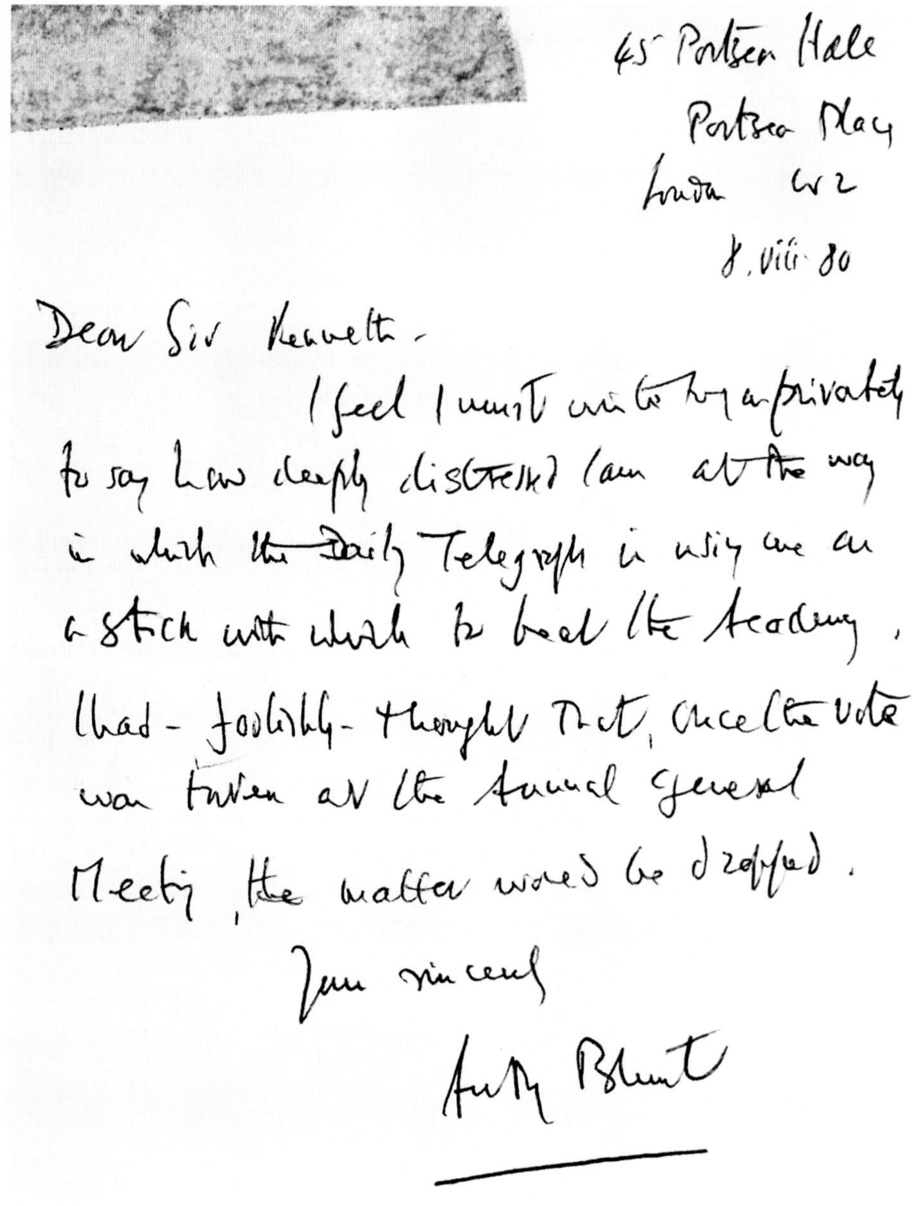
45 Portsea Hall
Portsea Place
London W2
8.viii.80

Dear Sir Kenneth,

I feel I must write to you privately to say how deeply distressed I am at the way in which the ~~Daily~~ Telegraph is using me as a stick with which to beat the Academy. I had – foolishly – thought that, once the vote was taken at the Annual General Meeting, the matter would be dropped.

Yours sincerely

Anthony Blunt

The 'matter' had certainly not been dropped – indeed it was being pursued through channels both private and public. W. Sidney Allen FBA was a linguistics scholar at Trinity College, Cambridge – the college from which Blunt had resigned his Honorary Fellowship at the end of 1979. Frustrated that Blunt had not now acted similarly to save the Academy further embarrassment, Allen wrote to Dover on 7 August **[40]** stating his own intention to resign at the end of the year if 'this creature' had not yet been shamed into quitting. Allen copied this letter 'for information' to some like-minded Fellows (certainly including Plumb and Norman Gash).

Professor W. Sidney Allen FBA

40: W. Sidney Allen to Kenneth Dover, 7 August 1980.

TRINITY COLLEGE
CAMBRIDGE
CB2 1TQ

7 August 1980

To the President of the British Academy

Dear Sir Kenneth,

I did not vote on the Blunt affair, in the perhaps naïve expectation that the man would have enough vestiges of honour to resign his fellowship on seeing the embarrassment his continuation was causing — as he had already done in respect of his honorary fellowship of my college (though in that case he presumably knew that he was otherwise likely to be expelled).

I do not see how I can remain a member of an academic body which includes in its number this creature whose treachery has aided a régime notorious for the suppression of academic as well as other freedoms. It is possible that Blunt may even yet be shamed into behaving in this matter as if he were an honourable man, and I am therefore delaying my resignation until the end of the year. I am giving provisional notice now only because, if it becomes necessary for me to resign then, it might be felt that I was reviving a stale issue.

Yours sincerely,

W. Sidney Allen

Copy sent to PBA

Another Fellow was following a less discreet approach to oust Blunt from the Academy. In a letter published in the *Daily Telegraph* on 6 August, Robert Blake deplored 'the behaviour of the British Academy', but declared his intention not to resign in protest, believing 'that there is a rather better chance of preventing the repetition of such folly by staying than leaving'.

But he went much further in an article published two days later in the *Daily Mail* **[41]**, bearing a very pointed headline (which may not have been of his own choosing). Blunt, he wrote, had 'spied for a peculiarly odious regime, a grinding totalitarian tyranny which, if given half a chance, would quickly have extinguished everything that the academy stands for.' He compared the 'blinkered attitude of the eminent academics' with those athletes who, in spite of the Soviet invasion of Afghanistan, had ignored the British government's urging that they should boycott the Moscow Olympics (which had ended the previous weekend).

41: Article by Robert Blake in the *Daily Mail*, 8 August 1980.

British Academy of cowards

If they won't expel this traitor, who will they ever kick out?

by Lord Blake

Provost of Queen's College, Oxford, and one of the minority of fellows of the British Academy who voted to get rid of Anthony Blunt.

Anthony Blunt: Spied f

FELLOWS of the British Academy were asked to expel the Soviet spy Anthony Blunt because he was not 'a fit and proper person' to be a member.

But the motion at last month's annual meeting was defeated by nearly three to one.

The meeting refused even to accept an amendment which would have kept him on the list while 'deploring' his conduct.

So Academisian Blunt, as he would be called in the country which was once his spiritual home, remains undeplored and a full member of the body which does for the humanities what the Royal Society does for the sciences.

The academy is incorporated under a royal charter and is largely financed by a Government grant. It does not and could not be expected to take orders from the Government, but it has an official status which makes it different from a purely private body like a London club.

Its members are supposed to act with some sense of public responsibility.

It is fair to say that apart from a few ageing Cambridge Marxists, the majority of the fellows deplored Blunt's conduct. The argument which carried the day was that the academy exists solely for the recognition and promotion of learning. It follows from this that a person's behaviour in other fields is entirely irrelevant and is a matter of which the academy should take no notice at all.

On this argument, presumably the only misdemeanour for which a fellow could ever be expelled is some sort of fraud or chicanery in connection with his research—like the affair of Piltdown Man.

As one of the minority in favour not only of deploring but also expelling Anthony Blunt, I find this argument extraordinary.

This is not a matter of political persecution. I would certainly not want to expel someone because he was a Marxist, though I happen to think that Marxism is a very silly creed.

Essence

Nor is it relevant to bandy charges of 'McCarthyism,' as some academicians did and do. The essence of the evils connected with the late Senator was the smearing of innocent people who held liberal to Leftish opinions with the untrue charge of being spies or traitors.

Anthony Blunt is a self-confessed spy. There is no question of a smear. His guilt is admitted.

Equally meaningless is the cry of witch-hunt. The point to remember about that over-used phrase is that there are no witches to hunt. But there are spies. And Anthony Blunt was one of them.

What is more, he spied for a peculiarly odious regime, a grinding totalitarian tyranny which, if given half a chance, would quickly have extinguished everything that the academy stands for.

It is here that the blindness and irresponsibility of the majority of the fellows seems most striking. The institution to which they belong is devoted to freedom of inquiry and freedom to publish the results of inquiry.

How much of that freedom would have survived if there had been a Communist Government in Whitehall? What sort of freedom do Russian academicians have today? The truth is that one cannot completely dissociate learning from morality, any more than one can dissociate sport.

The blinkered attitude of the eminent academics is comparable to that of the athletes who went to the Moscow Olympics despite the invasion of Afghanistan — with this difference that sportsmen are not expected to do much thinking whereas academics are.

One cannot help wondering how far those who voted in the majority would carry this dissociation. It is a fair bet that if Blunt's treachery had been known at the time, he would never have been elected to the academy in the first place, whatever the arguments now used to prevent his expulsion.

It can no doubt be maintained that it is one thing to refrain from electing someone, another to remove him after he has been elected.

But if treason is not enough, what degree of crime is needed to make someone not a fit and proper person, to be a fellow? Are there no limits at all?

Suppose a fellow of the British Academy from the safe distance of a country which had no treaty of extradition with Britain gave a Press conference and declared that he had been responsible for the murders of Lord Mountbatten and Mr Airey Neave, would the academy take no cognisance of that interesting revelation?

I find it hard to believe that a motion to expel the person concerned would not be carried. But the logic of the pro-Blunt argument points the other way. It is simply incredible that a convicted terrorist would not be removed from the British Academy.

Why then, is treason not considered enough? I suspect that somewhere at the back of the minds of some of the elderly academics who voted against the motion was the question of what country was benefiting from Blunt's treason.

Ally

After all, it was a long while ago and there had been a time when Russia did seem a Utopia to a large section of the intellectual world, or at least an ally against the advance of Nazism and Fascism. There on the road to treason but for the grace of God some of them might have gone, too.

Blunt seemed in a sense 'one of us'—on the correct side if slight wrong-headed. I could not help wondering what would have happened if a fellow of the academy had been exposed as a former spy for Franco's Spain or Dr Strydom's South Africa or the Greece of the colonels.

My guess is that a motion to expel him would have been carried with ease—and rightly. The academy has done itself nothing but harm over the Blunt affair.

It is sad that a great institution should appear to the public either to have adopted a double standard of morality or to be indistinguishable from a group of ostriches.

Blake's article may have been more dramatic, but the circulating copies of W.S. Allen's letter were having more impact. Gash, who had been pondering how best to respond to the Blunt business, had gained a sense of Plumb's views from the newspapers. Spurred by the arrival of the copy of Allen's letter to Dover, on 9 August he wrote to Plumb **[42]** to say that he was 'much disposed to follow his example' of threatening to resign at the end of the year.[35]

Professor Norman Gash FBA

42: Norman Gash to J.H. Plumb, 9 August 1980.

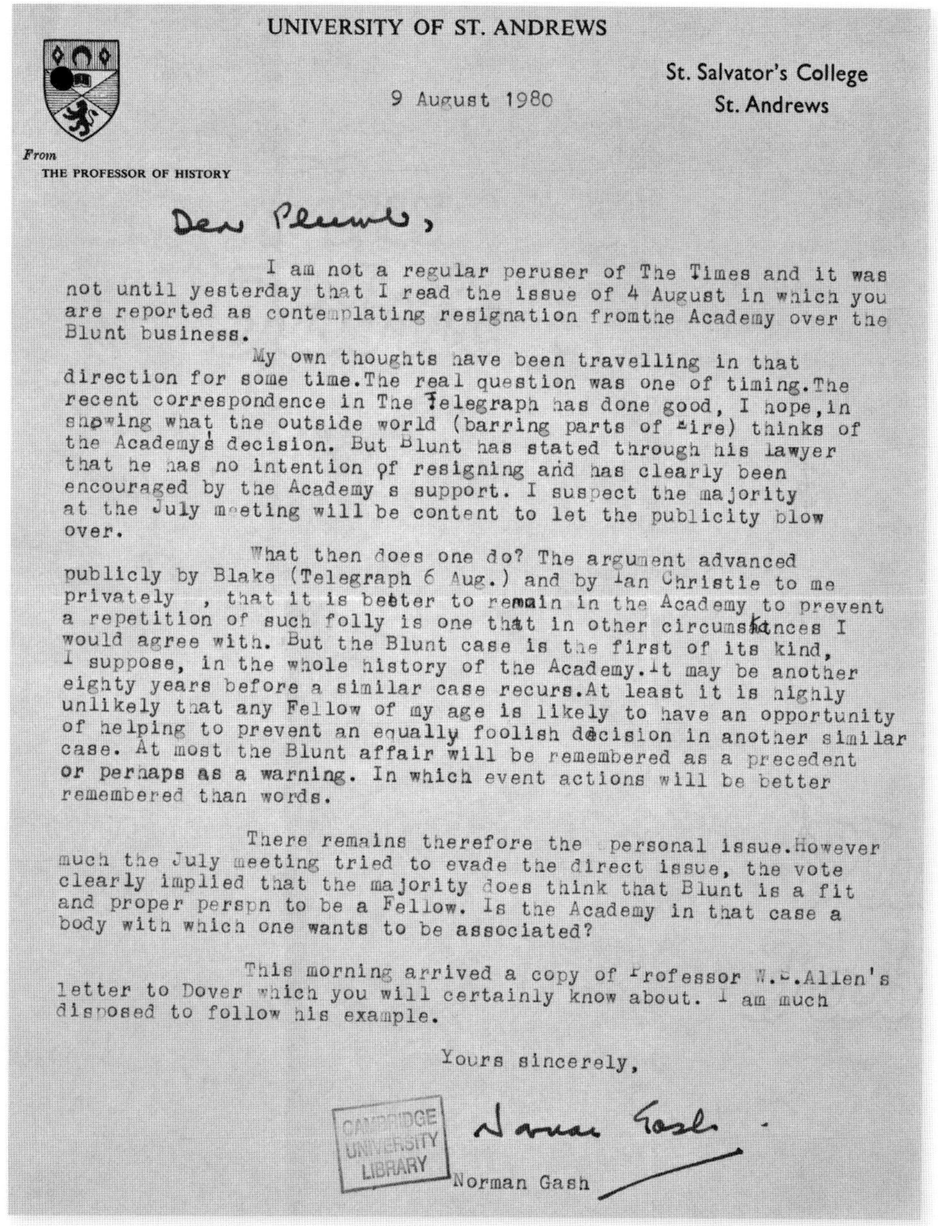

UNIVERSITY OF ST. ANDREWS

9 August 1980

St. Salvator's College
St. Andrews

From
THE PROFESSOR OF HISTORY

Dear Plumb,

I am not a regular peruser of The Times and it was not until yesterday that I read the issue of 4 August in which you are reported as contemplating resignation fromthe Academy over the Blunt business.

My own thoughts have been travelling in that direction for some time. The real question was one of timing. The recent correspondence in The Telegraph has done good, I hope, in showing what the outside world (barring parts of Eire) thinks of the Academy's decision. But Blunt has stated through his lawyer that he has no intention of resigning and has clearly been encouraged by the Academy s support. I suspect the majority at the July meeting will be content to let the publicity blow over.

What then does one do? The argument advanced publicly by Blake (Telegraph 6 Aug.) and by Ian Christie to me privately , that it is better to remain in the Academy to prevent a repetition of such folly is one that in other circumstances I would agree with. But the Blunt case is the first of its kind, I suppose, in the whole history of the Academy. It may be another eighty years before a similar case recurs. At least it is highly unlikely that any Fellow of my age is likely to have an opportunity of helping to prevent an equally foolish decision in another similar case. At most the Blunt affair will be remembered as a precedent or perhaps as a warning. In which event actions will be better remembered than words.

There remains therefore the personal issue. However much the July meeting tried to evade the direct issue, the vote clearly implied that the majority does think that Blunt is a fit and proper person to be a Fellow. Is the Academy in that case a body with which one wants to be associated?

This morning arrived a copy of Professor W.S. Allen's letter to Dover which you will certainly know about. I am much disposed to follow his example.

Yours sincerely,

Norman Gash.

Norman Gash

[35] Norman Gash had undertaken intelligence work during the war. He served in MI14 (the department concerned with intelligence about Germany), and focused on the Waffen SS: see B. Harrison and K.T. Hoppen, 'Norman Gash, 1912-2009', *Biographical Memoirs of Fellows of the British Academy*, xi (2012), p. 204.

Receipt of the copy of Allen's letter to Dover, followed by the letter from Gash, sent Plumb into his own whirlwind of correspondence on 11 August. He replied to Allen, saying that the approach he had taken had 'provided me with a way out of my dilemma and I shall follow suit.' Plumb went on to suggest that, if it could be made public that a number of Fellows shared those intentions, 'it might put sufficient pressure on Dover who, I think, has been very weak about the whole matter, to go and see Blunt and ask for his resignation.' Plumb then wrote his own equivalent letter to Dover **[43]**, warning him that, unless Blunt had been persuaded to resign his Fellowship by 31 December, he would himself resign at the end of 1980. And he advised Dover that he was not treating this stated intention as 'a matter of confidentiality'. He concluded by encouraging Dover to make a personal approach to Blunt, rather than going through 'intermediaries' (as Dover had done in March).

43: J.H. Plumb to Kenneth Dover, 11 August 1980.

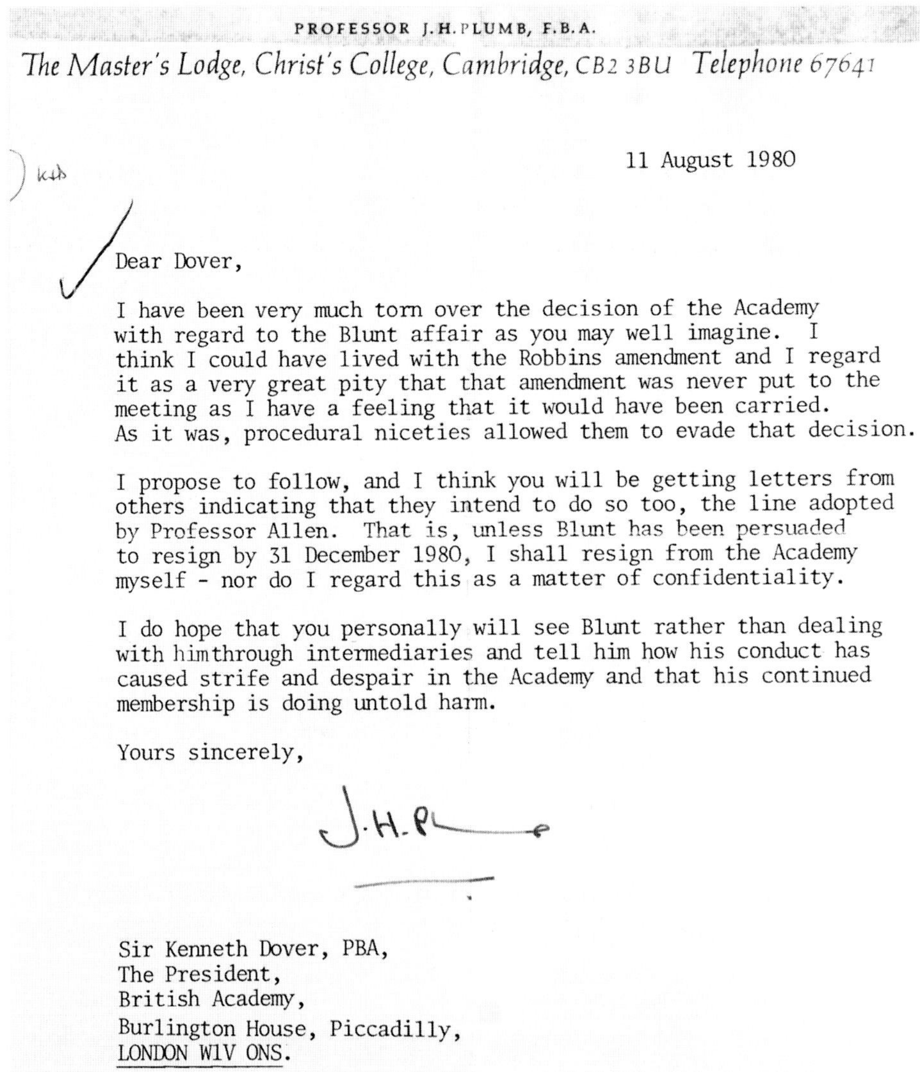

PROFESSOR J.H. PLUMB, F.B.A.

The Master's Lodge, Christ's College, Cambridge, CB2 3BU *Telephone* 67641

11 August 1980

Dear Dover,

I have been very much torn over the decision of the Academy with regard to the Blunt affair as you may well imagine. I think I could have lived with the Robbins amendment and I regard it as a very great pity that that amendment was never put to the meeting as I have a feeling that it would have been carried. As it was, procedural niceties allowed them to evade that decision.

I propose to follow, and I think you will be getting letters from others indicating that they intend to do so too, the line adopted by Professor Allen. That is, unless Blunt has been persuaded to resign by 31 December 1980, I shall resign from the Academy myself - nor do I regard this as a matter of confidentiality.

I do hope that you personally will see Blunt rather than dealing with him through intermediaries and tell him how his conduct has caused strife and despair in the Academy and that his continued membership is doing untold harm.

Yours sincerely,

Sir Kenneth Dover, PBA,
The President,
British Academy,
Burlington House, Piccadilly,
LONDON W1V ONS.

By permission of the Trustees of the Estate of Sir John Plumb

Plumb forwarded copies of his letter to Dover on to W.S. Allen, Norman Gash, Ian Christie, Robert Blake and John Ehrman. In a covering note to Gash **[44]**, he claimed that Allen's letter to Dover had persuaded him to send one of his own. If 'three or four of us' publicly threatened to leave the Academy, it might create enough pressure to force the resignation of 'that awful man'. And they should not be 'over-discreet' about it, so that Dover and the Academy could no longer 'hide … behind confidentiality'. To accompany the copies for Christie, Blake and Ehrman, Plumb dictated another short note **[45]**, encouraging them to 'follow suit': if they all threatened to resign, 'I think it would create an uproar'. The next day, he sent a copy of his letter to Dover to *The Times* and the *Daily Telegraph*.

45: J.H. Plumb to Ian Christie, 11 August 1980.

11 August 1980

Dear Ian,

I do hope you will be able to follow suit. I think this is the only way of pressuring the Academy into thinking again. If a man of your distinction were to join us, I think it would create an uproar. Norman Gash, I know, is going to do the same as myself and follow Allen's admirable lead.

Yours,

Dictated by the Master and signed,
in his absence, by his secretary

Professor Ian Christie,
10 Green Lane,
Croxley Green,
Hertfordshire WD3 3HR

By permission of the Trustees of the Estate of Sir John Plumb

44: J.H. Plumb to Norman Gash, 11 August 1980.

11 August 1980

Dear Norman,

Thank you very much indeed for your letter. I received a copy of Allen's letter when I returned here yesterday and it resolved in my mind about what should be my line of conduct and I propose to act, as you will see from the enclosed letter, in a similar way to Allen. On the other hand I think that if three or four of us, or even more, make it clear to Dover that we shall resign unless Blunt does, it might put some pressure on that awful man or even create pressure within the Academy for his resignation.

I think it very important that we should not be over-discreet about what we intend to do because the Academy loves to hide, and certainly Dover does, behind confidentiality. What I would like to see is a letter from Allen, myself and yourself and maybe some others to The Times saying what we intend to do unless Blunt agrees to resign. If he refuses still, I think my fellow-Academicians are welcome to him but I don't want to come across even his shadow.

Yours sincerely,

Dictated by the Master and signed,
in his absence, by his secretary

Professor Norman Gash, FBA,
Department of History,
University of St Andrews,
St Salvator's College,
St Andrews, Scotland.

By permission of the Trustees of the Estate of Sir John Plumb

Plumb's communication to Christie had the desired effect. Christie composed his own letter to Dover on 12 August **[46]**, threatening – like Allen and Plumb – a very public resignation from the Academy at the beginning of 1981 if the AGM's decision had not been somehow reversed. He meant to enclose (but forgot to do so) a copy of a draft article that he had sent to *Encounter*, laying out the arguments against Blunt for supporting a regime that had done 'untold damage to scholarship' in Eastern Europe and Central Asia. As an alternative to Plumb's suggestion that Dover persuade Blunt to resign in person, Christie proposed that the issue might be corrected through 'an Extraordinary General Meeting or a Referendum of the Fellowship'. And he was quite unapologetic about 'the publicity I have given to this matter. When a body of men in a public position commit an error of so appalling a nature, … the last thing they can expect is that it should be swept under the carpet.' He sent copies of this letter to both Plumb and Gash.

46: Ian Christie to Kenneth Dover, 12 August 1980.

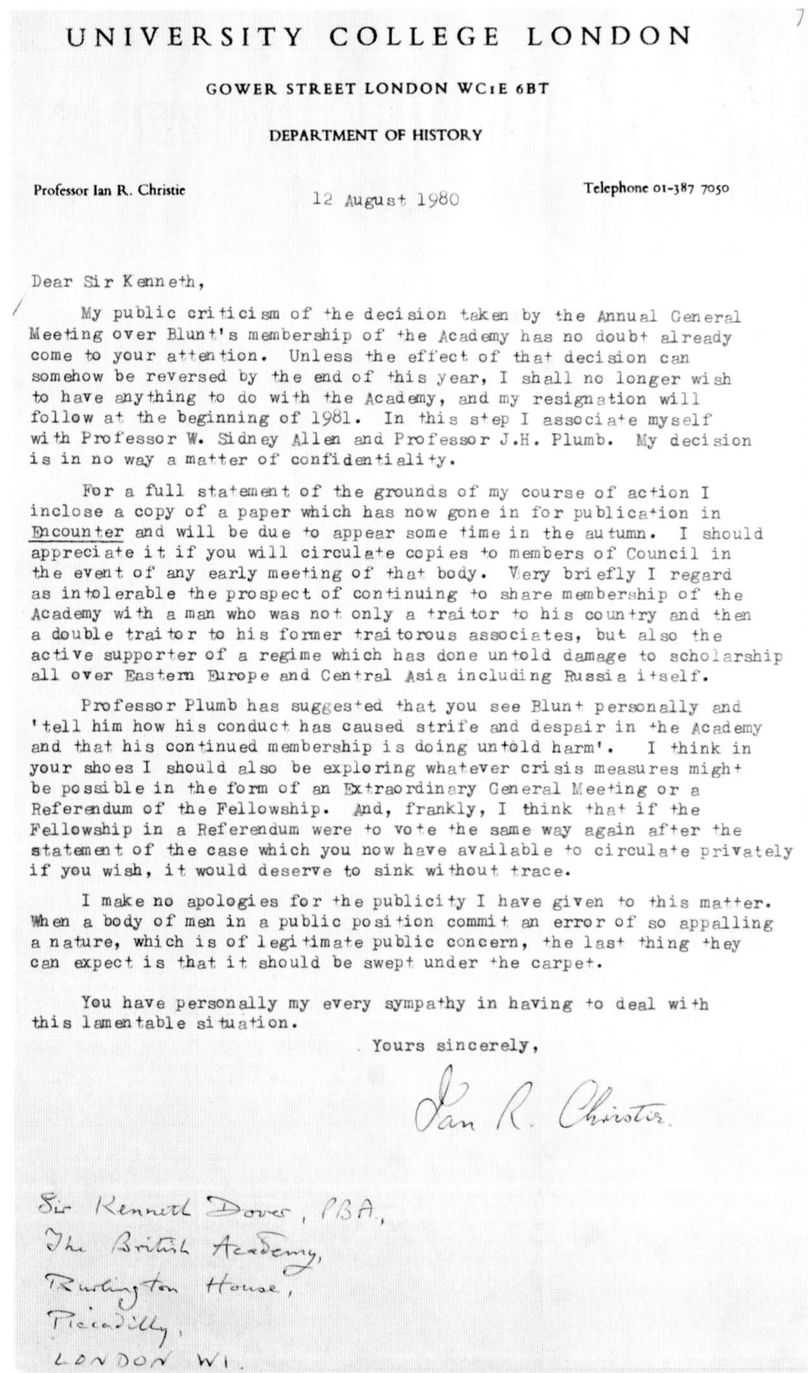

UNIVERSITY COLLEGE LONDON

GOWER STREET LONDON WC1E 6BT

DEPARTMENT OF HISTORY

Professor Ian R. Christie 12 August 1980 Telephone 01-387 7050

Dear Sir Kenneth,

My public criticism of the decision taken by the Annual General Meeting over Blunt's membership of the Academy has no doubt already come to your attention. Unless the effect of that decision can somehow be reversed by the end of this year, I shall no longer wish to have anything to do with the Academy, and my resignation will follow at the beginning of 1981. In this step I associate myself with Professor W. Sidney Allen and Professor J.H. Plumb. My decision is in no way a matter of confidentiality.

For a full statement of the grounds of my course of action I inclose a copy of a paper which has now gone in for publication in Encounter and will be due to appear some time in the autumn. I should appreciate it if you will circulate copies to members of Council in the event of any early meeting of that body. Very briefly I regard as intolerable the prospect of continuing to share membership of the Academy with a man who was not only a traitor to his country and then a double traitor to his former traitorous associates, but also the active supporter of a regime which has done untold damage to scholarship all over Eastern Europe and Central Asia including Russia itself.

Professor Plumb has suggested that you see Blunt personally and 'tell him how his conduct has caused strife and despair in the Academy and that his continued membership is doing untold harm'. I think in your shoes I should also be exploring whatever crisis measures might be possible in the form of an Extraordinary General Meeting or a Referendum of the Fellowship. And, frankly, I think that if the Fellowship in a Referendum were to vote the same way again after the statement of the case which you now have available to circulate privately if you wish, it would deserve to sink without trace.

I make no apologies for the publicity I have given to this matter. When a body of men in a public position commit an error of so appalling a nature, which is of legitimate public concern, the last thing they can expect is that it should be swept under the carpet.

You have personally my every sympathy in having to deal with this lamentable situation.

Yours sincerely,

Ian R. Christie

Sir Kenneth Dover, PBA,
The British Academy,
Burlington House,
Piccadilly,
LONDON W1.

I do not see how I can remain a member of an academic body which includes in its number this creature

W. Sidney Allen, 7 August 1980

... unless Blunt has been persuaded to resign by 31 December 1980, I shall resign from the Academy myself

J.H. Plumb, 11 August 1980

Unless the effect of that decision [at the AGM] can somehow be reversed by the end of the year, I shall no longer wish to have anything to do with the Academy

Ian Christie, 12 August 1980

By 13 August, Dover knew of Blake's article and Allen's letter, but he was not yet aware that similar letters were coming from Plumb and Christie (they had been sent to the Academy in London). But he reveals in 'Materials' that he had been telephoned by the classicist Robert Ogilvie FBA, a Professor at St Andrews, to warn him that Gash was trying to mobilise Fellows in Scotland to take action over the Blunt affair. So Dover arranged to meet Gash at St Andrews, 'to try to persuade him that he and his faction were behaving very badly'.

On the morning of 13 August, Gash had the advantage of Dover, in that he had seen the Plumb and Christie letters (the latter just arrived). Before the meeting started, Gash wrote to Plumb to confirm that he was ready to join in the threatened resignation approach, adding that he was about to have the opportunity to say so to Dover face-to-face.

'Materials' provides Dover's recollection of that meeting. Gash suggested that the AGM had been unrepresentative 'because it was "packed" with supporters of Blunt from London'. (According to Dover, only 48 of the 187 Fellows at the AGM were from London.) Gash went on to reveal that Plumb, Allen, Christie and himself 'were making public their intention to resign by the end of the year if Blunt had not done so'. At first Dover was 'strongly of the opinion that the threatened resigners were making asses of themselves'. But as the conversation continued, Dover was overtaken by 'an uncomfortable feeling' that 'the case against Blunt' had been 'quite inadequately presented at the AGM', and that within the Fellowship there might be 'widespread repentance, followed by a landslide of resignations which the Academy could ill afford'. So he told Gash that, because he owed Blunt a response to his letter of 8 August, he would take the opportunity to 'ask Blunt to consider the possibility of sparing the Academy further adverse publicity by resigning'.

After that meeting, Gash sent a second letter to Plumb **[47]**, to report the outcome. Gash wrote that he had told Dover he would resign at the end of the year if Blunt were still a Fellow. (Gash claimed that he hadn't mentioned Plumb or Christie, which doesn't tally with Dover's account.) Gash had urged Dover to see Blunt personally: now that Blunt had won 'his majority' at the AGM, 'it would be all the more to his credit if he voluntarily withdrew'. According to Gash, this approach had not occurred to Dover, who had said 'he would certainly think seriously about it.'

47: Norman Gash to J.H. Plumb, 13 August 1980.

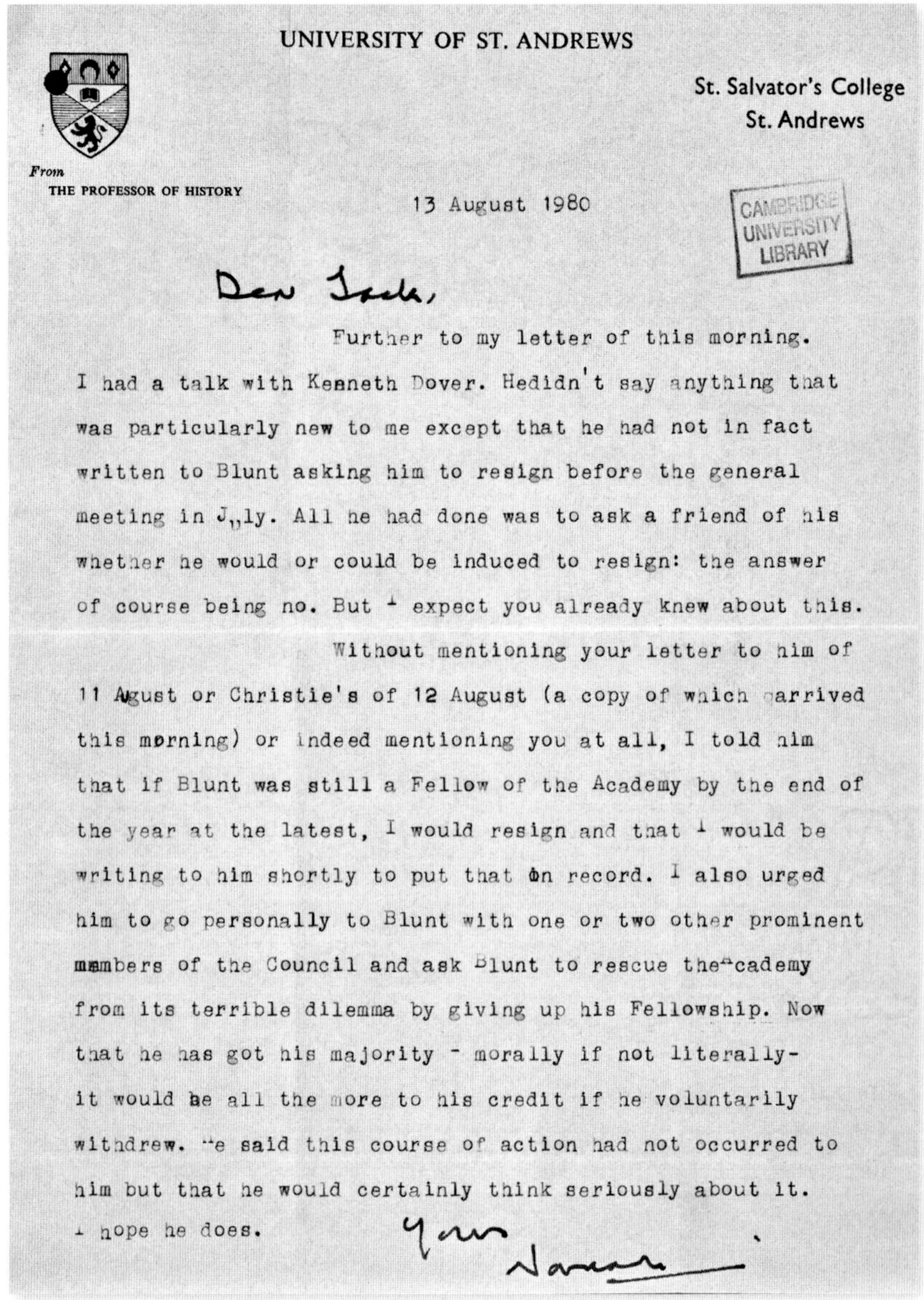

UNIVERSITY OF ST. ANDREWS

St. Salvator's College
St. Andrews

From
THE PROFESSOR OF HISTORY

13 August 1980

Dear Jack,

Further to my letter of this morning.

I had a talk with Kenneth Dover. Hedidn't say anything that was particularly new to me except that he had not in fact written to Blunt asking him to resign before the general meeting in July. All he had done was to ask a friend of his whether he would or could be induced to resign: the answer of course being no. But I expect you already knew about this.

Without mentioning your letter to him of 11 August or Christie's of 12 August (a copy of which arrived this morning) or indeed mentioning you at all, I told him that if Blunt was still a Fellow of the Academy by the end of the year at the latest, I would resign and that I would be writing to him shortly to put that on record. I also urged him to go personally to Blunt with one or two other prominent members of the Council and ask Blunt to rescue the Academy from its terrible dilemma by giving up his Fellowship. Now that he has got his majority - morally if not literally- it would be all the more to his credit if he voluntarily withdrew. He said this course of action had not occurred to him but that he would certainly think seriously about it.

I hope he does.

Yours
Norman

48: Kenneth Dover to J.H. Plumb, 14 August 1980.

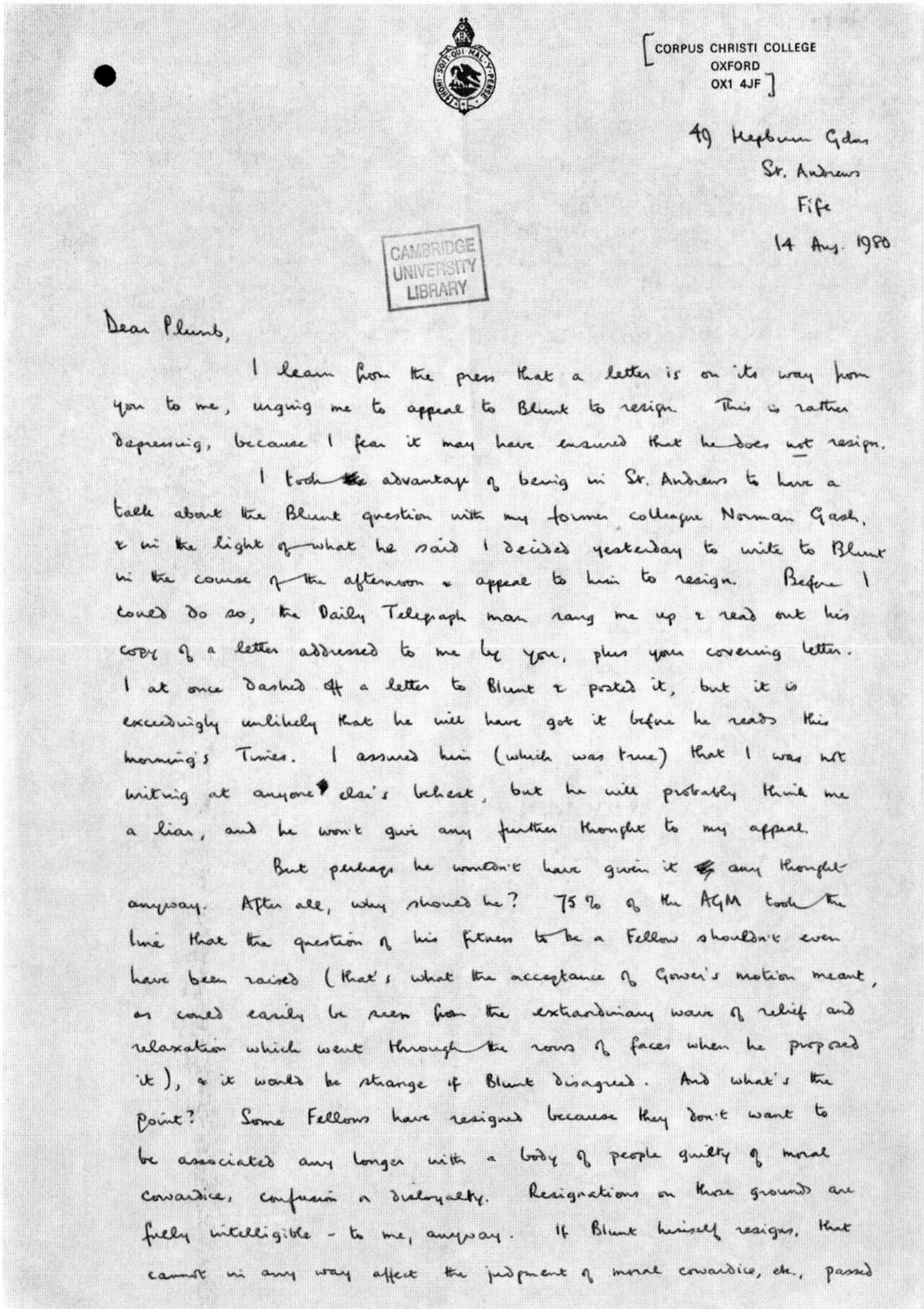

CORPUS CHRISTI COLLEGE
OXFORD
OX1 4JF

49 Hepburn Gdns
St. Andrews
Fife

14 Aug. 1980

Dear Plumb,

I learn from the press that a letter is on its way from you to me, urging me to appeal to Blunt to resign. This is rather depressing, because I fear it may have ensured that he does *not* resign.

I took ~~the~~ advantage of being in St. Andrews to have a talk about the Blunt question with my former colleague Norman Gash, & in the light of what he said I decided yesterday to write to Blunt in the course of the afternoon & appeal to him to resign. Before I could do so, the Daily Telegraph man rang me up & read out his copy of a letter addressed to me by you, plus your covering letter. I at once dashed off a letter to Blunt & posted it, but it is exceedingly unlikely that he will have got it before he reads this morning's Times. I assured him (which was true) that I was not writing at anyone else's behest, but he will probably think me a liar, and he won't give any further thought to my appeal.

But perhaps he wouldn't have given it any thought anyway. After all, why should he? 75% of the AGM took the line that the question of his fitness to be a Fellow shouldn't even have been raised (that's what the acceptance of Gower's motion meant, as could easily be seen from the extraordinary wave of relief and relaxation which went through the rows of faces when he proposed it), & it would be strange if Blunt disagreed. And what's the point? Some Fellows have resigned because they don't want to be associated any longer with a body of people guilty of moral cowardice, confusion or disloyalty. Resignations on those grounds are fully intelligible – to me, anyway. If Blunt himself resigns, that cannot in any way affect the judgment of moral cowardice, etc., passed

In 'Materials', Dover recounts what happened later on 13 August. As he was drafting a letter to Blunt, he was rung up by a reporter from the *Daily Telegraph*, who read out the substance of the 11 August letter from Plumb which was on its way to him. Dover then completed his letter to Blunt. He kept no copy, but 'it was something like: "It was very kind of you to write. I am going to make what may seem a rather bizarre and ungracious reply by asking you to consider the possibility of 'healing the wound' by resigning." I went on to point out that no one now could think that he was resigning under threat. … I decided to add another paragraph assuring Blunt that whatever he might read in the papers the next day, I was not writing at anyone else's command.'

The next day, 14 August, *The Times* carried an article headed 'More resignation threats over the Blunt affair', reporting that Plumb and Allen had written to Dover, and hinting that others might follow. And a letter by Gash published in the *Daily Telegraph* of 15 August warned that, with other resignations likely, 'the Academy will be facing the worst crisis in its 80-year history'.

Dover wrote to Plumb **[48]**, to say how depressed he felt to find out from the press about Plumb's letter – particularly because 'I fear it may have ensured that he [Blunt] does *not* resign'. And Dover said that he would not be prepared to ask Blunt to resign in person, because such a conversation with 'a man as intelligent as Blunt' would appear 'foolish'.

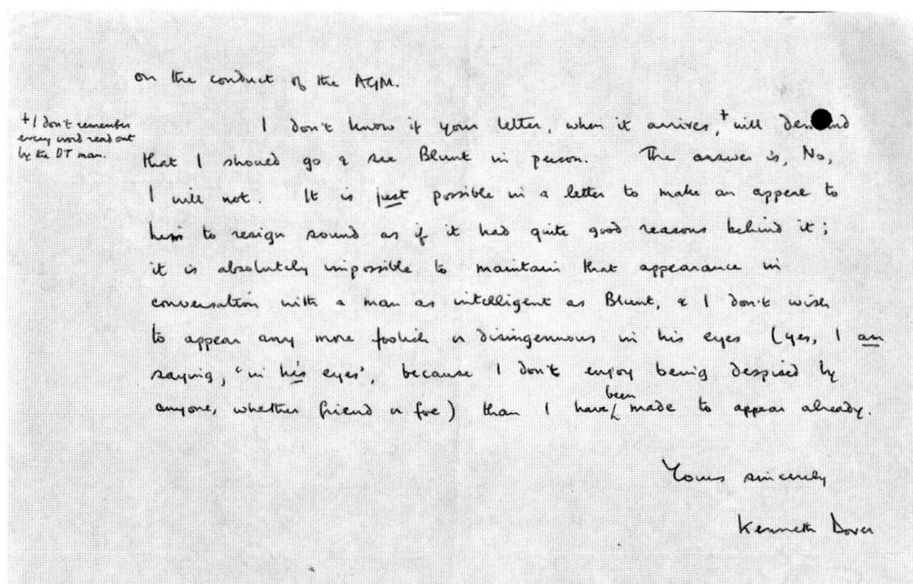

on the conduct of the AGM.

I don't know if your letter, when it arrives,[+] will demand that I should go & see Blunt in person. The answer is, No, I will not. It is *just* possible in a letter to make an appeal to him to resign sound as if it had quite good reasons behind it; it is absolutely impossible to maintain that appearance in conversation with a man as intelligent as Blunt, & I don't wish to appear any more foolish or disingenuous in his eyes (yes, I *am* saying, 'in *his* eyes', because I don't enjoy being despised by anyone, whether friend or foe) than I have been made to appear already.

+ I don't remember every word read out by the DT man.

Yours sincerely

Kenneth Dover

The press coverage on 14 August prompted new correspondence. The 92-year-old archaeologist Gertrude Caton Thompson FBA wrote to John Carswell **[49]** to say that, unless Blunt was 'induced to resign', she would 'feel it inappropriate to retain my fellowship' – something she was sorry to do 'so near the end of my journey'.

49: Gertrude Caton Thompson to John Carswell, 14 August 1980.

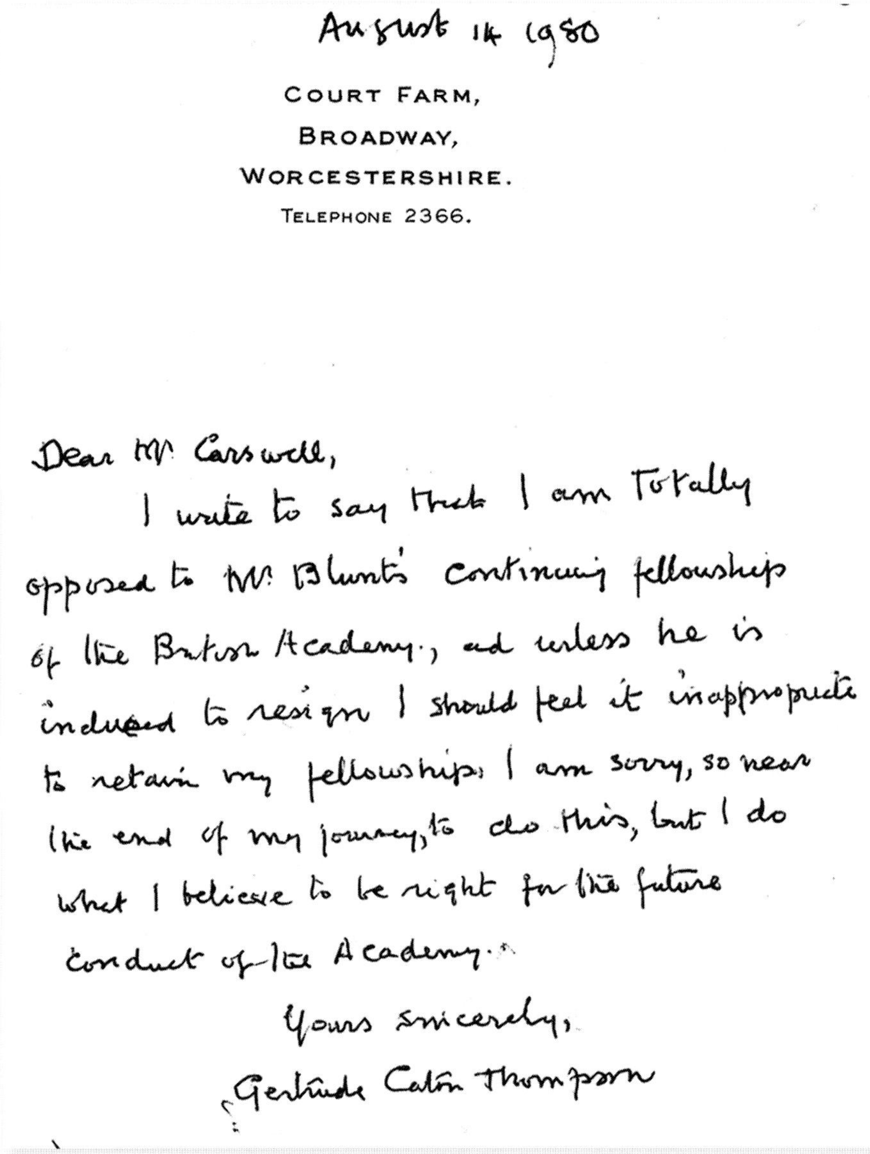

August 14 1980

COURT FARM,
BROADWAY,
WORCESTERSHIRE.
TELEPHONE 2366.

Dear Mr Carswell,

I write to say that I am Totally opposed to Mr Blunt's continuing fellowship of the British Academy, and unless he is induced to resign I should feel it inappropriate to retain my fellowship. I am sorry, so near the end of my journey, to do this, but I do what I believe to be right for the future conduct of the Academy.

Yours sincerely,
Gertrude Caton Thompson

On 14 August, John Ehrman wrote to Dover to argue that a referendum should be held to give Fellows 'a second bite at this particular cherry' – a postal vote on the 'Robbins amendment', followed (if that did not pass) by a postal vote on Council's original recommendation. 'We shall then know the Fellowship's real opinion.' Ehrman also wrote to Plumb, Christie and Blake to explain that he preferred for now to pursue this option, rather than threaten to resign. On 15 August, Blake wrote to Dover to say that he supported Ehrman's proposal for reopening the matter 'in some way which will ensure that *every* member of the Academy is consulted'. The medievalist Pierre Chaplais FBA wrote to Dover in a similar vein on the same day. On 18 August, Plumb signalled his own support for the idea, as a way of bringing more pressure on Blunt. And an article in the *Sunday Telegraph* of 17 August gave a public airing to the proposal for a referendum.

Mr John Ehrman FBA

Dr Gertrude Caton Thompson FBA

But events had already taken a new turn. As Dover was drafting a possible letter to send to *The Times* about the whole affair, Blunt telephoned him. Dover jotted down the substance of the call in a note to Carswell **[50]**. Blunt told Dover he would gladly resign if it would do the Academy any good, but the trouble was that there were Fellows who were determined to resign if he did.

On Sunday 17 August, Blunt rang again, and told Dover that he had decided to resign; his letter was on its way to the Academy **[51]**. He added that he had persuaded his friends not to resign in sympathy. According to 'Materials', Dover took a deep breath and said: 'Well … I am very grateful to you. I think … on balance … that this will be to the advantage of the Academy … will produce a better situation for the Academy.' Dover noted that he was 'absolutely sure' that he used the phrase 'on balance'.

50: Kenneth Dover to John Carswell, 15 August 1980.

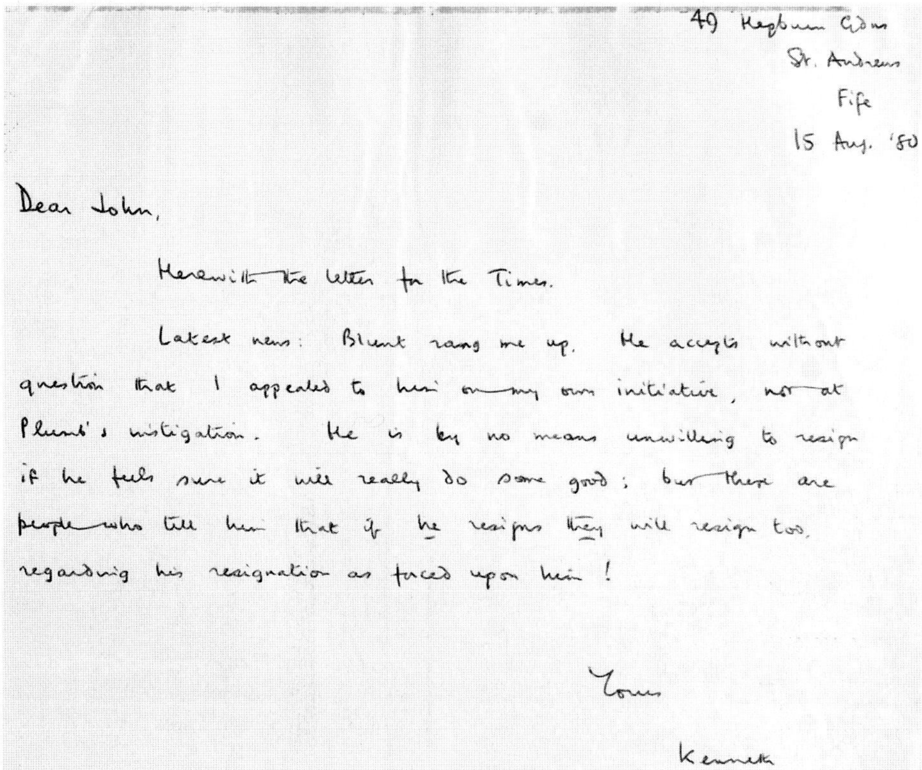

49 Hepburn Gdns
St. Andrews
Fife
15 Aug. '80

Dear John,

Herewith the letter for the Times.

Latest news: Blunt rang me up. He accepts without question that I appealed to him on my own initiative, not at Plumb's instigation. He is by no means unwilling to resign if he feels sure it will really do some good; but there are people who tell him that if he resigns they will resign too, regarding his resignation as forced upon him!

Yours

Kenneth

51: Anthony Blunt to Kenneth Dover, 17 August 1980.

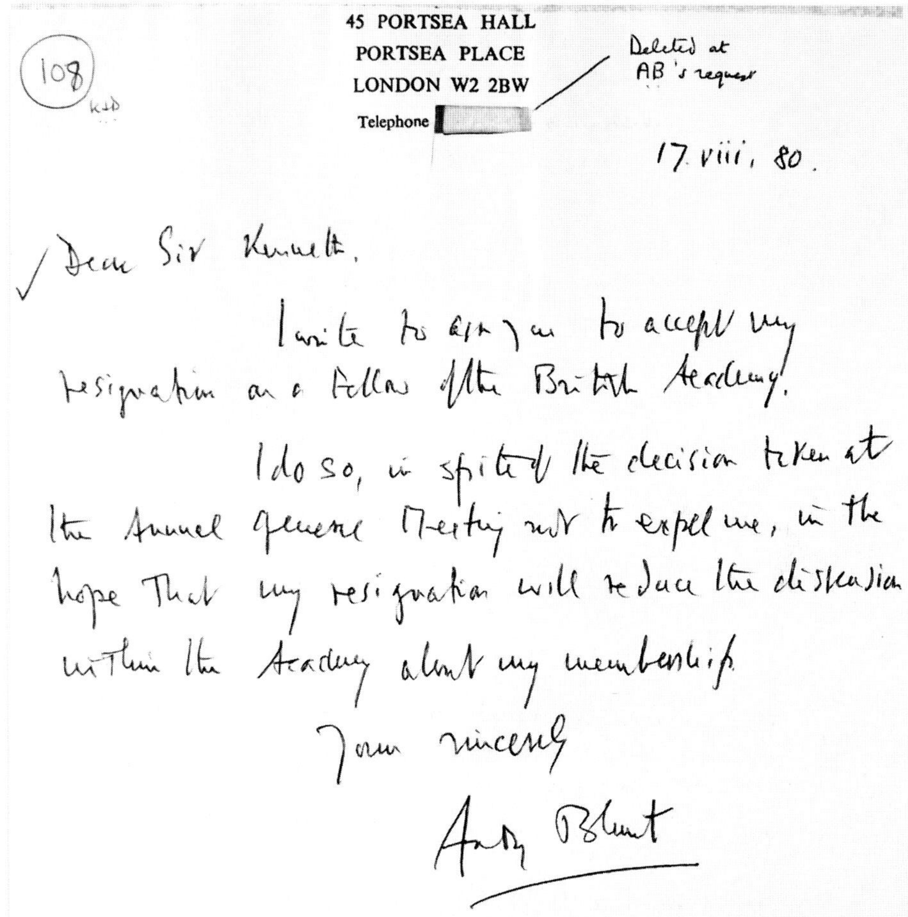

108 KJD

45 PORTSEA HALL
PORTSEA PLACE
LONDON W2 2BW
Telephone [redacted]

Deleted at AB's request

17.viii.80.

Dear Sir Kenneth,

I write to ask you to accept my resignation as a Fellow of the British Academy.

I do so, in spite of the decision taken at the Annual General Meeting not to expel me, in the hope that my resignation will reduce the dissension within the Academy about my membership.

Yours sincerely

Anthony Blunt

In the hope of averting any further public comments about referendums and resignations, Dover quickly passed on the news of Blunt's resignation to Gash, Plumb, Allen, Gurney, Ehrman and Christie.

On 19 August Plumb, Ehrman, Gurney and Allen **[52]** replied, indicating their satisfaction and relief at the new development. And Plumb sent a card to most of his co-conspirators, simply reading: 'I am delighted that our stand has forced Blunt to resign'. Ehrman wrote to Plumb admitting he was 'wrong in my estimate of Blunt's handling of this affair. I was confident he would swing off up to at least 15 resignations; and in point of fact I am wondering why he did not.'

52: W. Sidney Allen to Kenneth Dover, 19 August 1980.

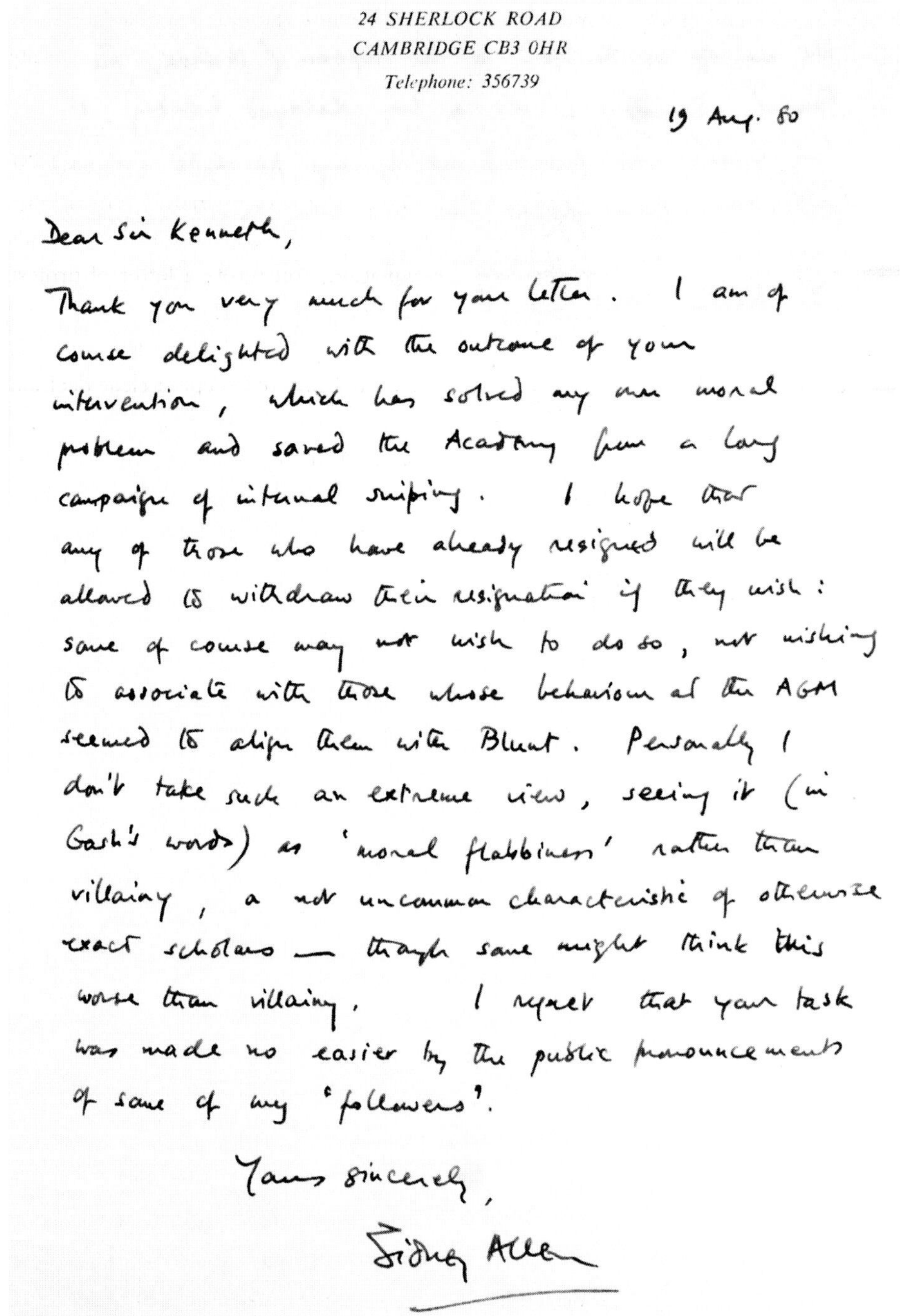
24 SHERLOCK ROAD
CAMBRIDGE CB3 0HR
Telephone: 356739

19 Aug. 80

Dear Sir Kenneth,

Thank you very much for your letter. I am of course delighted with the outcome of your intervention, which has solved my own moral problem and saved the Academy from a long campaign of internal sniping. I hope that any of those who have already resigned will be allowed to withdraw their resignation if they wish: some of course may not wish to do so, not wishing to associate with those whose behaviour at the AGM seemed to align them with Blunt. Personally I don't take such an extreme view, seeing it (in Gash's words) as 'moral flabbiness' rather than villainy, a not uncommon characteristic of otherwise exact scholars — though some might think this worse than villainy. I regret that your task was made no easier by the public pronouncements of some of my 'followers'.

Yours sincerely,

Sidney Allen

At this point Dover again seems to have misjudged how events might further unfold after Blunt's resignation, because he removed himself for the next few days to his son's house in Glenfarg (a small village 10 miles south of Perth), where there was no telephone.

Professor James Joll FBA

News of the resignation certainly provoked a response. The first to react was Blunt's close friend, the historian James Joll FBA, who had helped provide shelter for him in the aftermath of his unmasking. On the very day that Blunt had offered his resignation, Joll wrote a letter of protest to Dover **[53]**. He deplored the fact that the 'campaign' of a few Fellows who had been unwilling to accept 'a clear decision by a substantial majority' should have resulted in the request being put to Blunt. Joll revealed that he had only refrained from tendering his own resignation 'at the personal request of Anthony Blunt'.[36]

53: James Joll to Kenneth Dover, 17 August 1980.

The London School of Economics and Political Science
(University of London)

Copy

Houghton Street,
London, WC2A 2AE
Telephone: 01-405 7686

24 Ashchurch Park Villas,
London W12 9SP
(01-749-5221)

17 August 1980

Dear Dover,

I wa s very sorry to learn that Anthony Blunt had agreed to your suggestion that he should resign his Fellowship of the British Academy. I quite understand your reasons for wanting him to resign and his for agreeing to do so, but I am a fraid that it will appear to the outside world as the direct' result of a press campaign started by the statements and articles (one of them in the cheap press) of the two or three fellows unwilling to accept a clear decision by a substantial majority of those present at the Annual General Meeting on 3 J uly. It is obviously unfortunate that a decision of the Fellows taken after a thorough and serious discussion should appear to be so ea sily overturned by those who were not prepared to accept it.

There appears to be nothing which can now be done since Blunt has submitted his resignation, but I thought I should let you know how deeply I deplore that the decision to suggest to Blunt that he should resign was taken in these circumstances.

I should add that my first reaction, like that of at least one other Fellow, was immediately to send you my own resignation, and that I only refrained from doing so at the personal request of Anthony Blunt.

Yours sincerely,

James Joll

James Joll

By permission of Peters Fraser & Dunlop on behalf of the Estate of James Joll

[36] James Joll worked in intelligence during the war, including service in the Special Operations Executive: D. Blackbourn, 'James Bysse Joll, 1918-1994', *Proceedings of the British Academy*, 90 (1996), p. 415.

The Times and the *Daily Telegraph* carried articles on 19 August reporting Blunt's resignation, and associating it with the threatened resignations of Plumb and others. Disturbed by what he read, the philosopher John L. Mackie FBA wrote to express his 'strong disapproval' of Dover's action **[54]**, saying that it was inconsistent with his undertaking that he would 'defend in public what the Academy had done'. On the same day, the medieval historian Dorothy Whitelock FBA also wrote to express her sorrow that Blunt had been persuaded to resign.[37]

Mr John L. Mackie FBA

Professor Dorothy Whitelock CBE FBA

54: J.L. Mackie to Kenneth Dover, 19 August 1980.

UNIVERSITY COLLEGE
OXFORD
OX1 4BH
(0865) 41661

August 19, 1980

Sir Kenneth Dover
President of the British Academy

Dear Sir Kenneth Dover,

This morning's Times, in reporting Professor Blunt's resignation from the Academy, states that you wrote to Professor Blunt last week and that his action may have been prompted by your letter. It thus implies that you suggested that he should resign. It also implies that you did so at the request of three or four members who disagreed with the way the matter was dealt with by the Annual General Meeting. If these implications are correct, then I wish to express strong disapproval of your action, which is inconsistent with the intention of the clear majority of members present at the Annual General Meeting, and dubiously consistent with your own statement, made immediately after that vote was taken, that you would defend in public what the Academy had done.

Yours sincerely

J. L. Mackie

J. L. Mackie

[37] In her letter, Whitelock was equally perturbed by the throw-away claim in *The Times* report that, at the Academy's AGM, the Fellows had 'voted to move on to other business rather than decide the matter'. She sought to challenge this 'false impression', because she believed that, by 'declaring that it was not the business of the Academy to consider turning out Professor Blunt', the vote had very much been 'deciding the matter'.

Living up to his earlier utterances, A.J.P. Taylor went further and fired off a letter of resignation to Dover **[55]**. Instead of letting the decision at the AGM be the end of the matter, Taylor argued, Dover had allowed 'a small group of Fellows to thwart the wishes of a substantial majority'. He concluded: 'I will not be a party to a witch hunt'. That day's *Evening Standard* reported Taylor's resignation, and on 20 August *The Times*, the *Daily Telegraph* and the *Guardian* all carried stories with headlines quoting his 'witch hunt' phrase. The *Guardian* reported that Taylor had said 'his resignation would cause him no regret, since he would not be happy remaining in an institution which first voted not to expel Mr Blunt, and then brought pressure upon him to resign'.

Mr A.J.P. Taylor FBA

55: A.J.P. Taylor to Kenneth Dover, 19 August 1980.

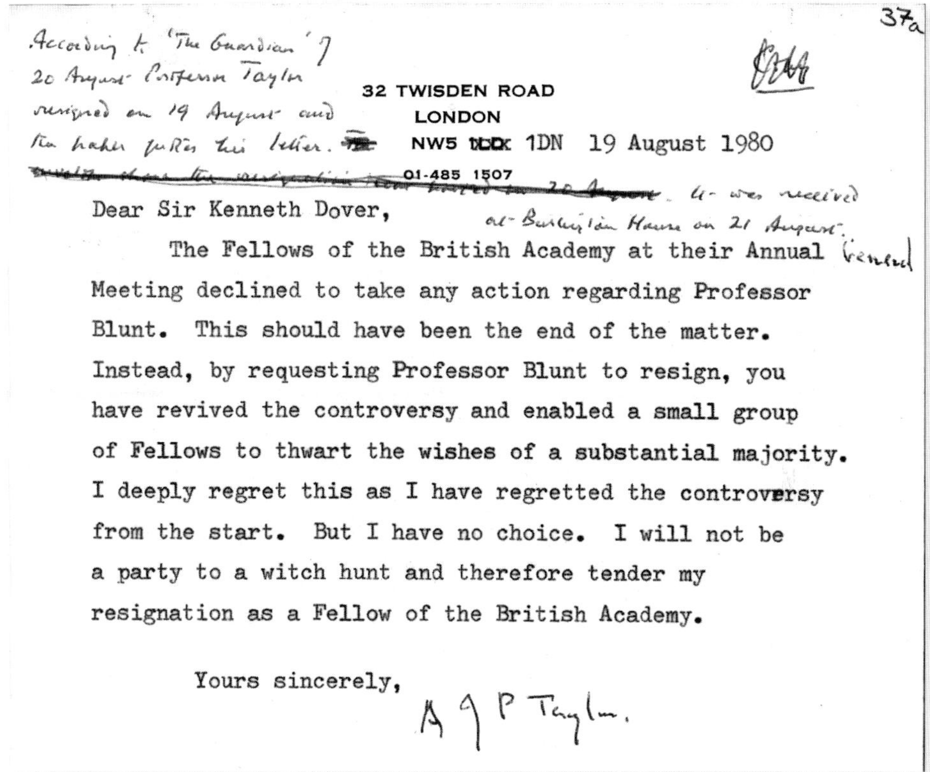

37a

According to 'The Guardian' 20 August Professor Taylor resigned on 19 August and then [illegible] this letter. It was received at Burlington House on 21 August.

32 TWISDEN ROAD
LONDON
NW5 1DN 19 August 1980
01-485 1507

Dear Sir Kenneth Dover,

The Fellows of the British Academy at their Annual General Meeting declined to take any action regarding Professor Blunt. This should have been the end of the matter. Instead, by requesting Professor Blunt to resign, you have revived the controversy and enabled a small group of Fellows to thwart the wishes of a substantial majority. I deeply regret this as I have regretted the controversy from the start. But I have no choice. I will not be a party to a witch hunt and therefore tender my resignation as a Fellow of the British Academy.

Yours sincerely,

A J P Taylor.

56: Helen Gardner to Kenneth Dover, 20 August 1980.

MYRTLE HOUSE, 12 MILL STREET, EYNSHAM, OXFORD. OX8 1JS
TELEPHONE (0865) 881497

20 August 1980

Dear President,

Let me begin by saying that this is not a letter of resignation, and also that I feel great sympathy for you in being involved in so distressing a business.

I was at Stratford at a Shakespeare Conference over the week end, and on Monday evening was at the theatre and, after the play ended, sat up after midnight talking over the play in the hotel bar. My housekeeper was telephoned by the International Radio Network, who wanted to speak to me, without saying who was calling, but said it was about Academy business and was urgent. She thought this meant that the call was from the Academy and gave them the address of my hotel. I heard in the morning from the night operator that I.R.N. had telephoned every half hour from 8-0 to midnight. I hope I need hardly say that, if I had been in my room and answered the call,I should have made no comment. Ihad no idea what it could have been about until I returned home last night and saw The Times.

If some senior member of the Academy, Lionel Robbins, or Isaiah Berlin, had gone to see Blunt privately, and persuaded him that, consoled by the large majority of members that had rejected the recommendation of Council, he should ~~xx~~ resign to save further dissension, I should not have been disturbed. What distresses me is that the President should, against the wishes of the large majority of Fellows present and voting at the meeting, have yielded to pressure from members of the minority, who had publicly announced their intention of resigning if the President did not do as they wished. I do not know how many of the ~~fnxtixx~~ fanatics on the other side, who would not accept Lord Robbins's ~~xxxxxxx~~ amendment since they thought it was not our business to deplore - a position that was logically proper but politically disastrous - will now think it their duty to resign with various public protestations of their high principles and integrity.

When I was telephones, first by Mr. Carswell and then by Lionel, and asked whether I would second an amendment - Isaiah having decided that for two ex-Presidents to speak against a Council recommendation would be impolitic - the formula that Lionel put

Helen Gardner, who had been recruited to co-sponsor the Robbins motion, wrote on 20 August to communicate how much the whole episode had caused her grief, including now being pestered by the media **[56]**. She bemoaned the behaviour of the 'fanatics' on both sides of the argument. The introduction of the word 'deplore' into the Robbins motion,[38] which had been done without her knowledge, had caused her to be 'attacked' by one set of Fellows before the AGM. Now she was distressed that 'the President should, against the wishes of the large majority of Fellows present and voting at the meeting, have yielded to pressure from members of the minority, who had publicly announced their intention of resigning if the President did not do as they wished'. It had always been an 'outrage' that Fellows 'should have been recommended "to put the boot in" on someone already lying on the ground'.

to me was 'While not in any way condoning....' I was not asked to agree to the change of wording , and by the time I received the papers with the word 'deplore' I could hardly withdraw my support. I was attacked by Richard Southern and others before the Encaenia luncheon and told that they intended to speak and vote against the amendment and, if that were lost, would then vote against the recommendation. I did my utmost to persuade them not to muddy the waters further and to respect the strength of feeling on the other side.

I hoped the size of the majority at the meeting would lay the matter to rest. I regarded it as fundamentally a vote of no confidence by the membership in the judgement of the Council. I felt this very strongly myself when I first heard of the Council's recommendation. If, when the scandal first broke last November , a special meeting of Council had been held and members circulated to express their views on Council's recommendation, and if the recommendation had been the same, I should still have thought it wrong and voted against it. I should not have thought it so ~~xxxxxxxxxxxxxxxxxx~~ disastrously wrong as I thought it was coming six months later. I thought it an outrage that the Academy should have been recommended to 'bring up the rear' and cast a last stone at a sufficiently disgraced and humiliated colleague, or, if a Scriptural reference is thought improper, should have been recommended 'to put the boot in' on someone already lying on the ground.

Yours very sincerely,

Helen Gardner

Helen Gardner

[38] See above p. 38 n. 17.

As some consolation for Dover, Trevor-Roper wrote more supportively **[57]**, appreciating the 'dreadful time' he had been going through. While he had not been in favour of expulsion, now that Blunt had chosen to resign, Trevor-Roper was happy to say 'good riddance'. He expressed the hope that 'the Academy will support you, and peace be restored.'

Lord Dacre of Glanton FBA (Hugh Trevor-Roper)

Dame Helen Gardner FBA

57: Hugh Trevor-Roper to Kenneth Dover, 20 August 1980.

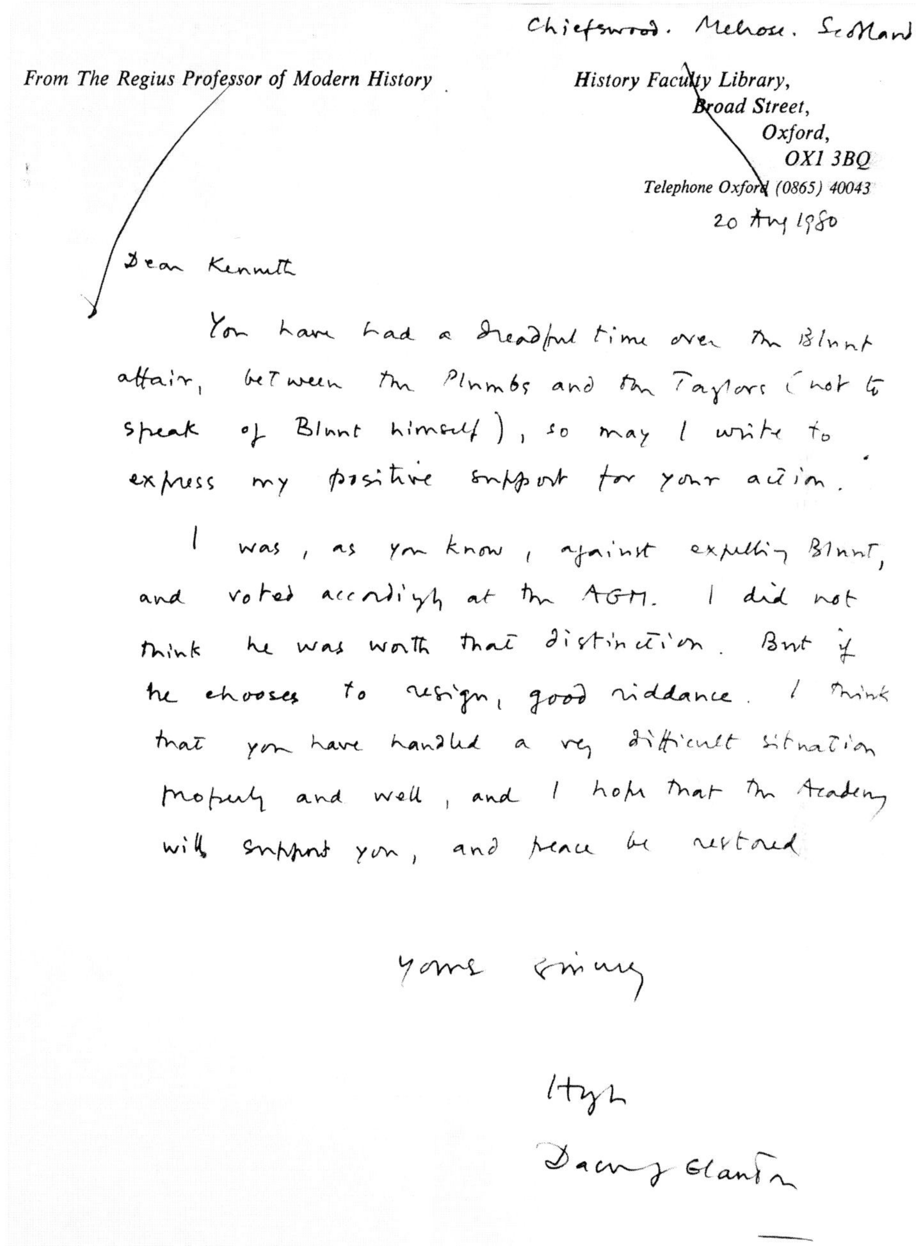

Chiefswood. Melrose. Scotland

From The Regius Professor of Modern History

History Faculty Library,
Broad Street,
Oxford,
OX1 3BQ
Telephone Oxford (0865) 40043

20 Aug 1980

Dear Kenneth

You have had a dreadful time over the Blunt affair, between the Plumbs and the Taylors (not to speak of Blunt himself), so may I write to express my positive support for your action.

I was, as you know, against expelling Blunt, and voted accordingly at the AGM. I did not think he was worth that distinction. But if he chooses to resign, good riddance. I think that you have handled a very difficult situation properly and well, and I hope that the Academy will support you, and peace be restored

Yours sincerely

Hugh

Dacre of Glanton

But Trevor-Roper's hopes for the restoration of calm were a little premature. On 20 August, Peter Brown left John Carswell a note about a phone call he had taken from the ancient historian Moses Finley FBA. Finley had said that Fellows were upset because the only things they knew about the Blunt affair were coming from 'misinformation in the press'. Finley was especially worried by the phone calls he was getting from 'many outsiders, younger scholars etc.', saying that the Academy was 'looking increasingly ridiculous'. He therefore urged the Academy, as a matter of urgency, to send Fellows a circular which would clarify the situation.

Dover's current remote location was inevitably hampering his communication with the Academy's offices in London. He admits in 'Materials' that this 'put an unreasonably heavy burden on John Carswell, who had to deal with reporters' questions and imagine what I might have said if the reporters had been able to get at me.' Peter Brown recalls his impression that Dover and Carswell 'were not singing from the same hymn sheet': 'when the press rang through and said do you want to comment on this, that or the other, Carswell did, and then had to report to Dover, who clearly said "I wouldn't have said that".'[39] Although Carswell was in telephone contact with Blunt over what could be said to the press, Dover afterwards thought that Carswell had got one or two details wrong about exactly when and how Blunt had been asked to resign.[40]

But, by one means or other, an initial reaction to A.J.P. Taylor's 'witch hunt' accusation was communicated on 20 August, so that it could be reported in the papers the following day. Dover was quoted as saying: 'There was no pressure. I do not see how he could be hounded out because once a decision had been taken not to expel him, he could not be forced to retire. ... The number of people who said they would resign was not very large. I wrote to him [Blunt] because this was in the air, and it seemed right to consider the possibilities.'[41]

Carswell also issued a briefing note to the broadsheet newspapers in the early evening of 20 August, to alert them to that fact that a 'considered statement' from the President on the 'full circumstances' surrounding Blunt's resignation was forthcoming.

One further focus of speculation was addressed on 20 August. The Academy had received numerous press questions about the future of the four Fellows who had resigned in the aftermath of the AGM. Carswell sent out a memorandum, in Dover's name, to Crook, Bawden, Skeat and Roberts, outlining the Academy's stance. The note said that it would be impertinent on Dover's part to suggest any course of action to those who had resigned. If any individual 'on reflection' did wish to withdraw his resignation, the Academy had no 'ready-made procedure' for dealing with it, but it would be surprising 'if Council wanted to be legalistic or bureaucratic about it'.

Dover's 22 August 'Note' of explanation about 'the resignation of Professor Blunt' was addressed to the whole Fellowship of the Academy, but was also sent to the press **[58]**. It chronicled Dover's version of events, from his receipt of Blunt's letter of 8 August, to the public announcement of Blunt's resignation on 18 August.

[39] Peter Brown interview, 12 February 2018.

[40] The level of press attention on the British Academy during the Blunt affair had an impact on all members of its staff. Jane Lyddon, then Assistant Secretary (Overseas), recalls 'answering the phone one day, as we all did (there were two outside lines, answerable from any phone), and finding a *Guardian* journalist on the other end, and telling him that if they were going to report the story they might at least do it accurately – I was a *Guardian* reader and very disappointed by the inaccuracies. He was deeply taken aback. I then put him through to Peter Brown, mindful of the fact that no younger member of staff was well-advised to speak to any journalist at all!' (E-mail correspondence, 30 March 2020.)

[41] Kenneth Dover quoted in *The Times*, 21 August 1980; similar wording appeared in the *Daily Telegraph* and the *Guardian*.

58: Kenneth Dover's note to the Fellowship on 'The Resignation of Professor Blunt', 22 August 1980.

THE BRITISH ACADEMY
BURLINGTON HOUSE, PICCADILLY
LONDON, W1V ONS
TELEPHONE: 01-734 0457

22 August 1980

Note to the Fellowship by the President
of the British Academy

<u>The Resignation of Professor Blunt</u>

The sequence of events during the last three weeks is insufficiently known to Fellows, and several misapprehensions are current, some of them generated in the heat of sensational discussion in the press. Remarks have been attributed to me which I do not recall making and do not think I made. What happened was this:

1. On 11 August I received a letter from Professor Blunt, dated 8 August, in which he told me something of what he felt about the situation and the way in which the press was using him "as a stick to beat the Academy". I wrote to thank him on 13 August, and went on to suggest that he "give serious consideration" to the possibility of resigning. I commented briefly on what I regarded as relevant aspects and possible consequences of resignation.

2. I had already reflected on this damaging controversy as it developed and the amounts and kinds of good or harm which might be done to the Academy by different courses of events. I never doubted for a moment that the vote on 3 July was an absolutely firm, clear, and decisive refusal to pronounce on a person's fitness to be a Fellow in the light of non-scholarly misconduct. While I had become aware, on 7 August, that some Fellows were saying that they would resign if Professor Blunt did not, I would not have been influenced by this in putting any such proposal to Professor Blunt had I not in any case been called upon to write to him. It was in the light of the public controversy as a whole, that I concluded that in replying to him I ought to ask him to consider resignation.

3. I must state emphatically that I consider myself absolutely free to ask anyone to consider anything, provided that my request does not convey any kind of threat. Up to 3 July I had consistently refused to ask Professor Blunt to resign (the <u>Sunday Telegraph</u> of 17 August was quite wrong about that, and I have written to the editor), because the threat of expulsion hung over him. After 3 July the situation was entirely altered. It seemed to me that there was now no threat, overt or covert, which I could possibly bring to bear on Professor Blunt even if I wanted to. No doubt there was a likelihood that attacks on him in the press would continue for some time if he did not resign, but he did not need me to tell him that, and in any case it was not in my power to control what people wrote to newspapers. If I had known on 13 August that some Fellows were seriously suggesting the holding of a referendum, in the hope of reversing the decision taken on 3 July, I would not have asked

.../2

2

Professor Blunt to consider resigning, even though I could not have believed that Council would accept the idea of a referendum, which is not provided for in our constitution. Obviously a request by the President of an Academy to consider a possibility can be thought to carry intimidating weight or to constitute 'pressure' - if it is written (e.g.) to a Senior Research Fellow; but hardly if it is written to someone older, more distinguished, and of longer standing as a Fellow than the President himself.

4. Before I finished writing my letter to Professor Blunt I was rung up by a man on the <u>Daily Telegraph</u>, who read out to me a letter which, he said, was on its way to me from Professor Plumb saying he and certain others would resign if Professor Blunt did not. I did not alter what I had already said in my letter to Professor Blunt, but I added a sentence to assure him that I was not writing to anyone else's order, whatever might be said in next day's papers.

5. On 15 August Professor Blunt rang me up to tell me that he was giving my letter careful consideration. He accepted my assurance that I had not written at the behest of others, and reaffirmed his wish to act in the best interests of the Academy, but told me that there were Fellows who, if he resigned, thought they should resign in sympathy, acting as if resignation had been forced upon him. It seemed to me that he and I were essentially agreed in finding that view surprising.

6. On 17 August Professor Blunt rang me up to say that he had decided to resign and that his letter of resignation was on its way. It was subsequently agreed that it would be desirable to announce it as soon as possible. We did not discuss the terms in which it should be announced, that being a matter entirely for Professor Blunt.

7. Next day I received Professor Plumb's letter and letters from some other Fellows, of whom one put forward a plan for a referendum and another told me of his intention to publish a piece in <u>Encounter</u>. Professor Blunt's resignation was made public later in the day.

I am sending copies of this to the Press and to all those who were on the Fellowship Roll at the time of the Annual General Meeting.

K.J. Dover
22.8.80

59: Arnold Taylor to Kenneth Dover, 23 August 1980.

TEL. WORMLEY (042.879) 2069

ROSE COTTAGE
LINCOLN'S HILL
CHIDDINGFOLD
SURREY GU8 4UN

23 August, 1980

Dear President,

<u>The Academy and Professor Blunt</u>

May I send this brief note of thanks and appreciation for your 'Note to the Fellowship' of 22nd August. Most of us, I think, would have been content to guess, but can now see, with what impartiality and good sense this unhappy affair has been handled. Certainly at least one Fellow marvelled at the restraint and patience with which on July 3rd you presided over what must surely have been the most difficult and trying AGM ever to have fallen to a chairman's lot.

I forebore to speak on that occasion, but should have felt constrained to do so if the Council's motion had looked like being carried. I abhor treason as deeply as anyone, but I was one of those who felt and still feel that what would have been seen as a corporate act of retribution by the Academy would have been wrong. My own view was and is that our only right guide in the matter must be 1 Cor. 13, but I am afraid I hadn't the courage to get up and say what would only have sounded trite in that assemblage; besides, there were too many others anxious to give expression to extreme views on one side or the other.

Please, no answer to this; it is meant to be no more than an acknowledgement of your 'Note', and I do not wish to add one iota to the appalling burden of correspondence that the affair must have caused you. The resignations are a pity and in some cases much to be regretted, but I do not think the Academy can have any reason to reproach itself.

Yours sincerely,

Arnold Taylor

Sir Kenneth Dover,
Corpus Christi College,
Oxford.

Dover's note prompted an influx of correspondence. Of the letters he received, six were critical, but 20 were broadly supportive – combining sentiments of sympathy for Dover's predicament with relief and hope that the affair had been brought to a conclusion. One such letter was from the architectural historian Arnold Taylor FBA **[59]**:[42] he was glad that the AGM had not committed 'a corporate act of retribution' against Blunt, but he now commended Dover on the 'impartiality and good sense' he had shown in this 'unhappy affair'.[43]

[42] Arnold Taylor had his own experience of intelligence work in the war, serving in the RAF's aerial photographic interpretation branch: see A. Saunders, 'Arnold Joseph Taylor, 1911-2002', *Proceedings of the British Academy*, 138 (2006), p. 366.

[43] The philosopher Karl Popper FBA wrote on 23 August 1980 to say that he found Dover's note to the Fellowship 'excellent and completely convincing in every point'. In contrast, writing on 6 September 1980, the historian Christopher Hill FBA questioned Dover's 'complete impartiality on the issue': what Dover had done 'seems to me to conflict with the spirit of the decisive vote taken' at the AGM, with 'divisive consequences for the Academy'. Later venting his annoyance in 'Materials' at Hill's view that he had not displayed 'complete impartiality', Dover mused: 'it is hard, I suppose, to be so far up Stalin's arse for so long without suffering some impairment of vision.'

The letter from the historian Geoffrey Elton FBA displayed a refreshing balance and perspective **[60]**. He said that the whole affair had been 'a prime example of the academic skill in making mountains out of molehills or finding issues of principle in the most unpromising corners.' He even suggested that, through the press coverage of this 'good silly-season subject', 'a great number of people have now heard of the Academy who had never before done so'.

Professor Geoffrey Elton FBA

60: Geoffrey Elton to Kenneth Dover, 24 August 1980.

CLARE COLLEGE
CAMBRIDGE
CB2 1TL
0223 358681

24 August 1980

The President
The British Academy
Burlington House
Piccadilly
London W1V 0NS

Dear Sir Kenneth,

Thank you very much for your circular letter of the 22nd. I am sure you did not expect replies, but I feel moved to write, in the main in order to assure you that there are other reactions to the whole Blunt business than those that seem mostly to have beset you. I cannot believe that I am alone in judging this to be a prime example of the academic skill in making mountains out of molehills or finding issues of principle in the most unpromising corners. Or in thinking that you have throughout behaved with exemplary propriety.

Because of a longstanding lecturing engagement I could not attend the AGM; had I been there, I think I should not have felt called upon to vote at all. I did regret that Council had ever put up that famous motion (though I was aware of the pressures to which they had been exposed), not because I have the slightest sympathy with Blunt, who deserves none, but because Council seemed to me to have no chance at all of getting it passed. The predictable knee-jerk reaction of liberal sentiment was bound to see to that. I was, however, slightly astonished by the passionate reactions to a majority vote: those resignations seemed to suggest that one could not remain a fellow of the Academy if on some issue that one elected into importance other fellows disagreed with one. If we all refused to belong to bodies that include people we disapprove of, existence would become very peculiar; do those resigners really have no doubts whatsoever, even on political grounds, about, for instance, other fellows of their own Colleges? Equally, I find it difficult to believe that my remaining a fellow signifies that I hold the highest opinion of the scholarly standing of every co-academician. Life, I confess, does not look like that to me or to make such impossible demands.

The people who cry witchhunt are demonstrating only a willingness to allow mischievous slogans to take the place of five minutes of thought.

All of which suggests that if some people wish to resign, for this or that reason, the decision - which of course must be theirs - need not perhaps cause the rest of us to lose a second's sleep.

I am not even sure that the publicity in the press - happily picking up a good silly-season subject - is all that unfortunate. At least a great number of people have now heard of the Academy who had never before done so. That anyone involved with the press would be misquoted and misrepresented was one of the minor certainties of life; that some (I mention no names) would enjoy the experience was not much more uncertain.

I think that Blunt should have resigned long since, of his own free will, or under a bit of pressure - pressure applied, however, when his misdeeds first became known and not at a late stage. That he has done so now is satisfactory; that some people find this an occasion for publicising their consciences is sad. But the losers in the business are neither the Academy nor its President.

Yours sincerely
Geoffrey Elton
G.R. Elton

By permission of the Royal Historical Society

Slightly less level-headed was the letter written by Richard Cobb **[61]**. Cobb had been somewhat out of the loop on holiday in Shrewsbury, and had only learned of recent developments – including A.J.P. Taylor's resignation – through some newspaper cuttings he had been sent. When he was then contacted by a *Guardian* journalist, who was also a former pupil, he said 'on impulse' that he too would submit his resignation. This was reported in the *Guardian* on 22 August. Cobb now wrote to say that, although he felt he had 'acted rightly', he regretted the manner in which his resignation had been made public.

61: Richard Cobb to Kenneth Dover, 26 August 1980.

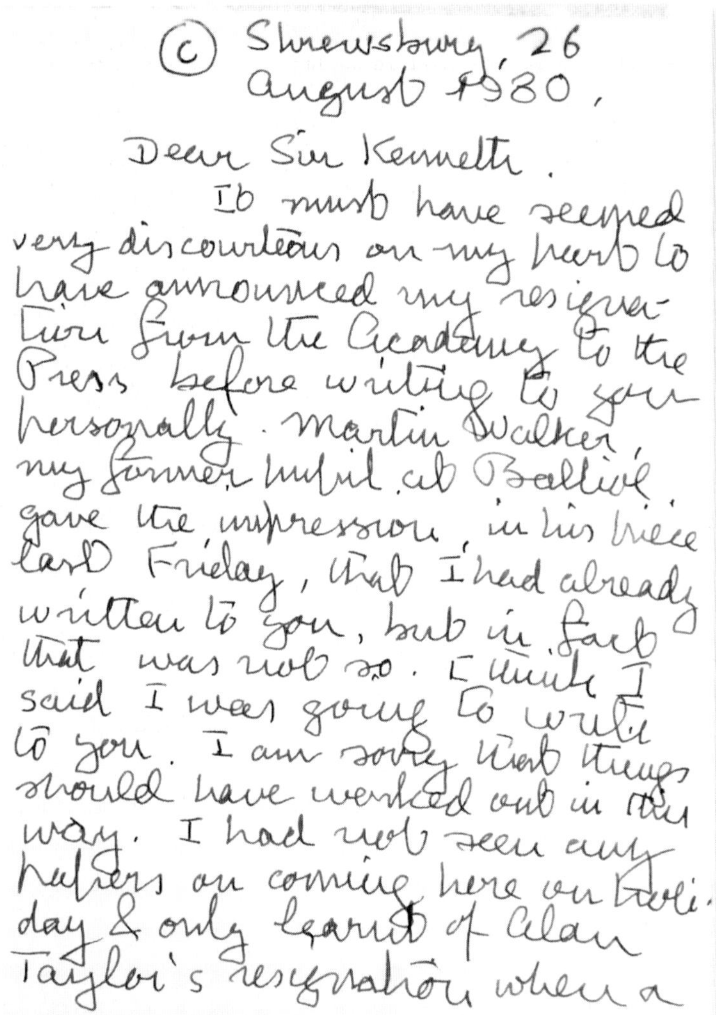

(c) Shrewsbury, 26
August 1980,

Dear Sir Kenneth.

It must have seemed very discourteous on my part to have announced my resignation from the Academy to the Press before writing to you personally. Martin Walker my former pupil at Balliol gave the impression, in his piece last Friday, that I had already written to you, but in fact that was not so. I think I said I was going to write to you. I am sorry that things should have worked out in this way. I had not seen any papers on coming here on holiday & only learnt of Alan Taylor's resignation when a

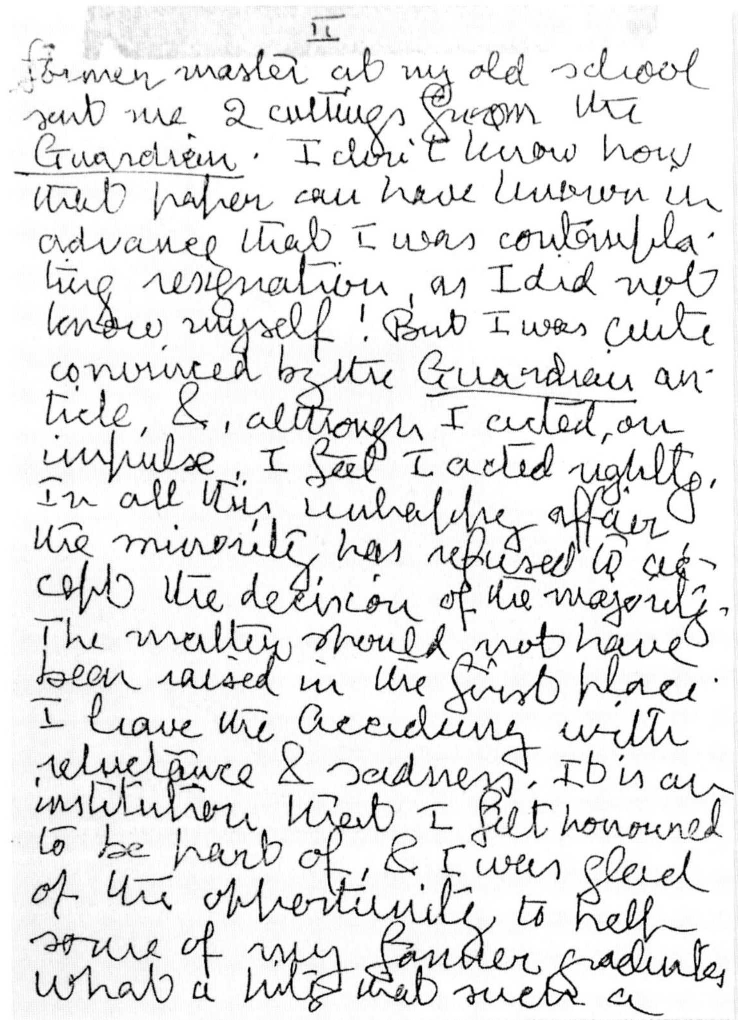

II

former master at my old school sent me 2 cuttings from the Guardian. I don't know how that paper can have known in advance that I was contemplating resignation, as I did not know myself! But I was quite convinced by the Guardian article, &, although I acted on impulse, I feel I acted rightly. In all this unhappy affair the minority has refused to accept the decision of the majority. The matter should not have been raised in the first place. I leave the Academy with reluctance & sadness. It is an institution that I felt honoured to be part of, & I was glad of the opportunity to help some of my former graduates. What a pity that such a

III

distinguished academic body should be forced into the rôle of a Court of Moral Inquisition! I am sure, too, that Professor Blunt resigned only under strong pressure, with a minimum of common sense on the part of the minority the whole business could have been avoided; I hope at least that your holiday has not been blighted by all this publicity. Publicity is the last thing I sought.

Yours sincerely

Richard Cobb

(Worcester College)

A few days later, Cobb wrote again to Dover **[62]**. He said he had returned from holiday to find 'voluminous mail' from colleagues asking him to withdraw his resignation – including one that appeared to be 'a message from Professor Blunt'. Cobb admitted that he would have acted differently if he had been in Oxford and 'able to consult my friends'. He asked: 'Could my action be dismissed as a piece of August Folly, forgiven and, I hope, forgotten?' (It was.)

62: Richard Cobb to Kenneth Dover, 31 August 1980.

From the Professor of Modern History

Worcester College Oxford OX1 2HB

Sunday, 31st August 1980

Answered

Dear Sir Kenneth

I returned from holiday in Shrewsbury yesterday and collected a voluminous mail in College. It contained two very friendly letters from my two Regiuses (Regii?), Hugh and Michael, asking me to withdraw my resignation. And I have had several other letters to the same effect, including one from Francis Haskell with what appears to be a message from Professor Blunt. I find their arguments quite convincing, and, if it is not too late, I would like to withdraw my resignation, and ask to be re-admitted to the fold. I should add, in my own defence, that I never read the papers while on holiday, and would have known nothing about recent developments, had not Stacy Colman, a former Classics master, put extracts from the Guardian through my door. And it was these - and the fact that Martin Walker, who covered the affair - was a former pupil of mine at Balliol - that drove me into rather unconsiddered action. I don't think it would have happened, had I been in Oxford and able to consult my friends. I certain did - and do - feel a strong sense of grievance about the rearguard action of the minority; but, as Hugh says, that is no reason to place myself outside a body that I admire and am proud to be part of. I felt saddened after I had got in touch with Walker, and refused to write a piece for his paper and to appear on some wretched TV programme. I did not seek publicity, which is something I hate. Could my action be dismissed as a piece of August Folly, forgiven and, I hope, forgotton? I really am very contrite, but also very hearetned by the kindness of my friends. I don't know whether I should write to the Guardian? But I would be happy if the Academy were to publicise my decision. I shall write and explain to Alan Taylor why I have changed my mind. Apparently he has found the whole episode fun, but I certainly did not. Many apologies. I should not have acted so impulsively; but these things do happen, and I had been feeling increasingly resentful at the efforts to re-open the matters decided at the AGM last month. I hope the whole episode may soon be forgotton.

Yours sincerely

I am sending this off before the mad month of August is out.

Richard Cobb

(Richard Cobb)

Cobb wasn't the only Fellow changing his mind. On 30 August, Jim Gower – the Fellow who had moved 'next business' at that pivotal moment in the AGM – drafted a letter of resignation from the Academy **[63]**. He expressed his lack of confidence in Council, and his disappointment that it had not censured those Fellows who had sought to get their way by threatening resignation.

Professor L.C.B. 'Jim' Gower MBE FBA

Gower never sent this letter to Dover. But on 2 September he sent a copy to Lionel Robbins, seeking his advice. He wrote: 'having slept on it, I'm not sure whether or not to send it. ... I don't like remaining in a body which seems to be riddled with the worst sort of academic bitchiness. On the other hand resigning achieves nothing – except to relieve one's feelings.' Gower didn't resign – and Dover never knew that it might have been a possibility.

At the beginning of September, Dover turned again to the four Fellows – Skeat, Roberts, Crook and Bawden – who *had* resigned in July: he admits in 'Materials' that he felt he would have 'brought off a coup' if he could somehow get them back. None of them chose to change their minds. In his reply to Dover **[64]**, Crook expressed his conviction that 'a man ought to be consistent in his actions and decisions'. He also did not want anyone to think 'that my resignation was an attempt to blackmail the Academy into changing its properly arrived at decision', and he disowned the behaviour of those Fellows who had indeed attempted to get their way by threatening to resign. Bawden similarly wrote to say that it would be 'quite inconsistent' on his part to resume his Fellowship. (He would later have a change of heart, and would be re-elected a Fellow in 1985.)

63: 'Jim' Gower to Kenneth Dover, 30 August 1980 (unsent draft).

Draft

26 Willow Road,
Hampstead,
LONDON NW3 1TL

Sir Kenneth Dover,
The President,
The British Academy,
Burlington House,
Piccadilly,
LONDON W1V ONS

30th August, 1980.

Dear President,

I was abroad at the time of the events referred to in your note of 22nd August and have, therefore, only just caught up with them. Having done so I have regretfully decided to resign from the Academy.

My reasons are:-

(a) The way that this matter has been handled throughout by the Council has sapped my confidence in them.

(b) The conduct of certain Senior Fellows in seeking to achieve their aims by whipping up press publicity and threatening to resign if they don't get their way seems to me to be deplorable. I have always understood that seeking to influence the decisions of a body of which one is a member by threatening to resign is quite improper; yet, in this case, it seems to have escaped the Council's ~~censure and, indeed, to have~~ achieved the aim of one faction by securing Professor Blunt's resignation despite the clearly expressed view of the meeting that he should not be asked to do so.

Holding these views the only decent course is to resign. I do so with reluctance since, as you will gather from what I have said, I have no wish to appear to be associating myself with Professor A.J.P. Taylor or for that matter with Professor Blunt for whom I hold no brief. Nor do I propose to make any public announcement unless you wish me to do so as the only way of preventing correspondents to continue to apply the suffix FBA to me. I should, however, be grateful if, when Fellows next are circulated, a copy of this letter could be enclosed so that they may know my reasons for leaving them.

I hope you will not regard this letter as in any sense a personal criticism of you in what must have been a singularly difficult and embarrassing situation.

Yours sincerely,

Professor L.C.B. Gower

64: John Crook to Kenneth Dover, 7 September 1980.

200

No answer [illegible]

TEL. NO. 61621

ST. JOHN'S COLLEGE
CAMBRIDGE CB2 1TP

7.9.80

Dear Kenneth,

I'm sorry: I've been away. Your letter of 2 Sept. exhibits once more the great personal kindness you've shown to the lost sheep, or at least this one, all along.

Alas — for me — I think the answer is "thank you warmly, but no". As I wrote to you, my reasons for resigning were partly gut reasons and partly an argument; and though I still wouldn't like to put my hand on my heart as to which was uppermost in my decision to take that step, the argument was one of consequence and importance in my mind. And it is still my belief that the decision taken by that overwhelming majority of Fellows present & voting implied overwhelming acceptance of a view of the relation of scholarship to the polity in general that I cannot join in upholding.

I think, too, that a man ought to be consistent and consequent in his actions and decisions. I know obstinacy is no virtue, and perhaps that is all I am exhibiting. But to ask to be put back now might suggest (to anyone interested enough in these little matters; and I expect someone will do a Doktorarbeit on it all in 100 years' time) that my resignation was an attempt to blackmail the Academy into changing its properly arrived at decision. You and I know that that would

2

TEL. NO. 61621

ST. JOHN'S COLLEGE
CAMBRIDGE CB2 1TP

have been a silly thing for me to hope to achieve, since the guns I carry are not of the necessary calibre. But I should like it to be on record that I do not believe it was right for Fellows of the Academy, after the decision of the Academy, to attempt to secure the reversal of that decision by threats of resignation, and I would not have been one of such Fellows. I resigned, tout court. I must now live with the consequences of my decision.

I'm afraid you will have had a very vexing summer, full of academics behaving as tiresomely as only academics can. Please accept my very best wishes for calmer things to come.

Yours sincerely

J A Crook

As an academic controversy and major news story, the Blunt affair was now at an end – though it would continue to rumble on as Dover, several Fellows, one former Fellow (A.J.P. Taylor), and one future Fellow (George Steiner) exchanged rival accounts and views in the pages of *Encounter* and other periodicals over the next twelve months.[44] Perhaps fittingly, it is Kenneth Dover who has had the last word. The final text in his collection of 'Materials for a History of the Events Leading to the Resignation of Professor A.F. Blunt' is his own 'Retrospect' **[65]**, a 24-point reflection on what had happened and why he had acted the way he had, composed for the benefit of posterity in May 1981.

[44] Ian R. Christie, 'A Confusion of Fellows', *Encounter*, October 1980, pp. 30-2; Kenneth Dover, 'The "Blunt Affair", Again', *Encounter*, November 1980, pp. 40-2; George Steiner, 'The Cleric of Treason', *New Yorker*, 8 December 1980, pp. 158-95; Hugh Lloyd-Jones, letter 'On Expelling Blunt', *Encounter*, January 1981, p. 95; Norman Gash, 'Over There: A Scholar and a Traitor', *Policy Review*, no. 15, winter 1981, pp. 153-60; A.J.P. Taylor, 'Postscript to the "Blunt Affair": Expelling a Spy', *Encounter*, June 1981, pp. 93-4, with 'Reply' from Kenneth Dover, p. 94; F.A. Mann, 'The Blunt Affair', *Encounter*, September 1981, pp. 92-3.

65: 'Retrospect' by Kenneth Dover, 12 May 1981.

RETROSPECT

1. I have always felt, and still feel, that a nation which fails to tear a traitor to pieces is doomed.

2. I have always believed, and still believe, that a nation which gives precedence to the word of the law over irrational feelings deserves respect and is likely to receive it.

3. There was only one justification for expelling Blunt: that he had worked treacherously for the supremacy of a totalitarian nation which has consistently frustrated and persecuted scholarship, and by so doing he tried to defeat the purposes for which the Academy exists.

4. This justification was not mentioned either on Council or at the AGM. I did not think it right to reveal even on Council, let alone at the AGM, that I myself considered it a justification.

5. By 3 July I was indifferent to the outcome, aware that I could not defend ~~the~~ Council's resolution on grounds of which I approved, very well aware that the proposal to expel Blunt stood no chance at all, and suspecting that even Robbins' motion would not command a majority.

6. My job as President was to take whatever course of action seemed most likely to be to the advantage of the Academy. In August my two objects were:
(a) to reduce to a minimum the number of resignations, and
(b) to curtail the period for which the issue of Blunt's fellowship provoked comment and correspondence in the press.

7. I was not at any stage willing to make false statements or to commit injustice in furtherance of my objects.

8. I did not at any stage consider that Blunt deserved to be treated with consideration if the interests of the Academy required that he should be sacrificed. There was no need to be rude to him, and I certainly would not have deceived him or broken a promise to him, but no degree of harshness towards him was unjust.

9. I was always willing that criticism of the Academy should be diverted on to me personally, and that I should be criticised within the Academy for action which would in the long run be to the Academy's advantage.

10. The resignations of Roberts, Skeat, Crook and Bawden are understandable, but I am not altogether in sympathy with them.

11. The threats of resignation made by Plumb, Gash, Allen and Christie were disgraceful and inexcusable, and if they have earned the hostility and contempt of many other Fellows they have only themselves to blame.

12. ~~If~~ When a terrorist threatens to kill a planeful of hostages if we do not yield to his disagreeable but (let us say, for argument's sake) practicable demands, we usually yield, attaching some value to the lives of the hostages. This is not a condonation of terrorism, but a consequence of weighing the alternatives. (11) and (12) must be considered together.

13. Knowing that the Plumb faction was resolute and determined to organise support, and knowing also that

(a) Gurney was looking for some such organised support to join, and

(b) Bawden's resignation had not been an immediate reaction to the AGM but the product of three weeks' reflection,

I judged that if Blunt did not resign the number of resignations by 1 Jan. 1981 might be well into two figures.

14. In view of (4) above, I judged that some Fellows would change from a pro-Blunt to an anti-Blunt attitude in the light of Christie's article.

15. As time passed, more people were likely to commit themselves to positions from which they could not easily withdraw.

16. Gash's notion that the AGM was 'packed' with Blunt-supporters from London was nonsense, and the idea that a referendum of the whole Fellowship could overturn the verdict of the AGM was quite unjustified. However, these considerations did not invalidate (13)-(15); only small numbers were involved, but even a handful mattered to me in the light of (6)(a).

17. IF ONLY the letter written to me by Blunt on 8 August had not reached me until after 13 August, then I would have

(a) written only to thank him, saying nothing about resignation;

(b) let my letter go in to the <u>Times</u>; and

(c) composed a memorandum for circulationto the Fellowship, arguing in reasonable and pacific terms against the Plumbfaction, persuading others not to join it, and saying that Council would consider a referendum only if a significant number of Fellows informed me that they had changed their minds since the AGM.

18. As it was, I wrote to Blunt as I did because

(a) considerations (6), (8), (9), (13), (14) and (15) were in my mind;

(b) the last post from St Andrews was due to go in an hour, and

(c) this was the very last moment at which I could decently mention resignation to Blunt; the news from the <u>Telegraph</u> reporter about Plumb's letter meant that the press would refer to the letter ~~that~~ next morning, and after that I could not expect Blunt or anyone else to believe that I had written to him in consequence of my own train of thought.

19. The attainment of the objectives I had set myself was flawed by Taylor's resignation, and I was deceived in my wild hope that I could somehow get back Roberts, Skeat, Crook and Bawden, but the nett total of resignations was smaller than it would have been if Blunt had not resigned, and the interest of the popular press in the affair did not last beyond the end of August.

20. That being so, I would not, even if I could, undo what I did on 13 August. I did the right thing for the right reasons.

22. I handled the matter badly. I was guilty of an error of judgment in

(a) failing to realise that my suggestion to Blunt possessed a certain <u>auctoritas</u>, and consequently

(b) underestimating the reactions which the resignation would provoke.

23. If my judgment had been better, I would have

(a) written a longer and chattier letter to Blunt, making it much clearer that I wrote as an individual, not as President, and

(b) kept a copy of the letter for circulation to the Fellowship if a circular should be rendered necessary by misrepresentations in the press, and

(c) gone down to London for 18-20 August, instead of inconsiderately making myself inaccessible for much of that period of three days and leaving the Secretary to deal with problems for which I had not adequately briefed him.

24. When I composed this Retrospect two days ago, and when I revised it yesterday, I began by stating my feelings on treachery and my belief about law, but I forgot to say anything at all about forgiveness, which, as I said in my unpublished letter to the <u>Times</u> and my piece in <u>Encounter</u>, was an important determinant of the AGM's decision. In fact I don't forgive easily; but I have done so just often enough to discover that forgiveness is a profoundly liberating experience. If the AGM had said firmly and openly that it forgave Blunt his collaboration with a regime hostile to scholarship, had declared its hatred of treachery, and had made it plain that ~~it was~~ forgiveness ~~which~~ was ~~the~~ its motive for giving precedence to the letter of the bye-laws and charter over feelings about treachery, that would have been a decision which I could have defended with pride, conviction and fervour. To disguise the will to forgive under vulnerable reasons is not good enough.

K J Dover

12 May 1981

Epilogue

By the time Dover completed his 'Retrospect' in May 1981, his presidency was running down and running out, which meant his compilation of the Blunt 'Materials' was not only a personal act of closure and catharsis, but was also part of the process of clearing up his accumulated Academy business. In November 1980, Dover had informed Council that 'he would not stand for re-election to a fourth and final year of office', on the not-entirely-convincing grounds that he had been invited to lecture in Japan. Corpus Christi College would allow him to go on leave, but he did not think he could 'decently offload all my presidential commitments to the Academy on to my Vice-Presidents'. It was, he later recalled, 'not a difficult decision.' The Blunt affair, he admitted, 'had undoubtedly imposed a strain on me which diminished the charms of office by comparison with a trip to the Far East.'[1] Accordingly, Dover's term of office ended in the summer of 1981, which meant he became the only post-war President of the British Academy who did not serve out the full four-year term that had become customary. He also remains the only President to have analysed his own performance in the post, as he did in his 'Retrospect' on the Blunt affair. In it, he claimed he had 'handled the matter badly', although it is not entirely clear whether that comment relates to a specific point in his self-analysis, or to his conduct of the whole business. There was criticism from some Fellows that he had failed to provide strong leadership or make his own views clear, and he can certainly be faulted for not having dealt personally with Blunt in March 1980, in the aftermath of the second meeting of the Academy's Council which had discussed the matter.[2] Yet it can also be argued that Dover had dealt with the matter rather well, at least according to the criteria he set out in 6 (a) and (b) – reducing to a minimum the number of resignations, and limiting the period that the Blunt issue made headlines in the press. Blunt was not expelled, but he did eventually resign. Only five other Fellows did so too, and by the end of 1980 the press had lost interest in the Academy (although not in Blunt himself). The 'terrible damage' that Richard Cobb feared the Academy would suffer 'as an institution' did not happen.[3]

Yet at the same time, Dover's position, as set out in his 'Retrospect', does seem oddly confused and contradictory: displaying at least as much woolliness as wisdom after the events. His first observation, 'that a nation which fails to tear a traitor to pieces is doomed', would have done credit to Professor J.H. Plumb in his most vengeful mode, yet Dover deeply disapproved of Plumb's position and of his behaviour throughout the Blunt affair. It is also surprising that Dover should have begun his 'Retrospect' by writing about how he *felt*, since he was a lifelong believer in the primacy of reason and thought over feelings and emotions, as he made plain in his second observation. Although he set out his own justification for expelling Blunt from the Academy, Dover gave no explanation as to why he thought it right not to reveal his views to Council or the Fellowship, and it seems strange, in the light of his own strongly-stated opinions, that he was 'indifferent to the outcome' of the AGM. Dover's closing panegyric on the importance of forgiveness also sits uneasily with his opening denunciation of traitors, and this makes it difficult to understand how he would have been prepared to defend 'with pride, conviction and fervour' a decision that the AGM might have taken to pardon Blunt for 'his collaboration with a regime hostile to scholarship', not least since this was the very reason he had earlier given as to why he thought Blunt should be expelled.[4] This all seems very jumbled: perhaps a sign that Dover had been ill-served by his lifelong lack of interest in ancient Greek philosophy. He was also certainly correct in censuring himself for his un-business-like habits: in not keeping copies of important letters, and for 'inconsiderately' making himself inaccessible for three days in August

[1] BA MS: Council Minutes, 7 November 1980, p. 6; Keith Thomas interview, 4 November 2019; K. Dover, *Marginal Comment: A Memoir* (London, 1994), pp. 206-07.

[2] See page 34.

[3] R. Cobb to H. Trevor-Roper, 10 September 1980, in T. Heald (ed.), *My Dear Hugh: Letters from Richard Cobb to Hugh Trevor-Roper and others* (London, 2011), p. 83; Sir Michael Howard, e-mail, 27 October 2019; Keith Thomas interview, 4 November 2019. The six Fellows who resigned were Theodore Skeat, Colin Roberts, John Crook, Charles Bawden, Blunt himself, and A.J.P. Taylor—though it bears repeating that Bawden was later re-elected.

[4] See document 65.

1980, when he should have taken charge in London, instead of leaving the Academy's Secretary, John Carswell, to cope as best he could.

***

Dover was concerned with analysing his own performance as President, but the longer perspective of forty years also allows for some broader reflections on some of the Fellows who were most prominently involved in the Blunt affair. Perhaps the most significant is that there was no simple left-right split: partisan political opinions did not necessarily determine Fellows' views of Blunt, or of what, if anything, the Academy should do about him. It was unsurprising that Eric Hobsbawm, also a Cambridge Apostle and a member of the Communist Party, should have been one of Blunt's supporters, and opposed to his expulsion. But Hugh Trevor-Roper (by then re-branded as Lord Dacre of Glanton) was also against, although he 'despised' Blunt, and so was Michael Howard, neither of whom were men of the Marxist left.[5] Howard had seen active military service during the Second World War, and had been awarded the Military Cross, yet soon after Blunt had been unmasked, he wrote to *The Times*, defending the decision of the security services not to prosecute in 1964, and he was also willing to forgive what he regarded as Blunt's youthful folly, even though he had been 'as amazed by the revelation as everyone else.'[6] On the other hand, Robert Blake, who had been taken a prisoner of war on the fall of Tobruk, but later escaped and worked for MI6, was determined that Blunt should be expelled, although unlike some others, he did not threaten to resign if Blunt did not do so. Despite their different views of politics and of history, Hobsbawm and Trevor-Roper got on well. Howard, Blake and Trevor-Roper were even closer friends, and all of them had connections with Christ Church, Oxford, where Trevor-Roper and Howard had been undergraduates, and where Blake was a Student (i.e. Fellow) from 1947 to 1968. Trevor-Roper and Blake had lunched together before the Academy's AGM, but they diverged sharply in their views of Blunt, and Blake regarded the meeting's decision to move on to the next item of business as 'disgraceful and discreditable'.[7]

The campaigning camaraderie between Lord Blake and J.H. Plumb also seems odd at first sight. Blake was a lifelong Tory and the biographer of Disraeli, who took the Conservative whip in the House of Lords. Plumb, by contrast, had been a Communist in the 1930s, wrote an incomplete life of Walpole, and was a strong supporter of Harold Wilson's in the 1960s and early 1970s. Yet he, too, was deeply hostile to Blunt: as Isaiah Berlin recalled, 'I was shocked by the fact that [Plumb] was so nasty. This wasn't *odium academicum*: it was *odium personali* [sic].'[8] He certainly had some scores to pay off. In pre-war Cambridge, where he had arrived as a graduate student with an external London degree from University College, Leicester, Plumb had wanted to be elected to the Apostles, and he had once been invited to Blunt's rooms at Trinity, where his recently-acquired Poussin was hanging over the mantelpiece. 'I don't know if I didn't smell right, or what', Plumb later recalled, on more than one occasion, 'but I was never asked again.'[9] That rejection had clearly rankled and festered across the years, and Plumb was undoubtedly out for retribution. But there was more to his vengefulness than that, for by the late 1970s, Plumb had moved politically well to the right. Disappointed by his failure to obtain a peerage in Wilson's resignation honours list of 1976, he soon shifted his political allegiance to Margaret Thatcher; and having written the television scripts and the book *Royal Heritage*, celebrating English and British monarchs as patrons and collectors, to mark the Silver Jubilee of Queen Elizabeth II in 1977, Plumb had begun to ingratiate himself with royalty, especially Princess Margaret.[10] Since neither Thatcher nor Elizabeth II thought well of Blunt's treachery, Plumb clearly hoped that his campaign to get him out of the Academy might earn him their approval and approbation.

It did at least earn him the gratitude of Lord Blake. '*You* are', Blake wrote to him in late August 1980, 'the person who deserves full credit over the Blunt affair', and he congratulated Plumb, 'most warmly on what you have done.' He had certainly done a great deal to organise and mobilise the malcontents, and his archive contains extensive correspondence, not only with Blake, but also with Christie, Ehrman and Gash. Moreover, Plumb had cherished hopes that he might succeed Dover as President, which might in turn have revived his chances of obtaining the peerage he craved from a grateful government and also some mark of recognition from a no-less appreciative sovereign.[11] But Plumb's victory over Blunt proved to be pyrrhic. Dover's 'Retrospect' made plain his loathing and rage at Plumb and his co-conspirators, for deliberately seeking to overturn the majority vote at the AGM that Blunt should not be expelled, and for making the Academy's private business public by writing and talking to the newspapers. This view was widely shared among the Fellowship, and there were also Fellows such as Hobsbawm and Trevor-Roper

[5] A. Sisman, *Hugh Trevor-Roper: The Biography* (London, 2010), p. 449-50; H. Trevor-Roper to H. Lloyd Jones, 27 July 1980, in R. Davenport-Hines and A. Sisman (eds), *One Hundred Letters from Hugh Trevor-Roper* (Oxford, 2013), pp. 249-51. See also documents 3 and 11.

[6] A.J.P. Taylor MS 1/3: M. Howard to Taylor, 18 February 1980. See also Howard's letter to *The Times*, 21 November 1979. M. Howard, *Captain Professor* (London, 2006), p. 191.

[7] R. Shannon, 'Robert Norman William Blake, 1916-2003', *Proceedings of the British Academy*, 153 (2008), pp. 101-2; *Daily Telegraph*, 6 August 1980; see document 31.

[8] M. Carter, *Anthony Blunt: His Lives* (London, 2001), p. 492.

[9] D. Cannadine, 'John Harold Plumb, 1911-2001', *Proceedings of the British Academy*, 124 (2004), pp. 276, 298, 302; N. McKendrick, *Sir John Plumb: The Hidden Life of a Great Historian: A Personal Memoir* (Brighton, 2019), pp. 179-80.

[10] J.H. Plumb and H. Weldon, *Royal Heritage: The Story of Britain's Royal Builders and Collectors* (London, 977).

[11] Plumb MS: Lord Blake to J.H. Plumb, 20 August 1980; Annan MS 5/1/805: J.H. Plumb to Lord Annan, 30 November 1990. See documents 42-48.

who knew of Plumb's Communist past, and who were further annoyed at the way he was trying to cover his earlier tracks. Isaiah Berlin's later verdict was damning: he thought Plumb 'an ignoble character.'[12] To make matters worse for Plumb, the person who *did* follow Dover as President of the Academy was Owen Chadwick, whom Plumb disliked for his religious faith and envied for his worldly success, securing the Regius chair at Cambridge that Plumb himself had vainly coveted, and being awarded the Order of Merit while President. Throughout the Blunt affair, Chadwick had impressed many members of Council with his moral authority and hostility to witch-hunts, and he did much to bring the Academy together once it was over.[13]

Isaiah Berlin's part in these proceedings was characteristic. He had known Blunt since the 1930s, and was aware of his double life, but he was against expelling him from the Academy.[14] He had initially agreed to co-sponsor with Lionel Robbins the amendment to be put at the AGM, 'deploring' Blunt's treachery, but not recommending expulsion. Yet at almost the last minute, Berlin pulled out, ostensibly on the grounds that it was inappropriate for a former President to be so ostentatiously involved, but more likely because, as so often, he sought to avoid controversy and keep his head down.[15] But Robbins, another former President, suffered from no such constraints and inhibitions. He, too, 'deplored' Blunt's conduct, but he was a lifelong friend, and for many years had chaired the Courtauld Institute's Board of Management; Blunt was deeply grateful to him for standing by him at such a testing time.[16]

'Daily Telegraph' cartoon of 13 August 1980: the British Academy was not used to this level of press attention.

A.J.P. Taylor, ever the wayward self-publicist, held an impromptu press conference on the steps of Burlington House after the AGM, at which he had clearly intended to resign, if the meeting had voted to expel Blunt. It was, he insisted, the Academy's duty to 'tolerate the intolerable', a remark which drew Dover's ire and contempt. Although, following Blunt, Taylor did eventually resign, in protest at the 'witch-hunt' which he believed had forced Blunt out, he later made inquiries as to whether he might re-join the Academy, but by then he was over seventy, which at that time was the upper age limit at which anyone could be elected a Fellow. 'Ah well', Taylor responded, 'I do these things, it is part of my life.'[17] One casualty of Taylor's resignation was his friendship with Professor Ian Christie, whom he had taught at Oxford and had remained in touch with ever since. But in a letter to the *Daily Telegraph*, Christie rejected Taylor's claim that he and his colleagues had been engaging in a 'witch-hunt', and urged Taylor to withdraw his resignation. There was no further contact between the two men.[18]

Behind the Fellows themselves throughout the Blunt affair was the figure of John Carswell, Secretary to the Academy from 1978 to 1983, and thus its chief executive (the first holder of such a full-time post had been appointed only in 1969, in succession to Mortimer Wheeler). Carswell had been educated at St John's College, Oxford, saw war service in the army, and thereafter joined the civil service, rising to become Under Secretary at the Department of Education and Science and Secretary to the University Grants Committee, before moving to the Academy. He was also a notable historian of eighteenth-century Britain and a member of the Garrick Club.[19] Carswell was deeply troubled by the adverse publicity which the Blunt business brought down on the Academy, which he believed was motivated by 'class hatred, philistinism, anti-elitism and anti-establishmentism'. He heard reports that Margaret Thatcher was wondering why, in the aftermath of her November unmasking of Blunt, her government was giving the Academy any money at all, and at lunch at the Garrick, Carswell encountered Sir Michael Havers, the Attorney General, in the men's lavatory, who told him that 'Blunt has blood on his hands, a lot of blood.'[20] Carswell definitely wanted Blunt out, to preserve the good reputation of the Academy, but he did not accept Dover's private reasons for expulsion,

[12] D. Thorpe (ed.), *Who Loses, Who Wins: The Journals of Kenneth Rose*, vol. ii, *1979-2014* (London, 2019), pp. 360-1. See document 3.

[13] Peter Brown interview, 18 February 2018.

[14] Berlin MS 103: A. Blunt to Berlin [?late October 1934]; 105-6, Blunt to Berlin [?January-June 1937]; 108, [?October 1936-June 1937]; I. Berlin to B. Williams, 14 March 1980, in H. Hardy and M. Pottle (eds), *Affirming: Isaiah Berlin letters, 1975-1997* (London, 2015), p. 126.

[15] Robbins MS 9/4/6: I. Berlin to Lord Robbins, 5 June 1980; see document 22; Keith Thomas interview, 4 November 2019; Peter Brown interview, 18 February 2018. For Berlin's alleged 'cowardice' in avoiding public controversies, see M. Ignatieff, *Isaiah Berlin: A Life* (New York, 1999), pp. 257-8.

[16] Robbins MS 9/4/6: A. Blunt to Lord Robbins, 4 July 1980; see document 29.

[17] A.J.P. Taylor to E.H. Taylor, 24 November 1979, in E.H. Taylor (ed.), *A.J.P. Taylor: Letters to Eva, 1969-1983* (London, 1991), p. 405; H. Trevor-Roper to A. Sisman, 21 June 1991, in Davenport-Hines and Sisman (eds.), *One Hundred Letters*, pp. 375-6; C. Wrigley, 'Alan John Percivale Taylor, 1906-1990', *Proceedings of the British Academy*, 82 (1993), pp. 519-20; K. Burk, *Trouble-Maker: The Life and History of A.J.P. Taylor* (London, 2002), pp. 339-43; A. Sisman, *A.J.P. Taylor: A Biography* (London, 1994), pp. 389-93; Peter Brown interview, 18 February 2018. See document 55.

[18] *Daily Telegraph*, 25 August 1980; J.H. Burns, 'Ian Ralph Christie, 1919-1998', *Proceedings of the British Academy*, 105 (2000), pp. 378-9.

[19] Among his many books were: J.P. Carswell, *The South Sea Bubble* (London, 1960); idem, *The Descent on England* (London, 1969); idem, *From Revolution to Revolution: English Society, 1688-1776* (London, 1973).

[20] Peter Brown interview, 18 February 2018.

namely Blunt's 'transfer of allegiance to a system which negates the Academy's objects.' After all, Carswell opined, the Academy had sometimes elected as Corresponding Fellows 'persons whose allegiance is to systems like the one Blunt supported.' For him, it was Blunt's 'concealment of his true character and affiliations over a very long period, including the time at which he was elected [a Fellow]', which was the 'decisive' matter. If 'that secret had been known at the time', Carswell believed, Blunt 'would never have been elected to the Academy in the first place as a "fit and proper person".'[21]

***

Even though Blunt's double life was acknowledged in certain quarters, it was completely unknown in others, and the revelations came as a great shock to those who considered themselves his friends and who thought they had understood him well. This was quintessentially so in the case of the art historian Ellis Waterhouse, himself a Fellow of the Academy, who had been at school with Blunt at Marlborough, and who had edited the *Festschrift* to mark his sixtieth birthday. In a warm and affectionate preface, Waterhouse had praised Blunt's 'qualities of intellect and moral integrity'. He had also noted there that 'perhaps not all our friends of [the 1930s] turned out in the end altogether as one would have wished', completely unaware that those words applied to no one more fully than to Blunt himself. Waterhouse was so furious that Blunt had not told him beforehand that he initially refused to speak to him, and Blunt was visibly shaken by his rejection. He later relented and visited Blunt when they discussed art-history matters, but relations were never fully restored and the old intimacy was gone forever.[22] Another art historian and Fellow who had worked closely with Blunt was George Zarnecki. He had fled the Nazis in the 1930s, and had been Deputy Director of the Courtauld, where gossip about Blunt's mysterious life was widespread among the students. But Zarnecki had had 'no conception whatever of this part of Blunt's life', and was 'completely shattered' by what he took as a 'personal betrayal.'[23] Elsa Scheer, his former secretary at the Courtauld, with whom he had worked for more than thirty years, also 'cut off all connection' with Blunt; he found it a 'great sadness.'[24]

After his unmasking, Blunt lived on in obscurity and disgrace, supported by friends who stood by him, and by some Fellows of the Academy who thought he had behaved well, but shunned by those who could not countenance his treachery and deceit.[25] He continued to work at the Courtauld, the Warburg, the British Library and the British Museum, and delivered occasional lectures. He travelled to Italy, completed a *Guide to Baroque Rome*, which was largely ignored in the British press, began work on a book on Pietro da Cortona, and remained a frequent contributor to the *Burlington Magazine* and other periodicals.[26] Urged on by friends such as Lord Rothschild's wife Tess, Blunt wrote a memoir, which remained unpublished, and was subsequently deposited in the British Library, where it was only made available in 2008, twenty-five years after his death. Sir Robert Armstrong, the Cabinet Secretary, was relieved to discover that it contained no 'unwelcome' surprises or revelations.[27] Blunt wrote it 'for my friends who have stood by me with unbelievable affection and loyalty', and 'for those members of the public … who want to know the truth about my life and action', as opposed to 'the versions that have been served up to them by the press – I do not say "the gutter press" because that would imply that some parts of the press were not in the gutter.' He admitted that his decision to join the Communist Party, and to throw in his lot with Soviet Russia, while motivated by his belief that 'the cause of anti-fascism was of paramount importance', had been 'naïve politically', and was 'the biggest mistake of my life.' He conceded that his feelings for England 'had changed during the war', that the Labour victory in 1945 meant 'permanent changes for the better were on the way,' and that he might 'be able to put the whole thing behind me and return to normal existence.' He recognised that Stalin's regime 'had degenerated into a tyranny as bad as Hitler's', and that the application of Marxism to art history 'could only be made to seem to work by a great distortion of the facts.' But he 'found it unthinkable' that he would denounce his friends, and it 'never occurred' to him to do so.[28]

Blunt also admitted that following his unmasking, he had thought 'very seriously' about suicide. But he considered it a 'cowardly solution', and in any case, he still wanted to do more work and write more books. (Ironically, it was his late-life partner, John Gaskin, who had attempted suicide in January 1980, and he eventually succeeded in

[21] BA: Carswell Blunt Affair file, Bundle 1, item 50: J.P. Carswell, Handwritten notes on the Blunt affair [undated].

[22] E. Waterhouse, 'A Personal Preface', in E. Waterhouse (ed.), *Studies in Renaissance and Baroque Art presented to Anthony Blunt on his sixtieth birthday* (London, 1967), p. x; Carter, *Anthony Blunt*, p. 484.

[23] Peter Brown interview, 18 February 2018; P. Crossley, 'George Zarnecki, 1915-2008', *Biographical Memoirs of Fellows of the British Academy*, xii (2013), pp. 446-7.

[24] BL Add MS 88902/1: Blunt, unpublished handwritten memoir [c. 1982], f. 127.

[25] Rylands MS 3/50: A. Blunt to G.H.W. Rylands, 28 December 1979; 3/259/4, R. Lehman to Rylands, 3 January 1980; Lehmann MS 2/56, A. Blunt to R. Lehmann, 27 December 1980.

[26] BL Add MS 88902/1: Blunt unpublished handwritten memoir [c. 1982], f. 127; Carter, *Anthony Blunt*, p. 496. Blunt's late-life publications are listed in E. Hasloch, 'Bibliography of the major writings of Anthony Blunt since 1969', *Burlington Magazine*, September 1983, pp. 548-9. Blunt handed his unfinished manuscript on Pietro da Cortona to a young German scholar, Jorg Merz, who eventually published *Pietro da Cortona and Roman Baroque Architecture incorporating a draft by the late Anthony Blunt* (London, 2008).

[27] The National Archives of the UK (TNA) PREM 19 3942: Sir Robert Armstrong, minute, 23 June 1987; D. Plante, *Becoming a Londoner: A Diary* (London, 2013), p. 425.

[28] BL Add MS 88902/1: Blunt, unpublished handwritten memoir [c. 1982], f. 135; Add MS 88902/2: Blunt, notes from typed manuscript [c. 1982], ff. 22, 41-42.

killing himself eight years later, throwing himself under a train.)[29] But Blunt was rapidly ageing under the pressure of disgrace and dishonour, he was suffering from both angina and cancer, and he died in London following a heart attack in March 1983, aged seventy-five, the very same month that his fellow spy, Donald Maclean, expired in Moscow. The obituaries in the British newspapers, and the letters that followed, were again unforgiving. 'Quiet funeral for Blunt' (at Putney Vale Crematorium, where the press outnumbered the mourners), as reported in the *Guardian*, was the least censorious. 'Fourth man Blunt dies in disgrace', noted the *Observer*; 'Blunt, the high-class spy dies in disgrace' agreed the *Sunday Times*; while 'Art historian who spied for Russia', was the verdict of *The Times*.[30] In the *Daily Telegraph*, the journalist Godfrey Barker not only denounced Blunt as a traitor, but also claimed that his reputation as an art historian had been inflated by students still in 'academic servility' to him: he had been deeply mistaken about Russia in the 1930s, and much of his work on Poussin had been no less wrong in terms of chronology, and was also lacking in visual sensitivity and perception.[31] It was left to Kerry Downes, a professor in the art history department at Reading University, to put the contrary case. 'As director of the Courtauld Institute', he wrote in a letter to the *Guardian*, Blunt had 'contributed immensely and uniquely, by authority and by example, to the development of art-history in post-war Britain, as his many former pupils, all over the art world today would show and, if honest, be proud to acknowledge.'[32]

Blunt's estate was valued at more than £850,000, perhaps £2.5 million in today's currency, a significant sum for an academic whose parents had been well-connected but not well-off. He left his library, architectural drawings and copyrights to the Courtauld, made some small personal bequests, and bequeathed everything else, apart from one item, to John Gaskin. The exception was the Poussin, *Eliezer and Rebecca*, his best-loved picture, which had so dazzled and intimidated the young J.H. Plumb in Cambridge in the 1930s, and which, as a final act of atonement, Blunt wanted to leave to the nation. His executors hoped it would be accepted in lieu of death duties, but the government procrastinated over the offer for more than a year, before deciding the picture was insufficiently pre-eminent to meet the usual criterion of acceptance in lieu. Margaret Thatcher was emphatically against, minuting 'No' on a submission from Robin Butler, her Private Secretary.[33] In the end, Michael Jaffé, who was Director of the Fitzwilliam Museum in Cambridge and eager to acquire a Poussin for his collection, scraped together the money and bought it for £192,000. Thus did Blunt's prize possession, made possible by Lord Rothschild's gift, and which had started him out on his career as an art historian, return to Cambridge. The painting still hangs in the Fitzwilliam, but there is no way of knowing, from the caption, the name of the art historian and spy to whom it had once belonged. When Jaffé showed Queen Elizabeth II around the Fitzwilliam Museum, she paused at the painting which she remembered from lunching with Blunt, but all she said was 'Poor Anthony', an observation that might be interpreted in a variety of ways (as was that of the Queen Mother, who according to Kenneth Rose 'did not like to hear Blunt disparaged, even after he had been exposed by Mrs Thatcher as a Soviet spy').[34]

In Blunt's case, the protracted imbroglio at the British Academy added to his late-life woes, and he was clearly disappointed that he had to resign his Fellowship, which he greatly valued; in Dover's case, Isaiah Berlin thought he had been 'rather destroyed by the awful time he had' over it (he also thought Dover neither 'well-known enough or, indeed, quite grand enough' for the Order of Merit).[35] Having relinquished the Academy presidency one year early, Dover duly departed for his overseas lecture tour, thereafter returning to Oxford, where he retired from Corpus in the summer of 1986. He decamped with some relief to full-time living at St Andrews, where he had been elected chancellor of the university in 1981, a post which he held until 2005. He also continued his foreign travels, to China and Japan, and there were repeated journeys to Stanford (1987-92) and Cornell (1984-89), where he was a visiting professor. He remained academically active, publishing two volumes of collected papers, *Greek and the Greeks* (1987), and *The Greeks and their Legacy* (1988), which displayed many of the special aspects of his scholarship, among them 'his liberal, rationalistic temperament, his impatience with obfuscation or nonsense, whether modern or ancient, and especially with the complex of ideas which he sees as Platonic and then Christian, including the belief in the goodness of God and in life after death.'[36] In 1993 Dover published his long-planned edition of Aristophanes's *Frogs*, and was awarded the British Academy's Kenyon Medal for achievement in classical studies. His final book, *The Evolution of Greek Prose Style* (1997), fittingly reflected his lifelong fascination with historical linguistics, word-order, vocabulary and rhythm. It was also appropriate that Dover's last major publication, rounding off his oeuvre, was a revised edition of *Greek Word Order* (2000), appearing forty years after the original work, which was his first book.

Such a lengthy and fulfilled old age was very different from Blunt's brief and disgraced twilight years. But there was one further controversy, which arose from the

[29] BL Add MS 88902/2: Blunt, notes from a typed manuscript [c. 1982], f. 68; Carter, *Anthony Blunt*, pp. 487-88, 498. The cause of Gaskin's death was given as 'blunt force trauma'.

[30] *Sunday Times*, 27 March 1983; *Observer*, 27 March 1983; *The Times*, 28 March 1983; *Guardian*, 31 March 1983.

[31] *Daily Telegraph*, 4 April 1983. This was also the argument made in P. Kidson, 'Anthony Frederick Blunt, 1907-1983', *Biographical Memoirs of Fellows of the British Academy*, xiii (2014), pp. 28, 37.

[32] *Guardian*, 29 March 1983.

[33] TNA PREM 19 3942: M.E. Brown to R. Butler, 26 April 1984; R. Butler to Prime Minister, 17 May 1984.

[34] Carter, *Anthony Blunt*, pp. 498-99; Plante, *Becoming a Londoner*, p. 444; Rose, *Who Loses, Who Wins*, p. 427.

[35] See document 30; I. Berlin to E. Adeane, 4 May 1993, in H. Hardy and M. Pottle, *Affirming*, p. 456.

[36] D.A. Russell and F.S. Halliwell, 'Kenneth James Dover, 1920-2010', *Biographical Memoirs of Fellows of the British Academy*, xi (2012), p. 171.

publication of Dover's puzzling and disquieting autobiography, *Marginal Comment*, in 1994. For not only was it almost entirely devoid of those 'humane and benign qualities' which many friends and colleagues admired in him, but it was also widely condemned, for its exhibitionism, its vain pursuit of notoriety, and its egotistical coldness. Dover noted that he had considered suicide on several occasions (something he had in common with Blunt). He provided much embarrassing information about his sexual urges and performance: how he had passed up the opportunity 'to have an adulterous affair' with a much younger woman; how at sixty-four he and his wife had enjoyed 'some of the best fucks of our life'; but how thereafter he had 'had to come to terms with a recalcitrant and unimaginative penis.'[37] Yet the part of the book that seemed most insensitive and caused the greatest offence was the chapter in which he described his relations with Trevor Aston, a brilliant historian, but a wayward Fellow of Corpus, struggling with severe psychological problems and increasingly erratic in his behaviour. Dover had gone to great pains to help his unhappy colleague, but to no avail, and he reluctantly concluded that the only solution was to do what he could to help precipitate Aston's suicide: 'how', as he put it, 'with brutal candour…to kill him without getting into trouble.' Aston had, eventually, taken his own life; but Dover's unrelentingly unsympathetic account caused Aston's friends great distress, and soured Dover's relations with Corpus to such an extent that he seriously considered resigning his Honorary Fellowship and had to be dissuaded from doing so. Few autobiographies, and even fewer academic life-writings, have stirred up such a public storm, as a result of which Dover was interviewed by Anthony Clare for the BBC Radio 4 programme *In the Psychiatrist's Chair.*[38] It was a distinction he surely shared with no other President of the British Academy.

***

Sir Kenneth Dover died in 2010, by which time the Blunt affair, and his own autobiographical idiosyncrasies, were long behind him (and long behind the Academy, too). There remained the matter of the 'Fifth (and final?) Man', who was first mentioned in the newspapers just before Christmas 1979, at the very height of the Press excitement over the Blunt affair. He was named as John Cairncross, and although not explicitly described as the 'Fifth Man', it was reported that he had been 'talent-spotted' for the Communist cause by Blunt.[39] Like Burgess, Philby and Blunt, Cairncross had been an undergraduate at Trinity College, Cambridge where, like Blunt again, he had excelled at modern languages. (One of his brothers, Sir Alec Cairncross, was equally clever, and became a distinguished economist and Fellow of the Academy.) John Cairncross came top in the examinations for both the home civil service, and the Foreign Office and Diplomatic Service, was initially seconded to the Cabinet Office, worked at Bletchley and for MI6 during the war, where he passed many more documents to the Russians than Blunt, and in 1945 was transferred to the Treasury, where he continued to spy for the Russians. Following the defection of Burgess and Maclean, Cairncross had come under suspicion, along with Blunt. He was forced to resign from the civil service, went to live abroad, and eventually owned up to his clandestine activities in the early 1960s. But once again, there was no likelihood of prosecution, since he had confessed on foreign soil. Only in 1982 did the security services discover the full extent of Cairncross's perfidy, and it was not until 1990 that he was outed in the media as the 'Fifth Man', to which he publicly admitted the following year. Although there was continuing media speculation as to who further traitors might be, the hunt for any 'Cambridge spies' beyond the so-called 'Magnificent Five' was effectively over.[40]

Even though he had done more damage to the national interest, the slow-motion revelations about Cairncross attracted far less public attention than Blunt's sensational public unmasking. Unlike Blunt, Cairncross was lowly-born, he was neither an Apostle nor gay, he had never been closely enmeshed in the upper echelons of the establishment, and he had no royal connections. He returned to Britain for his final months, lived in obscurity in the west country, assisted with a ghost-written autobiography, and died in 1995.[41] But while Blunt is long since dead, he has remained a figure of continuing fascination and notoriety, and has been the subject of many subsequent fictional portrayals. *Blade on the Feather*, written for television by Dennis Potter, was an early example, transmitted in mid-October 1980, not long after the Blunt affair at the Academy had ended. It starred Donald Pleasance as Professor Jason Cavendish, a patrician, Cambridge-educated art historian, who was clearly modelled on Blunt, and it addressed familiar issues of loyalty and patriotism, betrayal and falsehood. Yet Cavendish's explanation of why he spied for Russia bore little resemblance to Blunt's, and may have owed more to Le Carré. 'I was born into a class', Cavendish observed, 'that loves only what it owns. But we don't quite own enough of it any more … I suppose we were all riddled with disappointment.' For Blunt, by contrast, embracing Communism had been the best way to oppose Hitler, a justification he repeated at the controversial *Times* news conference; even though he also

[37] Dover, *Marginal Comment*, pp. 220-21, 242-43.

[38] Dover, *Marginal Comment*, pp. 228-29; Russell and Halliwell, 'Kenneth James Dover', pp. 166, 172-73.

[39] *Sunday Times*, 23 December 1979; *The Times*, 24 December 1979.

[40] *Sunday Times*, 14 October 1990, 22 September 1991; *The Times*, 15 October 1990; J. Cairncross, *The Enigma Spy: the story of the man who changed the course of World War Two* (London, 1997); C.M. Andrew and O. Gordievsky, *KGB: The Inside Story of its Foreign Operations from Lenin to Gorbachev* (London, 1990), pp. 210, 253, 406; C.M. Andrew, *The Defence of the Realm: The Authorized History of MI5* (London, 2010), pp. 421-41, 706-07.

[41] R. Davenport-Hines, *Enemies Within: Communists, the Cambridge Spies and the Making of Modern Britain* (London, 2018), p. 517; *The Times*, 9 October 1995; *Independent*, 10 October 1995.

remarked on one occasion that he had become a spy 'for the hell of it, I suppose.'[42] The next television rendition was *Blunt*, transmitted in January 1987, with Ian Richardson in the title role, and drawing extensively on the writings of Goronwy Rees. As with his earlier depiction of Le Carré's Bill Haydon, Richardson's Blunt was cold, detached and duplicitous, and the story focused on his role in helping engineer the defection of Burgess and Maclean in 1951.[43]

Soon after John Cairncross had been outed as the 'Fifth Man', the BBC transmitted Alan Bennett's *A Question of Attribution*, in October 1991. Blunt was played by James Fox ('people find me cold'), and Queen Elizabeth II by Prunella Scales ('facts not chat'). Originally produced as a stage play, Bennett described the piece as an 'inquiry in which circumstances are imaginary but the pictures are real', and it was set in the late 1960s. By then, Blunt had confessed, and the Queen knew, but having been granted immunity, he was still the surveyor of her pictures.[44] It begins at the Courtauld Institute, where Blunt is in conversation with a man from the security services, in which the subjects of art and spying are constantly mixed up. 'Appearances deceive,' Blunt remarks at one point – a comment about art which could equally well apply to spying. Blunt's next, unexpected encounter is with Queen Elizabeth II among the pictures of the Royal Collection in Buckingham Palace, where they stand before a triple portrait, previously thought to have been by Titian, but no longer attributed to him. 'Portraits,' the Queen observes, are supposed to 'show what one is really like. The secret self.' 'We don't know,' she goes on, addressing Blunt, 'whether you have a secret self.' As for the particular canvass: 'If something is not what it is claimed to be,' inquires the Queen, 'what is it?' In her view, the answer is simple: it is 'a fake'. Blunt demurs, preferring the word 'enigma'. 'That is,' the Queen retorts, 'I think, the sophisticated answer.' 'Be careful,' she concludes, as Blunt climbs a ladder to inspect the painting more closely, 'one could have a nasty fall.' As Blunt admits once the Queen has left: 'I was talking about art. I'm not sure that she was.' Back at the Courtauld, Blunt delivers a lecture in which he explains that the painting once misattributed to Titian was originally just a double portrait. Only after it was cleaned was the third man revealed, and only when it was later x-rayed, did a fourth man and a fifth man come to light.[45]

Bennett's own double depiction, of Blunt and the Queen, was far from unsympathetic: but in exploring the issues of forgery, concealment, deception, misattribution and unmasking, he was also drawing attention to the similarities between art and spying (even though most art historians are not spies and most spies are not art historians). In his *roman à clef*, *The Untouchable* (1997), John Banville looked at the connection more frequently made in Blunt's case between the secret lives of gay men and the secret lives of spies.[46] The central character is Victor Maskell who, like Blunt, is an art historian, gay and a spy. Like Blunt again, Maskell has been stripped of his knighthood and publicly disgraced, and is 'untouchable' in two senses, being both beyond the reach of the law, yet also shunned and shamed by former friends. There is little by way of plot to the book, as Maskell reflects on his life to a young biographer, Serena Vandaleur, admitting that sex with men and spying were both activities that appealed on account of their clandestine thrills – 'the aphrodisiac properties of secrecy and fear' – rather than because they were ever serious ventures. Yet even those illicit excitements eventually turned sour. For Maskell, when gay sex was legalised it became less enthralling, and the documents that he passed to the Russians turned out to be of little importance.[47] Banville decided to write the book having seen Blunt smile to himself, when not aware of being on camera, just before giving his press conference in the offices of *The Times*, following his unmasking by Thatcher. It was, Banville later explained, the reaction of a man who survived many interrogations by the British secret service. 'Do these people', Blunt's smile seemed to suggest, 'really imagine they will get anything out of me, a man who has spent decades being grilled with scant success by the best spy-catchers in the land?' It was at that moment, Banville recalled, that 'I knew I would have to base a novel on this man.'[48]

As Blunt and his contemporaries recede from memory into history, the fictional renditions of their lives and activities have become increasingly fanciful. This is well exemplified in the case of Peter Moffatt's *The Cambridge Spies*, a four-part BBC docu-drama shown on television in May 2003, the first episode of which began with the disclaimer 'certain events and characters have been changed for dramatic effect.' Indeed, they had been. Blunt, Burgess, Maclean and Philby were much in evidence, but their connections were seriously jumbled, as were their varied relations with the secret services, and despite the title, John Cairncross scarcely appeared. Moreover, the whole

[42] D. Cannadine, *The Decline and Fall of the British Aristocracy* (London, 1990), pp. 500-01; Carter, *Anthony Blunt*, p. 491; S. Willmetts and C. Moran, 'Filming Treachery: British Cinema and Television's Fascination with the Cambridge Five', *Journal of British Cinema and Television*, x (2013), p. 61.

[43] *The Times*, 13 November 1986, 12 January 1987; *Guardian*, 10 January 1987; *Sunday Times*, 18 January 1987; J. Oldham, '"The trouble with treachery nowadays": Revisiting the Age of Treason in Philby, Burgess and Mclean and Blunt', *Journal of British Cinema and Television*, xv (2018), pp. 407-15.

[44] *The Times*, 2 December 1988, 26 July 1991, 21 October 1991; *Guardian*, 21 October 1991; *Independent*, 21 October 1991; *Financial Times*, 23 October 1991.

[45] A. Bennett, *Plays 2* (London, 1998), pp. 309-51; N. Cloarec, 'The Secret Life of Secret Agents: Alan Bennett and John Schlesinger's *An Englishman Abroad* (1983) and *A Question of Attribution* (1991)', *Revue LISA*, xiv (2016), pp. 1-13; Willmetts and Moran, 'Filming Treachery', pp. 66-67.

[46] George Steiner discussed both of these connections with spying, namely art and homosexuality, in his withering excoriation of Blunt: 'The Cleric of Treason', *New Yorker*, 8 December 1980, pp. 158-95.

[47] P. McGrath, 'The Fourth Man', *New York Times*, 8 June 1997; J. Banville, *The Untouchable* (New York, 1998 edn), p. 321.

[48] J. Banville, 'Omens and poetic licence', *Guardian*, 25 February 2006.

production was distorted by a roseate, amnesiac, nostalgic glow, making it seem more like an undercover version of *Brideshead Revisited*. Miranda Carter, whose biography of Blunt had appeared two years before, was even more damning: 'just an expensive soap', she concluded.[49] Most recently, Anthony Blunt has appeared in the latest instalment of *The Crown* (2019), where he is depicted as blackmailing Prince Philip on the basis of evidence he had linking the prince to the Profumo affair. But as Hugo Vickers has pointed out, it was well known at the time that Stephen Ward, who was at the centre of the affair and subsequently committed suicide, had made sketches of the prince, and Vickers is surely correct in dismissing this piece of dramatic invention as 'ludicrous'.[50] These ever more inventive fictional renditions of Blunt certainly testify to his continuing posthumous newsworthiness, but in none of them so far has the British Academy, or the controversial Annual General Meeting, received any notice or attention.

***

In any case, since Blunt's time, the Academy has itself changed considerably.[51] The Fellowship is much larger, numbering more than one thousand, and is drawn from across the whole of the United Kingdom. It is no longer the male-dominated club that it still resembled in the late 1970s and early 1980s, one indication of which is that it regularly elects virtually the same proportion of women Fellows as of men. The subjects it represents have themselves evolved and developed, and more new Sections have been added, among them Management and Business Studies, and Culture, Media and Performance. In the current climate of opinion, some aspects of Fellows' private lives, especially concerning their personal conduct and sexual relations, are no longer as off-limits as they were widely believed to be at the time of the Blunt affair.[52] Thanks to its enlarged number of Corresponding Fellows, the work of its overseas Institutes, its engagement with other academies in north America, Europe and Asia, and the many global projects it helps to fund and oversee, the Academy's international range and reach are greater than ever before. (It is significant that during the many discussions of Blunt's conduct, no Fellow seems to have mentioned the Academy's growing connections with eastern Europe, Russia and China.) As the champion of the humanities and social sciences, the Academy has established a much higher profile, in Whitehall and Westminster, in the media and with the public, its publications range from studies of the Irish border problem, co-authored with the Royal Irish Academy, to research papers on the future of business corporations, and it hosts a programme of lectures, seminars, conferences and events far more extensive than in the days of Gollancz and Kenyon.[53] It also provides a significant element of the United Kingdom's research funding, from small research grants and postdoctoral fellowships to senior research fellowships and professorships. In electing its Fellows, the Academy continues to insist on academic excellence, but in proclaiming the importance of research and evidence-based learning as public benefits and cultural necessities, it is much more outward looking than it was forty years ago.[54]

As a (largely) state-funded body, there has also been a growing recognition of the need to bring the insights of the subjects the Academy represents to bear on its own history, activities and practices, and beyond the particularities of the fortieth anniversary of the Blunt affair, that commitment to transparency must be the greater justification for the publication of this book. The four epigraphs with which it begins have a certain appropriateness to the events described in the pages that follow, but they also express opinions that might be questioned in the light of those occurrences. Macaulay may have been correct in his disdain for the hysteria and hypocrisy of what we would now term 'moral panic'; yet however 'ridiculous' such episodes might seem, they often reflect deeper anxieties, in the case of Blunt's treachery, about a nation being undermined and betrayed from within by conspiracies of spies and homosexuals, and covered up by the establishment.[55] E.M. Forster's famous antithesis between loyalty to friends and fidelity to country, and his preference, shared with Blunt, for the former over the latter, possesses a certain polarised plausibility; but concern for the well-being of friends surely implies a concern for the safety and survival of the country in which they might be living.[56] Henry Kissinger (and others) have no doubt been justified in noting the bitterness and pettiness of many academic quarrels; but as with the Blunt affair, great matters and significant issues are often also involved, and when they are, there is invariably scope for legitimate differences of view. Geoffrey Elton was not the only person to suggest that the Blunt imbroglio meant that for a time more people had heard of the British Academy than ever before; but it is much more well-known and widely-recognised today, and for very different and far better reasons.[57] What would Sir Kenneth Dover – and the one-time *Sir* Anthony Blunt *FBA* – think of the Academy now?

[49] M. Carter, 'Cambridge Spies? The truth is far more interesting', *Daily Telegraph*, 10 May 2003; Willmetts and Moran, 'Filming Treachery', p. 60.
[50] H. Vickers, 'Royal affairs', *The Times*, 18 November 2019.
[51] Keith Thomas interview, 4 November 2019; Onora O'Neill interview, 9 January 2020.
[52] Keith Thomas interview, 4 November 2019; Robin Jackson interview, 24 October 2019.

[53] G. Anthony, *Brexit and the Irish Border: Legal and Political Questions* (London and Dublin, 2017); M. D'Arcy and F. Ruane, *The Belfast / Good Friday Agreement, the Island of Ireland Economy and Brexit* (London and Dublin, 2018); C. McCrudden, *Brexit, Rights, and the Ireland-Northern Ireland Protocol to the Withdrawal Agreement* (London amd Dublin, 2018); *Reforming Business for the 21st Century: A Framework for the Future of the Corporation* (London, 2018).
[54] Onora O'Neil interview, 9 January 2020.
[55] J. Scott (ed.), *A Dictionary of Sociology* (New York, 2014), p. 492; Robin Jackson interview, 24 October 2019.
[56] N. Annan, *Our Age: Portrait of a Generation* (London, 1990), pp. 311-27.
[57] Dawn Adès interview, 30 October 2019. See document 60.

Indexes

of individuals and institutions related to the British Academy and the matter of Anthony Blunt 1979-1980

Fellows and staff of the British Academy

Some other individuals, institutions, etc.

Academic and cultural institutions

Books

'Cambridge Five', other members

Intelligence services

Newspapers and magazines

Political figures

Television